THE ULTIMATE SCHOOL COUNSELOR'S GUIDE TO ASSESSMENT & DATA COLLECTION

Sandra (Sandi) Logan-McKibben, PhD, NCC, NCSC, ACS, BC-TMH, is a clinical assistant professor and the School Counseling Track Coordinator at Sacred Heart University. Prior to earning her doctorate, she worked as an elementary and middle school counselor in Southern California; was the district-level Tobacco Use, Prevention, and Education (TUPE) Coordinator; and was a site supervisor for practicum and internship students. Working with a caseload of over 1,200 students split across multiple school sites, she has plenty of experience with overcoming challenges and barriers within the field. She understands the importance of developing and implementing a data-driven, comprehensive school counseling program.

Her scholarly interests include school counseling supervision, school counseling leadership, and data-driven decision-making. In additional, she has contributed to multiple editorial boards as a peer reviewer for *Teaching & Supervision in Counseling, Journal of Specialists in Group Work*, and *The Professional Counselor.* She has served in multiple leadership roles with state and national counseling associations, including California Association of School Counselors, Chi Sigma Iota International, and is past Assistant Chair for the Board of Directors of the Florida School Counselor Association. She has earned notable awards, including Chi Sigma Iota International's Outstanding Doctoral Student, Florida Counseling Association's Member of the Year, and Florida School Counselor Association's School Counselor Advocate of the Year.

Dr. Logan-McKibben has taught undergraduate courses in family–school collaboration and stress and anxiety management, as well as master's and doctoral-level courses in counselor education and supervision. She also was a co-primary investigator for a United States Department of Education-Office of Special Education Programs collaborative training grant ($2,250,000) designed to improve collaboration and strengthen professional development opportunities for school counselor and school interventionist trainees.

Jenna Marie Alvarez, PhD, LSC, LPC, is an assistant professor-Educator and the School Counseling Track Coordinator at the University of Cincinnati. Prior to earning her doctorate, she worked as an elementary school counselor in Central Ohio. While there, she had a caseload of approximately 600 students and was the sole school counselor for her building. Her experiences include creation of a schoolwide reading program that utilized a registered therapy dog to help emerging readers build skills and reduce anxiety. She also created multigrade-level leadership teams to promote student leadership and student collaboration. Prior to becoming an elementary school counselor, she worked as an intervention specialist at the middle and high schools within the district in which she became a school counselor.

Her research interests focus on professional school counseling with the hope of decreasing the achievement gap for marginalized students. Dr. Alvarez achieves this goal through research collaborations that contribute to evidence-based practices that are applicable and accessible to school counselor practitioners. Specifically, her research has examined the role of school counselor trainees who work with students with disabilities. She has expanded her research to explore the overall impact of trauma on students and the effectiveness of trauma-informed care as it relates to the school counselor role.

Her commitment to creative teaching was recognized with the 2020 University of Cincinnati College of Education, Criminal Justice, & Human Services Golden Apple for Teaching Award for Counseling Education. Dr. Alvarez has taught master-level courses for both school and mental health counselor trainees in counselor education. In addition she is a licensed mental health counselor with community and hospital internship experience. She serves as a peer reviewer for the *Journal of School Counseling* (JSC) and the *Journal of College Counseling* (JCC). Recently, she joined the advisory council for the Evidence-Based School Counseling Conference (EBSCC).

THE ULTIMATE SCHOOL COUNSELOR'S GUIDE TO ASSESSMENT & DATA COLLECTION

Sandra (Sandi) Logan-McKibben, PhD, NCC, NCSC, ACS, BC-TMH

Jenna Marie Alvarez, PhD, LSC, LPC

SPRINGER PUBLISHING

Springer Publishing Company, LLC
11 West 42nd Street, New York, NY 10036
www.springerpub.com
connect.springerpub.com

Acquisitions Editor: Rhonda Dearborn
Compositor: S4Carlisle Publishing Services
ISBN: 978-0-8261-8553-2
ebook ISBN: 978-0-8261-8554-9
DOI: 10.1891/9780826185549

Additional Resources: the Assessment Instruments and Results Reports, can be accessed by visiting the following url: http://connect.springerpub.com/content/book/978-0-8261-8554-9

21 22 23 24 / 5 4 3 2 1

Names: Logan-McKibben, Sandra (Sandi), author. | Alvarez, Jenna Marie, author.
Title: The ultimate school counselor's guide to assessment & data
collection / Sandra (Sandi) Logan-McKibben, PhD, NCC, NCSC, ACS, BC-TMH, Jenna Marie
Alvarez, PhD, LSC, LPC.
Identifiers: LCCN 2021027880 (print) | LCCN 2021027881 (ebook) | ISBN
9780826185532 (cloth) | ISBN 9780826185549 (ebook)
Subjects: LCSH: Student counselors. | Educational counseling—Research. |
Educational statistics—Data processing. | Student records—Data processing.
Classification: LCC LB1027.5 .L5794 2022 (print) | LCC LB1027.5 (ebook) |
DDC 371.4/22—dc23
LC record available at https://lccn.loc.gov/2021027880
LC ebook record available at https://lccn.loc.gov/2021027881

Printed in the United States of America.

To all the practicing school counselors and school counselors-in-training for the work that you do to make a difference in the lives of students, families, and fellow colleagues, each and every day. Thank you!

To our mentors for providing us with inspiration and guidance.

To my husband, Bradley, thank you for your never-ending love, support, and motivation.

—Sandra (Sandi) Logan-McKibben

To my husband, Joe, and to my children, Ceci, Cruz, and Colson, thank you for your unconditional love and support throughout this process.

—Jenna Marie Alvarez

CONTENTS

SPRINGER PUBLISHING CONNECT™

Additional Resources: The Assessment Instruments and Results Reports, can be accessed by visiting the following url: http://connect.springerpub.com/content/book/978-0-8261-8554-9

FOREWORD

As a graduate student or early-career school counselor, I can only imagine running far and fast from a book on assessment and data collection. At the same time, these topics may seem intimidating: Drs. Logan-McKibben and Alvarez are the best possible guides for your journey. These authors possess the ultimate combination of professional credentials and accessible, warm dispositions, which is needed to cover this content in a comprehensive and meaningful way. What they have to offer in this very easy-to-read text just makes good sense because they have tied it to many of the concepts, documents, and sources with which school counseling professionals are already familiar. In addition to being scholars and counselor educators with extensive knowledge, Dr. Logan-McKibben and Dr. Alvarez each have one of the most prized possessions of writers on these topics: real-world experience.

Once a school counselor, always a school counselor. When those of us like Sandi, Jenna, and myself, leave the K-12 arena for higher education, we are always looking for ways to contribute back to where we once were, to make the journey a little easier for those coming down the path next. I imagine Sandi and Jenna wrote this text because it was one they knew they could have used as school counselors; indeed, I could have used it! Writing this foreword for these two friends is an honor; we share a respect for how hard it is to be a school counselor and what a powerful job it is. As I write this, I am wearing a sweatshirt Jenna alerted me to that says "Female Genius" on the front. All three of us own one, as do some of our other colleagues. These sweatshirts were created by students from the Women in Business club at Indiana University in 2019 as backlash to a male professor at the same university who took to social media to question the value of women in higher education. Perhaps the best part of the story is that the proceeds of the sweatshirt sale went to a local nonprofit that supports girls' development, specifically to be "strong, smart, and bold." Sandi and Jenna embody these same qualities as women, professionals, and scholars—they are strong, smart, and bold. Writing a book, especially one on topics that are not always readily received by your target audience, is nothing short of arduous. Doing the majority of it during a pandemic is grueling. Once you read this text, whether just that portion that you need at a specific point in time, or its entirety, you, too, will feel strong, smart, and bold—ready to tackle the next challenge in your school counseling program.

Context is always an important factor in school counseling because our profession seems to change slowly yet also needs to meet societal demands that are in constant flux. The authors provide considerable historical context about how and why assessment and data are vital to school counseling practice, especially as they haven't always been. Readers will appreciate the bigger picture in some chapters if they want to have a more holistic view of the role of these topics. The real star of the text, I believe, is Chapter 4. Sandi and Jenna have done such time-intensive work here to give readers what they really want: the go-to assessments, many of them FREE, for use in school counseling programs. Graduate programs may point school counselors in training to a few of these resources, but are not likely to do so all at once or collect them together the way this chapter does, so conveniently categorized by the domains we know so well. Readers can appreciate the countless hours that went into sourcing these assessments, ensuring they are still active, contacting developers for permissions, and staying up to date on any developments that occurred while the text was written. As a counselor educator, I know how valuable this chapter alone is for me in teaching my students about assessment. Knowing these assessments exist and are more easily accessible than you thought will save you time, save you from recreating the wheel, and put more credible tools in your back pocket than many of the things you can find on random websites or that you might make up on your own (although they outline the merits in those too!). You'll be glad to know you can use many of these instruments over and over again as you change schools or evolve your program.

The Ultimate School Counselor's Guide to Assessment and Data Collection delightfully fills a unique gap in our profession. Addressing assessment by specifically highlighting formal and informal tools and tying them to data collection brings the whole picture of program evaluation into clearer and, more important *easier* focus for school counselors. Two cherished friends created this labor of love with a great deal of thoughtful effort. I can assure you of this because I know they want to support your success as a school counselor and support your school counseling program's success. Sandi and Jenna have been where you are and know the desire to work smarter, not harder, as a school counselor on the programmatic things so that the focus on students remains the priority. They also understand that assessment and data give you the language you often need to advocate to stakeholders and leverage the support you need to push progress forward. I hope you'll agree with me that conceptually and practically, readers will have much to gain from this text in its parts and as a whole. Sandi and Jenna would love to hear what you think about the book, too—yes, *really*! Trust me, and reach out to them with your questions, comments, examples, and ideas.

—Erin Mason, PhD, LPC, CPCS

PREFACE

This first edition of *The Ultimate School Counselor's Guide to Assessment and Data Collection* is the result of the professional observations and experiences of the authors and those whom they have supervised and trained. What is highlighted in the field and supported by research is that school counselors-in-training are not getting adequate knowledge and training in assessment and data collection relevant to their specialty area. While counselor preparation programs frequently require a course in counseling assessment, school counselors-in-training often report dissatisfaction with the relevance of what is covered, as the content is not focused on what school counselors actually see and use in practice. Further, practicing school counselors often express confusion in not knowing what assessments may be best suited to the work, which could be related to lack of knowledge or lack of accessibility of such instruments. Prior to the writing of this book, no resource existed that focuses on the concept of assessment specifically for school counselors and provides them with formal and informal assessments that offer opportunities for data collection that, in turn, inform one's data-driven, comprehensive school counseling program (CSCP). Whether one is concerned with individual student data, school-level data, school counseling program-level data, or the school counselors' practices or beliefs, this professional resource offers a unique opportunity to meet the call of school counseling professionals for a book that offers guidance and access to instruments that focus on multiple levels of data.

When speaking with many practicing school counselors, both novice and experienced, they note that *assessment* and *data* sound scary and seem like they are efforts that take considerable time. Yet, the word *data* is mentioned 29 times in the *ASCA Professional Standards and Competencies*, and the word *assessment* 12 times. We cannot hide from the fact that we have professional and ethical responsibilities to be data driven. This very notion was the impetus for us to write this book. We want practicing school counselors and those in training to have the knowledge necessary to be a data-inspired and data-driven school counselor who develops and implements a comprehensive school counseling program that meets the needs of its students. When scanning Facebook groups specifically for school counselors, these are just a few of the postings seen in the last year:

- "What data do you collect from working with students individually?"
- "I have a budget of zero. How can I use assessments when they all seem so costly?"
- "My principal asked me to find a universal screener, and she wants us to start implementing ASAP. HELP?!"
- "Where can I find a pre–posttest for my bully prevention curriculum?
- "What is the best way to create a pre–posttest for all 378 sixth graders at my school?"
- "Does anyone have a needs assessment they are willing to share?"
- "I don't know where to start. What is the best social-emotional learning (SEL) assessment to use?"
- "Our district is looking at implementing a districtwide suicide assessment protocol. What do you use?"
- "I'm looking for data-collection tools to use during my core curricular classroom lessons."
- "Any ideas on how to easily track data from small groups?"
- "What data do you use to justify your position?"

GOAL OF THIS BOOK

The Ultimate School Counselor's Guide to Assessment and Data Collection bridges the gap in knowledge and skills to allow school counselors to carry out their critical work in advocating for student success every day, based upon data. From this resource, we hope readers will gain the necessary attitudes, knowledge, and skills required to be a data-inspired and data-driven school counselor who serves as a leader and agent of change as a part of the development and implementation of a comprehensive school counseling program. One of the most salient and unique features of this book is that it offers readers actual assessments that can immediately be implemented in one's school. The contents of this book provide a unique opportunity for scholarly research to be accessible to the consumer (i.e., school counselors) thus bridging the research-to-practice and training gaps.

INTENDED AUDIENCE

The intended audience for this book is school counselors-in-training, practicing school counselors, those who serve in a district-level supervisory or coordinator position, as well as school counselor educators. Practicing school counselors may find this to be a helpful resource in the initial development of their data journey. Supervisors and coordinators might consider using this resource as a book to study for a professional development opportunity. You could consider facilitating school-level book studies, which could in turn provide you with relevant information about the future professional development needs of the school counselors you support. This book may be used as required or supplementary reading for school counselor educators (and thus their students) within a school counselor preparation program in classes, such as Introduction to School Counseling, Organization & Administration of Comprehensive School Counseling Programs, or for use during fieldwork experiences.

ORGANIZATION OF THE CONTENT

The chapters within this book are organized developmentally, starting with foundational and theoretical knowledge and moving toward application. Each chapter is written with the practicing school counselor in mind, using collaborative and inclusive language:

- Chapter 1 provides readers with a snapshot of the history of school counseling and introduces readers to the process of data collection and use of assessments.
- Chapter 2 highlights both formal and informal assessments and provides the reader with examples of how to connect assessments to CSCPs.
- Chapter 3 outlines the various approaches to CSCPs by addressing assessments and data collection in connection to the American School Counselor Association (ASCA) National Model.
- Chapter 4 allows readers to familiarize themselves with a variety of informal and formal assessments across the domains of academic development, career development, and social–emotional development.
- Chapter 5 focuses on understanding needs assessments and program evaluation to drive the development and implementation of a comprehensive school counseling program. Additionally, the chapter explains each type of data (process data, ASCA Mindsets & Behaviors data, outcome data) and illustrates examples of each type of data across school levels.
- Chapter 6 exposes readers to a variety of technological tools that can help in the assessment and data-collection processes and illustrates numerous accountability report formats.

Readers can access downloadable content that includes assessment instruments discussed throughout the book, as well as results reports discussed in Chapter 6. The instruments can be utilized for school counselors to make data-driven decisions, including decisions on core curricular classroom lesson topics, small group, and individual counseling pre–posttests. This online-only material can be accessed by visiting the following url: http://connect.springerpub.com/content/book/978-0-8261-8554-9

Overall, our intent is for this book to serve as a resource that can guide your assessment and data-collection efforts. It is our sincere hope that we can help you in your journey toward becoming a data-driven school counselor who implements a comprehensive school counseling program that positively contributes to student success across all domains—academic, career, and social–emotional development. Use of the information offered in this book serves as an opportunity to advocate for what is in the best interest of your own professional development, and by proxy, the best interest of your students' success.

—Sandra (Sandi) Logan-McKibben, PhD, NCC, NCSC, ACS, BC-TMH

—Jenna Marie Alvarez, PhD, LSC, LPC

ACKNOWLEDGMENTS

We are extremely grateful to the many individuals who directly or indirectly supported the development of this book. Our appreciation goes to those practicing school counselors and school counselors-in-training who had the opportunity to provide encouragement, insight, and feedback on our work:

- Nicole Buzainz
- Lisamarie Ferrer
- Olivia Gordon
- Shannon Inman
- Leah Lovely
- Jess McKee
- Daniela Nunez
- Nadine Press

We also wish to acknowledge the individuals and organizations that provided permission to use their instruments and examples of their data-driven work:

- Jasmine Arellano (Pomona Unified School District)
- Angela Cleveland (Counselors for Computing)
- Timothy Conway (Lakeland High School)
- Andrea Cordeiro-Benson (Blair Middle and High School)
- Dr. Matthew Corrigan (Seton Hall University) Paula Crutchley & Bethney Ahrendsen (Kuder)
- Erin Gibson (Boston Children's Hospital)
- Dr. Stanley Kutcher (Dalhousie University)
- Jodi Miller (WellCheq)
- Dr. Timothy Poynton (University of Massachusetts-Boston)
- Jennifer Schmid (Hillview Middle School)
- Leslie Martinez (University of La Verne)
- Greg Monaco (Monaco & Associates)
- Dr. Kelly Posner (Columbia University)
- Kathleen Rakestraw (American School Counselor Association)
- Dr. Russell Sabella (Florida Gulf Coast University)
- Dr. Christopher Sink (Old Dominion University)
- Steve Zaharakis (School Counselor Use-of-Time Analysis)

Also, we thank the entire Springer staff for their commitment and work on this project . . . especially during a pandemic!

I [Sandra] am eternally grateful to my husband for his unconditional support and encouragement through this project and just in life in general. I love you to the beach and back! I am extremely thankful for my parents, who instilled a passion for learning and exploring who and what I want to be . . . and for providing lots of laughter throughout life. And to my co-author, we can accomplish whatever we dream and we have some much to be thankful for, including our friendship.

I [Jenna] am beyond blessed to have the support of my family throughout the development of this book as it has been a labor of love. To my husband, Joe, thank you for always pushing me to achieve my goals. You encourage me daily to be the director of my own success. I appreciate this can-do spirit no matter what life has thrown at us. To my Alvarez trio, Ceci, Cruz, and Colson, you three are the fuel to my fire. I love you three to the moon and back. To my parents, Roger and Gail, thank you for teaching me early on what hard work looks like and how to be an impactful advocate. To my late grandmother, Goldie, your creativity lives on and is embedded in all elements of this project. To my dear colleague, friend, and co-author, thank you for your support and love throughout this project.

1

LANDSCAPE OF THE SCHOOL COUNSELING PROFESSION AND THE IMPORTANCE OF ASSESSMENT AND DATA COLLECTION

Introduction

The profession of school counseling has experienced significant shifts related to the role of a school counselor in making data-informed decisions. Sink (2009) explained that effective evidence-based programing derives from school counselors who possess an understanding of both qualitative and quantitative research methods. Development within the school counseling profession related to comprehensive school counseling programs (CSCPs) has begun to include data collection in combination with assessments that collectively inform programming. The American School Counselor Association (ASCA) recently released the fourth edition of the National Model. In this model, the process and purpose of data collection was streamlined to provide school counselors with recommendations of how to develop data-driven CSCPs (ASCA, 2019a). Other comprehensive models of school counseling exist and are explored within this book. Specifically, this book discusses models related to valid and reliable assessments and data-informed decisions for effective student programming.

Upon graduation, school counselors lack access to a wide variety of scholarly journals that often describe and provide valid and reliable instruments. Depending on the educational setting and the expectation of the counselor's role, school counselors are faced with budget constraints, which can prevent the purchase of valid and reliable instruments. A school counselor might decide to create an instrument to gather information for a CSCP. The absence of valid and reliable instruments could negatively impact a school counseling program (Scarborough, 2005).

Many school counselors report feeling inadequate and incompetent in their research and assessment skills associated with their role (Davis et al., 2005). Our professional organization, ASCA, recently updated the school counseling standards and competencies to reflect the increased importance of data-informed decision-making. According to the professional standards, school counselors are to use current and relevant research to address student needs through a CSCP (ASCA, 2019b). The inclusion of valid and reliable measures allows school counselors to address current professional standards and competencies in an efficient manner and identify barriers of closing the research-to-practice gap.

The Council for Accreditation of Counseling and Related Educational Programs (CACREP) standards require both faculty members and school counselor trainees to embrace a professional identity through affiliation with professional organizations that support the mission of school counseling (CACREP, 2015). Perera-Diltz and Mason (2010) noted that a part of school counselors' professional responsibilities must be addressing gaps between educational state mandates and their school counseling practice. Addressing these gaps is associated with being actively engaged with data, including collecting data and sharing results with key stakeholders (Perera-Diltz & Mason, 2010). This shift continues to be seen in the way school counselors operate. Since the inception of the first ASCA standards and National Model, our profession has seen shifts in how we approach school counseling program development. The ASCA National Model continues to reflect these shifts and includes a deiled section related to program planning. Within this section of the ASCA National Model, school counselors are provided with a framework to incorporate data into the informed decision-making process (ASCA, 2019a).

The aim of this book is to provide valid and reliable assessments to support the data-collection process by providing the reader with multiple approaches to CSCPs that support evidence-based school counseling practices. We will use these assessments to support evidence-based school counseling practices to help school counselors close practice gaps within each of their unique school systems. For example, we explore the development and use of the School Counseling Program Implementation Survey (SCPIS) as a tool for school counselors to better understand their program and its outcomes (Clemens et al., 2010). Additionally, we explore the research supporting the validity and reliability of the My Class Inventory-Short Form Revised and we discuss ways to incorporate this assessment into a CSCP (Mariani et al., 2015; Sink & Spencer, 2005, 2007). This chapter seeks to expand on the data-collection process to address the gaps associated with using valid and reliable measures for school counselors. We seek to provide school counselors with an exhaustive list of measures connected to the ASCA (2019b) professional standards and domains.

Gaps school counselors experience include training, confidence, and implementation of research-based initiatives, assessments, evidence-based practices, and CSCPs (Scarborough, 2005; Sink, 2009; Young & Kaffenberger, 2015). Counselor educators are in the position to address gaps associated with confidence by ensuring trainees incorporate assessments and other evidence-based practices while in a school counseling preparation program (Astramovich et al., 2005). Diversifying exposure to assessments in appraisal courses is an important first step in encouraging school counselor trainees to implement evidenced-based practices in the field.

Counselor educators can play a critical role in shaping how school counselor trainees perceive and approach their professional practice. For example, increased exposure to assessments related to the work of school counselors can help trainees form strong professional identities. Neukrug et al. (2013) found that clinical assessments were the most frequently taught assessments in counselor preparation programs. The authors attributed this finding to the fact that counselor educators have more experience in clinical settings versus school settings (Neukrug et al., 2013). Increased awareness of the importance and value of how school counselors can utilize assessments in practice could increase access to low-cost or no-cost measures suited for the school environment. For example, Tadlock-Marlo et al. (2013) recognized that clinically based multicultural assessments lacked the necessary components to address specific multicultural issues students face in schools. Therefore, it

Increased awareness of the importance and value of how school counselors can utilize assessments in practice could increase access to low-cost or no-cost measures suited for the school environment.

is imperative that school counselors have access to a wide variety of low-cost or no-cost school counseling assessments in order to fully support student needs.

Tadlock-Marlo et al. (2013) reiterated that one strength of many school counselors is their ability to advocate for students. Valid and reliable assessments, evidence-based practices, and CSCPs corroborate the advocacy efforts of school counselors. As a profession, and with guidance from ASCA, school counselors are becoming more data driven; however, gaps in training persist. School counselors can create data-driven, comprehensive programs within their schools through increased knowledge obtained from valid and reliable assessment data. School counselors must take responsibility for program development, employ their leadership skills to implement data-informed programming, and strive to meet and exceed the current professional standards and competencies related to data-driven, evidence-based practices (ASCA, 2016, 2019a, 2019b; Astramovich et al., 2005; Scarborough, 2005; Sink, 2009).

School counselors are encouraged by ASCA to follow the ASCA National Model, including counselor competencies and the ASCA Ethical Standards (ASCA, 2016, 2019a, 2019b). However, school counselor trainees in programs accredited by the CACREP are not required to demonstrate the ASCA competencies. Even further, the current CACREP standards do not explicitly address the ASCA National Model or require school counselor trainees to adhere to the ASCA National Model when creating a CSCP. The CACREP standards require both faculty members and school counselor trainees to embody a professional identity through affiliation with professional organizations that support the mission of school counseling (CACREP, 2015). Despite the lack of mandates, it is imperative that school counselors show competency with the ASCA National Model for the benefit of their students. To address the disconnect mentioned previously, an ASCA (2020a) position statement on school counselor preparation programs stated that school counselors should be prepared for the professional role when trained in a program that is committed to connecting curriculum to the ASCA National Model and standards. Additionally, to address the absence of the ASCA National Model within CACREP accreditation standards, ASCA partnered with the Council for the Accreditation of Educator Preparation (CAEP) to approve the ASCA Specialized Program Accreditation (SPA) standards in 2019. The ASCA SPA standards will be used in the review process for school counselor preparation programs starting in the fall of 2021 (CAEP, 2020).

In order to effectively use the ASCA National Model, data must be central to the creation and implementation of CSCPs, as evidenced by the need for valid and reliable data to inform working with diverse students. The ASCA National Model provides school counselors with tools and resources to serve students from diverse backgrounds (ASCA, 2019a). Also, ASCA continually releases position statements related to various elements of the school counseling profession. The position statements are published to educate school counselors and school counselor trainees on engagement with, support for, and advocacy of students from diverse backgrounds while implementing a CSCP. For example, the position statement, *The School Counselor and School Counseling Programs*, highlighted that valid and reliable data are foundational components for creating appropriate programming for students served by school counselors (ASCA, 2017). Data-driven CSCPs have not always been the expectation. In the next section, we discuss the historical underpinnings leading to our current need for data-driven CSCPs.

History of School Counseling

Vocational counseling emerged in the 1900s and is now considered professional school counseling (ASCA, 2019a). Prior to the 1920s, our professional roles were fulfilled by teachers and administrators (2019a). However, the school counseling profession shifted in the 1920s to focus on student health and wellness. At the time, the available training and funding focused on vocational guidance services, and not on training individuals to become school counselors. In the 1950s and 1960s, school counseling started to become a legitimate profession (Erford, 2019). School counselors were nonexistent in American schools until the 1950s and 1960s. In fact, many higher education institutions did not provide training programs for school counselors (Erford, 2019). In 1952, ASCA was founded, and became a sister organization with the American Counseling Association (ACA) in 1953 (Erford, 2019). As the ASCA's membership grew and the definition of school counselors as educators, first, and counselors, second became widely accepted, a separation between ASCA and ACA began to emerge. Both organizations functioned independently of each other and were formally separated in 2018 (Wong, 2018).

School counselors were originally referred to as *guidance counselors*. The use of the term *guidance* to refer to the profession of school counseling started to disappear in the 1980s (Erford, 2019). Extending on this point, Zyromski et al. (2019) sought to understand the impact title has on our profession. Zyromski et al. found that participants who were given a survey with the term school counselor scored significantly higher than those who were given a survey with the term *guidance counselor.* The researchers noted the impact that title has on professional confidence, no matter the years of experience (Zyromski et al., 2019). However, educators and the public often still use the term *guidance counselor* to refer to school counselors. Erford (2019) stated, "The term *guidance* was widely viewed as conveying the notion that the professional school counselor was primarily involved in a directive form of giving advice to students" (p. 7). Also, the term *guidance* does not align with the ASCA's professional identity and mission of school counselors (Dollarhide & Saginak, 2017). This professional identity shift is illustrated through the professional organization as ASCA has a published vision and a mission statement that align with the role of the counselor who is focused on social justice and advocacy for students and the school community. The vision statement created by ASCA embodies the heart of our profession, which is focused on using our professional skills and training to ensure the needs of all students are met (ASCA, 2020b).

The mission statement developed by ASCA highlights theimportance of school counselors being both professional and ethical within their mission statement (ASCA, 2020b). The mission statement embodies the vision of ASCA and continues to express the importance of professional identity through the association's goals and objectives. For example, ASCA provides school counselors with professional development that is relevant to our current practices and helps support student development (ASCA, 2020b). Additionally, aligning with the mission, vision, goals, and objectives, ASCA continues to advocate for the 250:1 ratio of students to school counselor, citing that the ratio not only allows school counselors the ability to focus on role-appropriate duties, but improves overall student success (ASCA, 2019a). With the continued advocacy efforts for the 250:1 ratio, other individual states may shift toward mandating ASCA's recommendations of a 250:1 ratio and evidence-based programs through CSCPs.

A school counselor is a leader who advocates for students to create systemic change while collaborating with teachers, administrators, parents, students, and other key stakeholders (ASCA, 2019a). In 1953, ASCA introduced *The School Counselor* journal, one of the many initiatives to create a solid professional identity for school counselors (Erford, 2019). Also, the U.S. Department of Education created the Pupil Personnel Services Organization in 1953. The introduction of the Pupil Personnel Services Organization increased the professional credibility of school counselors by officially housing the school counseling licensure process (Erford, 2019). Each of these steps by ASCA and the Pupil Personnel Services Organization moved the profession away from the *guidance* identity and toward-21st century school counseling focused on social justice (Erford, 2019).

In 1997, ASCA created a set of standards titled *The National Standards for School Counseling Programs*, which provided school counselors with a set of benchmarks to structure their school counseling programs (Erford, 2019). The first version of the ASCA National Model was developed in 2003.

The National Model serves as a foundational guide for counselor educators and practicing school counselors who are navigating the school systems within their professional role. The development of the ASCA National Model provided a blueprint for school counseling in the 21st century. In response to the evolution of the school counseling profession, three editions of the ASCA National Model have followed in 2005, 2012, and 2019.

Data collection and program evaluation are included in the initial development and re-evaluation stages as part of a CSCP. Whether a school counselor chooses to align their program with the ASCA National Model and Recognized ASCA Model Program (RAMP), the National Model and RAMP are considered the gold standard in our profession for engaging in program evaluation. By no means are we saying that you must do this, but rather, we want to provide you with all of the information. The National Model provides school counselors with a framework to sort through collected data relevant to their practice (Astramovich, 2016). Through our own personal experiences as school counselors, we recognize that organizing and making sense of the data can be overwhelming. However, learning how to implement a CSCP helps make the process of creating a data-driven school counseling program more manageable. School counselor trainees are taught various techniques to developing CSCPs using several data-collection methods. Nelson and Tarabochia (2020) speculated that, "The other 75% of school counselors may utilize another school counseling program model (e.g., state or local model), an ASCA model, or no program model at all" (p. 4). We feel it is important for us to touch upon various types of programming for CSCP within Chapter 3 to provide you with the tools to create a CSCP that works for your school. Throughout this section, we have discussed how our profession has evolved from guidance counselor to school counselor. In addition to the shift in our professional title, our work within the schools has shifted to serving all students through a data-driven CSCP.

As illustrated in Table 1.1, the perspectives of a guidance counselor versus a school counselor are quite different in nature due to their training and the focus or intent of their work. While school counselors do perform some of the responsibilities of guidance counselors, the role today is much more defined toward meeting the needs of all students through leadership, advocacy, collaboration, and systemic change, and the implementation of a CSCP.

Importance of Data Collection in School Counseling

In light of the current educational trends, it remains critical to have knowledge and awareness of assessment measures that best serve students and schools. School counselors must be data driven and utilize both formal and informal assessments to drive their CSCP. To have an effective counseling program that is evidence based, school counselors must possess an understanding of qualitative and quantitative research methods (Sink, 2009).

School counselors report feeling uncomfortable about data collection. Many school counselor trainees lack the confidence to conduct rigorous assessments and use assessment results to inform their school counseling practice (Davis et al., 2005). Particularly in urban settings, school counselors are shifting toward following the ASCA's National Model and standards for counseling (Eschenauer & Chen-Hayes, 2005). Further, school counselors are often not responsible for the administration and interpretation of assessments for special education eligibility, but their ability to comprehend the results and apply interpretations to specific interventions is vital.

Sink (2009) explored how school counselors can create comprehensive school counseling programs and found the use of data collection to be fundamental to establishing a CSCP. In fact, it is imperative that school counselors collect, review, and analyze data to make informed decisions when selecting appropriate programs and interventions. However, a nationwide survey of school counselors reported that

TABLE 1.1 PERSPECTIVES FROM A GUIDANCE COUNSELOR VERSUS A SCHOOL COUNSELOR

	GUIDANCE COUNSELOR	SCHOOL COUNSELOR
Role in academic development	"It is not my role to support students in developing academically; that's the teacher's job."	"My role as a school counselor is to support students in academic development through my CSCP. This can be done through activities such as academic advising, academic skills-based groups, interpreting academic data to actively collaborate with students, parents, and other key stakeholders to ensure all students have the opportunity to learn."
Role in career development	"I complete college paperwork and write academic letters and proctor the PSAT."	"I work with my students, parents, and other key stakeholders to provide meaningful opportunities for engagement to prepare students for the next steps. I make sure that real-world connections are made intentional to support students in making informed postsecondary choices. I work with community partners to provide my students with access to career mentors who represent the diverse population of our students."
Role in social–emotional development	"I engage in social–emotional development when a teacher can no longer handle the behavioral issues of a student. I pull that student into my office to do worksheets from a book written in 1995."	"In my role as a school counselor at Zan Elementary, I ensure that all of my classroom lessons and group lessons are aligned with the current ASCA Mindsets and Behaviors for Student Success that are connected to social–emotional development. I actively seek out national and state standards and evidence-based curriculum related to social–emotional learning. When I cannot find evidence-based materials, I look for best practice strategies. I also make sure that I am addressing these mindsets and behaviors when I am working one-on-one with students."
Student-to-counselor ratio	"I don't really understand the importance of a ratio; I just work with whatever students need my help."	"Working within the ASCA recommended ratio supports my efforts toward student success and implementation of a successful CSCP."
Intervention and student support	"My role is to provide counseling to those students who come to me and express that they want assistance."	"My role is to support all students toward achieving success by administering needs assessments, analyzing data, and consulting with key stakeholders to identity students in need of Tier 2 (secondary level) services. I do this by being actively involved in the MTSS team."
The ASCA National Model	"I know of the ASCA National Model, but I do not actively incorporate it into my day-to-day activities as I don't have time."	"I actively work to incorporate the ASCA National Model into my work as a school counselor. I first started with developing a vision and mission statement for my CSCP that is connected to my school and district's vision and mission statement."
Metrics of success	"I know I am doing a good job because students tell me so."	"I know that my students are different as a result of my counseling interventions and efforts, as evidenced by the data collected throughout the school year."
Closing the gap	"I work hard and care about all of the students, therefore any gaps are being addressed in our school."	"I utilize all available data to make informed decisions to select interventions that meet the unique needs of our students. I actively advocate for policy changes that discriminate against students."

ASCA, American School Counselor Association; CSCP, comprehensive school counseling programs; MTSS, Multi-Tiered Systems of Support; PSAT, Preliminary Scholastic Aptitude Test.

only 54% of those surveyed were involved in data-collection processes. About 32% of the school counselors in the survey shared the results of the data with key stakeholders within their school communities (Perera-Diltz & Mason, 2010). Zyromski and Mariani (2019) offer practical models to support a school counselor's implementation of evidence-based interventions through data collection to make informed decisions. School counselors' competence and confidence related to making data-informed program decisions is connected to training and professional development. Zyromski and Mariani (2019) discuss the process and logic models to help support school counselors to use data to select evidence-based interventions. The researchers demonstrated that school counselors can more effectively reach program goals when they combine these research models through demonstration with fictitious school examples. Later we expand on the process and logic models within this chapter to help readers gain a better understanding of the various ways to start the process of program intervention, selection, and evaluation.

Twenty-First Century and Social Justice School Counseling

School counselors play an important role as advocates for their students, especially contemporary school counselors who are focused on social justice. For example, researchers looked at the role school counselors play in reducing or eliminating barriers for students (Eschenauer & Chen-Hayes, 2005). Dollarhide and Saginak (2017) stated that, "Newer counselors are more activist-oriented toward and trained in leadership, advocacy, systemic change, while others still see their roles in older models of test-and-tell guidance, scheduling, and academic discipline" (p. 13). In the following sections, we discuss the components that make up a 21st-century school counselor. Specifically, we discuss how assessment, as well as data collection, play a critical role in advocating for change.

Virtual School Counseling

We would be remiss if we did not discuss virtual school counseling as it relates to the 21st century and social justice school counseling. School counselors are positioned within the school systems to collaborate and advocate for the needs of the student. Virtual school counseling helps to extend our position as school counselors. As many educational systems have experienced great shifts on the delivery of virtual learning, this provided an opportunity for school counselors to deliver services in a new way. With these shifts, school counselors have been able to leverage this position to advocate for students and families with regard to access to housing programs, technology assistance, food, and other community resources (Strear et al., 2021).

Given the global health pandemic caused by COVID-19, the American Academy of Pediatrics (AAP) released a position statement in support of schools returning to in-person instruction citing the critical importance of the academic, social–emotional, and mental health needs of students provided within school buildings (AAP, 2020). Organizations, such as ASCA and the National Association of School Psychologists (NASP), united to create a school reentry plan that centered around social and emotional learning as well as mental health support (ASCA, n.d.). The shifts to virtual school counseling stemmed from the global pandemic and unexpected closing of K-12 schools. Although the practice of virtual school counseling is a continued area of growth for our profession, we briefly discuss the state of virtual school counseling and provide resources for you to consider as you develop or refine your CSCP to embrace virtual services for students.

With the reopening of schools, came "road maps" or frameworks for school counselors to consider in relation to social and emotional learning in various learning formats. For example, the Collaborative for Academic, Social, and Emotional Learning (CASEL) released a road map for reopening schools that was centered around social and emotional learning to promote equity in services and start the healing process from the pandemic (CASEL, 2020). This road map provided an intentional framework highlighting critical steps to not only support students in their social and emotional learning, but to also sustain these practices (2020). This is a great example of how to shift your school counseling practice with intentionality. Outside of the pandemic, this document highlights strategies that we can apply to virtual school counseling moving forward. For example, the road map discussed the importance of obtaining input from key stakeholders related to needs of reopening schools. This applies to virtual school counseling practice; we would want to survey parents, students, and teachers on their needs, including technology needs related to participating in virtual school counseling services. Strear et al. (2021) addressed this exact point of moving forward with digital school counseling practices, noting that participants talked about how they shifted large in-person events (e.g., career nights) into virtual events. They noted that participants recognized that virtual school counseling created more access opportunities for students and families in multiple schools across one district (Strear et al., 2021). Another advantage of virtual school counseling could be collaboration among districts in more rural areas to combine resources, *both digital and school counseling*, to increase the availability of academic, career, and social–emotional large- and small-group lessons.

Currently, a universal working definition of virtual school counseling is unavailable. However, Goodrich et al. (2020) discussed the need for school counselors to integrate virtual school counseling services, such as individual and small-group services, within the ASCA National Model through videoconferencing applications (e.g., Zoom or Google Hangouts). It was noted that integrating technology into the practice of school counseling could help students foster a better understanding for how to set digital boundaries, learn or practice digital social skills, and teach social–emotional skills while engaging students in interventions (Goodrich et al., 2020).

Additionally, ASCA released virtual school counseling toolkits for elementary, middle, and high school grades. The elementary toolkit (ASCA, 2020c) includes on-demand links for *Second Step* lessons that are designed to help elementary students recognize their feelings. These are great resources that school counselors can use to blend asynchronous and synchronous learning. Asynchronous learning typically happens at a time that works for the student's schedule. Synchronous learning is real-time learning that is interactive and typically involves a videoconferencing platform. Elementary school counselors can have students view these on-demand lessons on their own time (asynchronous learning) and then come together to process reactions to the lesson and do breakout activities (synchronous learning). This is one example of how to flip traditional large- and small-group lessons into a virtual school counseling practice.

The shifts we have recently seen has placed a positive emphasis on serving all students regardless of the educational delivery model (face-to-face, remote, hybrid, etc.). School counselors are in positions to advocate for student needs, including trauma and access to virtual mental health services (ASCA, n.d.). For example, ASCA (n.d.) states that school counselors are trained to support students in times of transition while recognizing potential warning signs related to difficulty with transitioning, including transitions related to reentry to school. Additionally, school counselors were pushed to grow in virtual school counseling practices while recognizing the impacts and inequities of virtual learning for students (Strear et al., 2021). As we continue to move forward, school counselors need to consider and develop ways to implement their services within their CSCPs through a virtual platform.

ASCA National Model and ASCA School Counselor Competencies

The ASCA National Model provides school counselors with a foundation for how to operate. This model holds school counselors accountable for their role in the school setting. The National Model provides school counselors with evaluation templates and empowers them to create comprehensive school counseling programs through the collection and analysis of data (ASCA, 2019a). Aside from templates, the National Model encourages school counselors to think like project managers. For example, ASCA's National Model calls for school counselors to be "result oriented" with their programming and management of school counseling programs (ASCA, 2019a).

The ASCA National Model distinctly cultivates a framework for school counselors to create comprehensive counseling programs that ensure all students succeed (ASCA, 2019a). The biggest changes from the third to the fourth edition of the National Model are to the flagship quadrants that have been a foundational component of the National Model since its inception. The four quadrants of the National Model's third edition were *Foundation, Management, Delivery,* and *Accountability* (ASCA 2012, 2019a). The revised quadrants are *Define, Manage, Deliver,* and *Assess* (2019a). The change from *Accountability* to *Assess* shows a shifted focus toward the importance of program evaluation. The overarching goal of the National Model is to ensure that school counselor programs meet the needs of students. Therefore, this change in focus meets student needs by ensuring programs are consistently and properly evaluated.

A set of counselor competencies are included as a self-assessment method in the National Model to help school counselors benchmark their professional practice. The standards are also available as a stand-alone document. A set of draft standards were released in 2018 as a step toward updating the competencies. This update sought to reflect the current role of the school counselor. The final version of the standards was released in 2019 to coincide with the updated National Model (ASCA, 2018a, 2019b). The purpose of the *ASCA School Counselor Professional Standards & Competencies Assessment,* located within the ASCA National Model's fourth edition, is to provide school counselors with an interactive way to assess their skills and promote professional growth (ASCA, 2019a, 2019b). We encourage you to self-evaluate against these standards and competencies on an annual basis.

The competencies related to serving all students through direct and indirect service connects with the ASCA Ethical Standards (ASCA, 2016). The accountability-related competencies ensure that the school counselor adheres to the comprehensive school counseling program and analyzes data to evaluate programs and initiatives. For example, the standards help guide the school counselor toward self-assessments, peer consultation models, ethical decision-making models, and professional resources for support (ASCA, 2016).

The ASCA Ethical Standards require all school counselors to service all students regardless of background or abilities (ASCA, 2016). Also, school counselors must balance their adherence to confidentiality, their educational duties, and parental rights to be involved in a child's education (ASCA, 2016). Ethical standards for school counselors support effective interventions through school counseling programming, communication of key information related to the outcomes of CSCPs, and engagement in program evaluation. Collectively, school counselors ensure all student needs are being met (2016). Table 1.2 highlights the important differences between the current edition and the previous edition of the ASCA National Model, particularly in its emphasis on promoting data-driven school counselors.

Multi-Tiered Systems of Support

As the school counseling profession continues to evolve, we see school counselors becoming more involved in the Multi-Tiered Systems of Support (MTSS) approach to serving students. Our readers may be wondering why we are covering MTSS in a book devoted to assessment and data collection. Sugai et al. (2019) explained clearly, "School counselors who engage in MTSS expand their influence at the individual level through enhanced universal screening, progress monitoring, and selection and use of evidence-based counseling practices" (p. 2). There is a direct connection to our readers' work between the CSCP and MTSS approaches that intertwine programming, assessments, and data collection.

TABLE 1.2 ASCA NATIONAL MODEL LANGUAGE AND CONTENT SHIFT, FROM ACCOUNTABILITY TO ASSESS

<table>
<tr><td colspan="3">ASSESS (PREVIOUSLY ACCOUNTABILITY)
This component has been renamed to emphasize the ongoing formative assessment of the school counseling program to inform improvement to the design implementation of a school counseling program.
The fourth edition includes two sections:
▪ Program Assessment
▪ School counselor Assessment and Appraisal</td></tr>
<tr><th>THIRD EDITION TOPICS</th><th>FOURTH EDITION SECTION</th><th>FOURTH EDITION TOPICS</th></tr>
<tr><td>Program Assessment Analysis</td><td>Program Assessment</td><td>School Counseling Program Assessment Template
This assessment has been streamlined and simplified. It is designed to help school counselors assess their progress toward the design and delivery of a comprehensive school counseling program.</td></tr>
<tr><td>Results Reports</td><td>Program Assessment</td><td>Annual Results Reports
1. Classroom and Group Mindsets & Behaviors Results Report Analysis
2. Closing-the-Gap Results Reports Analysis
Tips are presented for analyzing participation, Mindsets & Behaviors and outcome data collected for these reports each year.</td></tr>
<tr><td rowspan="2">Results Reports</td><td>Program Assessment</td><td>Data Over Time
Tips are presented for analyzing achievement, attendance and discipline date over multiple years.</td></tr>
<tr><td>Program Assessment</td><td>Reporting Program Results
Tips are presented for sharing data about the impact of the school counseling program on achievement, attendance and discipline.</td></tr>
<tr><td>School Counselor Competencies Assessment</td><td>School Counselor Assessment and Appraisal</td><td>ASCA School Counselor Professional Standards & Competencies Assessment (2019)
The assessment is self-report of the acquisition of mindsets and behaviors school counselor need to meet the school counseling profession's rigorous demands and pre-K–12–student's needs.</td></tr>
<tr><td>School Counselor Performance Appraisal</td><td>School Counselor Assessment and Appraisal</td><td>School Counselor Performance Appraisal Template
The template for school counselor performance appraisal has been updated. It has been expanded to include examples of artifacts school counselors can present to demonstrate how they have met each standard.</td></tr>
</table>

Reprinted with permission from the American School Counselor Association.

For an in-depth exploration of MTSS, we have included *The School Counselor's Guide to Multi-Tiered Systems of Support* (Goodman-Scott et al., 2019) in our additional readings list. This edited book includes a comprehensive approach to the role of school counselors and MTSS. Our goal within this chapter is to briefly summarize MTSS, the school counselor's role, and the connection to your CSCP.

ASCA (2018b) argues that the National Model should be a framework for school counselors as they navigate their school community to help every student within their system succeed. School counselors have direct involvement with their administrators, teachers, and other key stakeholders. A way to ensure that school counselors are involved in a whole-team approach is through the collaborative implementation of MTSS (ASCA, 2018b).

There are three tiers of support within the MTSS approach. Directionally speaking, all students start at Tier 1 (primary level) receiving universal, classroom-based lessons from the school counselor that are connected to the overall needs identified in your CSCP. These needs are often found through school-wide needs assessments. In Tier 2 (secondary level), students who have been identified as needing additional supports receive small-group interventions or individual meetings from the school counselor. In Tier 3 (tertiary level), students could receive additional small-group interventions, short-term counseling, and/or coordination for additional outside counseling services. For an in-depth exploration of Tier 1, Tier 2, and Tier 3 interventions for school counselors, we have included *Hatching Results for Secondary School Counseling: Implementing Core Curriculum, Individual Student Planning, and Other Tier One Activities* (Hatch et al., 2019a) and *Hatching Tier Two and Three Interventions in Your Elementary School Counseling Program* (Hatch et al., 2019b) and to our recommended reading list. Hatch et al. created both of the aforementioned books to support school counselors serving students through each tier.

While we have outlined the three tiers of support within the MTSS approach, many professionals often still refer to Response to Intervention (RtI) aside from MTSS and generally apply RtI only to core academics. However, it is important to think of RtI as support services housed within MTSS that are applicable to how school counselors serve students. The most common language used to explain Tier 1 is primary level, universal interventions, universal instruction, core instructional interventions, or core classroom instruction, which means services that are intended for all students. Tier 1 involves the careful selection of evidence-based programs to support all students based on the available school-wide data or data that have been collected from needs assessments. The MTSS team would work together to select the best school-wide, evidence-based universal screener before implementation (Sugai et al., 2019). Later, in Chapter 4, we will discuss instruments that you may consider utilizing for screening, intervention, or programmatic decision-making. The MTSS team would review the school-wide data to make informed decisions on what programming is most appropriate. For example, if behavioral data show about 60% of office referrals stemmed from peer conflicts, peer fights and the needs assessment data show that 85% of the student population reports that peer conflicts, bullying, and peer relationships are a concern for students, this information would help the MTSS team narrow their focus on school-wide curriculum that supports peer relationships to help reduce peer conflicts and bullying. After implementation of the evidence-based curriculum, the MTSS team would assess the effectiveness of the program. Ideally, the team would see a decrease in office referrals for peer conflicts and physical altercations, as well as additional data on students' perceptions of peer relationships.

The second level of service is Tier 2; this level involves targeted interventions for students, often in small-group format. School counselors would collaborate in MTSS Tier 2 meetings to help identify students who are at risk and would benefit from additional targeted services (Olsen, 2019). Typically, these meetings occur on a regular basis and each member has an established role. The team members depend on the unique school system and involve members who bring key levels of expertise and skills (Olsen, 2019). I [Jenna] recall a situation where I organized an agenda and ensured that meetings stayed on track for my role as the school counselor on an MTSS team. Our principal would provide updates on school-wide data and any directives coming from the district office. Our two RtI teachers would provide updates on students currently being served in Tier 2 intervention groups for reading and math. Our school psychologist was involved to collaborate and provide consultation related to Tier 2 behavioral support. Additionally, our instructional coach helped bridge the gap between support services inside and outside of the classroom.

Olsen (2019) highlighted that school counselors can benefit from serving in this role as it aligns with our scope and practice, but it is important to address potential limitations when caseloads fall outside of the recommended 1:250 ratio. At the time, I had a caseload of 600 students as the sole elementary school counselor. The work I provided within Tier 2 seemed like an additional set of workload tasks. However, as time went on, the benefits of being actively involved in data review and decisions related to supporting at-risk students continued to outweigh the feelings of overload. In addition to selecting students for Tier 2 services, we should consider what other academic or behavioral services are needed for our students. For example, by serving on the Tier 2 meetings for students who qualified for Tier 2 reading supports, I noticed roughly 60% of those students were being referred to my office either by self-referral, teacher referral, or parent referral for feelings of performance anxiety.

My participation in the MTSS process directly influenced my CSCP and allowed me to examine my own data and see a connection to our academic Tier 2 data. Noticing this connection through the data, I sought out a therapy dog, Reese, who volunteered in our school along with her human mom, Debbie, to provide small-group reading support. Our students would actively read aloud to our therapy dog. Reese would simultaneously support the students' uneasy feelings associated with reading, which in turn built their reading confidence and growth. I am happy to report that Reese is still actively involved in the school counseling program long after my departure from the school. I share this example to demonstrate the substantial impact of data-driven school counseling practices on student outcomes. The example shows that we can continue to grow in our school counseling approaches by examining our existing data and recognizing that MTSS can be a valuable tool to support this growth.

School counselors also play a critical role in supporting students in Tier 3, which is known as the tertiary level or as intensive interventions. While this tier supports a small percentage of students within a school, services provided at this level are often quite intensive and individualized. Often, when we think of Tier 3, we might find ourselves positioned as a coordinator or advocate for services such as special education or community-based services. Advocating for students needing Tier 3 services involves looking at individual student data. School counselors attending student intervention team meetings to ensure students receive initial services is not sufficient. Students in these situations have most likely received previous interventions, but the data have shown a halt or decline in academic or behavioral progress. The school counselor's involvement through the MTSS team is critical because they may have experience with the parents or teachers who may have been resistant to qualifying the student for services. Our understanding of the data can help us advocate on behalf of the student to bridge the gap and help other key stakeholders make sense of the data.

We highlighted MTSS within this chapter to show the reader that it is a tool within the school system that uses the current data while providing a collaborative framework for collecting additional assessment data. School counselors' involvement in MTSS allows them to continue to improve CSCPs to meet student needs. The concept of MTSS is widely taught and understood by educators and administrators. However, an extension of this system that is unique to school counselors is that of the Multi-Tiered, Multi-Domain Systems of Support (MTMDSS), which was developed by Dr. Trish Hatch.

Multi-Tiered, Multi-Domain Systems of Support

Trish Hatch developed the Multi-tiered, Multi-domain Systems of Support (MTMDSS; 2017). The MTMDSS compliments the academic and behavioral focus of the MTSS model but extends the previously discussed model to include the career domain and to align with the role of the school counselor. This model recognizes the critical role that school counselors play in collaborating with key stakeholders through the MTSS process, while also integrating their unique role and responsibilities as a service provider (Hatch, 2017). Throughout Hatch's MTMDSS framework, the same tiered system is used to highlight the data collection related roles of the school counselor within each tier. Thus, Hatch (2017) explains which data should be used by school counselors to inform their programing.

School Safety

Continuing the conversation of MTSS and MTMDSS, it is important for us to discuss Positive Behavioral Interventions and Supports (PBIS) and Social and Emotional Learning (SEL) in relation to school safety. School counselors play a critical role in the assessment of crisis and trauma, which also contribute to the implementation of a CSCP that meets the needs of its students. The ASCA's position statement related to school safety and school crises highlights a direct connection not only to provide students with services, but also to be an active member of school safety planning (ASCA, 2019c).

In this position statement, ASCA also briefly mentions the importance of risk assessment screenings, while including a note of caution. The statement encourages school counselors to reference their ethical standards (ASCA, 2019c). Specifically, Standard A.9.b states that school counselors who choose to use a risk assessment must ensure that they report the information to parents in an accurate manner. This standard certifies that parents fully understand any assessed risk level and reinforces that school counselors always communicate the results of the risk assessment despite the findings (ASCA, 2016). When school counselors administer risk screeners or partner with school-based mental health providers to administer risk assessments, it is critical that they adhere to the ASCA Ethical Standards for the safety and well-being of students and faculty alike. Additionally, these ethical standards call for the implementation of valid and reliable assessments (ASCA, 2016). In a position statement about suicide risk assessments, ASCA reinforces the use of valid and reliable assessments in connection with school-wide screening programs, which are most often determined by departments of education for each state or by the local school district (ASCA, 2020d).

A PBIS framework is a school-wide system for supporting students' behavior. This framework provides a behavioral system for both rewarding desirable behaviors while managing undesirable behaviors through a whole-school approach. The goal is to help students increase their positive behaviors inside and outside of the classroom through adopting a school-wide acronym that concisely communicates the desired behaviors. It is important for school counselors to have an active role in the design, delivery, and management of their school's PBIS program. Goodman-Scott (2014) highlighted an elementary school that adopted the PBIS framework and demonstrated the process for rewarding positive behavior while addressing negative behavior and provided a list of classroom-managed behaviors and office-managed behaviors through examples.

In addition to the PBIS framework, data collection is a critical component used to keep track of the office referrals. For example, after reviewing PBIS data, a local elementary school found that office referrals increased around school breaks (Goodman-Scott, 2014). By analyzing this data, the PBIS team planned to increase their encouragement of positive behaviors through their reward system (2014). School counselors have an active role in analyzing the data collected through the PBIS framework. In Chapter 4, you are introduced to examples of assessments that you may consider administering with respect to student behavior and social–emotional development. These assessments are what enable school counselors to advocate for students at both the school and individual levels.

Utilizing SEL standards is fundamental in helping to support the holistic growth of all students. These standards have started to grab the attention of many state educational systems. For example, in 2019, the Ohio Department of Education (ODE) released statewide SEL standards aimed at supporting kindergarten through twelfth-grade students within developmentally age-appropriate bands.

The ODE recognized the connection of the new SEL standards with the need for trauma-informed schools. Thus, the ODE encouraged districts to evaluate current policies and procedures to remove SEL barriers for students (Ohio Department of Education [ODE], 2019a, 2019b). Additionally, districts are encouraged to include trauma-informed practices as a part of the Ohio Improvement Process (OIP). The OIP is coupled with the SEL standards and uses a PBIS framework (ODE, 2019c). Other states have also adopted a similar approach to SEL with a nationwide trend of school counselors actively seeking SEL assessments for their CSCPs.

When searching for assessments related to SEL standards, CASEL is a common web-based resource that provides free access to *Measuring SEL: Using Data Inspired Practice* (www.measuringsel.casel.org). This interactive guide walks users through selecting, preparing, assessing, and using SEL assessment data. Some of the assessments provided in this catalog have a cost associated with them, but others are free to use. Regardless of cost, the resources within the CASEL guide directly link to the program goals within your CSCP.

It is important that school counselors consider statewide and district-wide initiatives for school safety screeners, PBIS supports, and SEL standards. School counselors must also ensure their direct role of meeting student needs. School counselors can better ensure that student needs are being met by taking an active role in data collection, assessment, and analysis in connection with CSCPs. Additionally, an important component of a school counselor's position is to actively involve parents and caregivers in the assessment process.

School-Based Mental Health Services

School counselors need to understand the collaborative role they have with other school-based mental health providers. Appling et al. (2019) highlighted the value of collaboration between the roles of school counselors and mental health counselors. While there is limited research available about how these roles can actively collaborate together, it remains critical to discuss the possibilities associated with these collaborations as they pertain to assessment. School counselors can make timely and appropriate referrals to school-based mental health counselors using data collection and data analysis. Additionally, school-based mental health providers often have access to valid and reliable assessments or screeners through their agencies. School counselors and school-based mental health counselors can work collaboratively to support students.

Data-Driven Approaches

Currently, systematic, data-driven approaches to school counseling are in alignment within the ASCA National Model to help close the gap within school counseling services (ASCA, 2019a; Lee & Goodnough, 2019). Data-driven practices within the profession of school counseling are related to social justice, equity, and advocacy because implementing a data-driven school counseling practice means that school counselors are creating a more inclusive environment for all students. Opportunities for all students refer to the creation of opportunities that remove systemic barriers that prevent students from reaching their goals. These barriers include physical barriers, school-and district-level policy barriers, economic barriers, and many other forms of systemic barriers. It is important that school counselors continue to grow their data-collection skills to help all students gain access to resources in order to close the barrier gaps (Lee & Goodnough, 2019). We discuss access, attainment, and achievement data in detail in Chapter 2.

Evidence-Based Practice

Mariani and Perhay-Kuba (2019) explain that, "Evidence-based practice (EBP) refers to the utilization of treatments and interventions that have been field-tested and proven to benefit their intended recipients" (p. 267). Evidence-based school counseling refers to interventions (e.g., core curricular classroom lessons, group or individual counseling) that are created with research that demonstrates the intervention's effectiveness. Common questions about EBPs that school counselors ask include: Where do I locate evidence based programming? What costs are associated with evidence-based programming? How do I know if a program is evidence based? Throughout this book, we address these questions and provide some practical examples. We briefly describe the implementation of evidence-based programming. Our primary aim of this text is to provide strategies for how to understand and locate evidence-based programming for your CSCP.

While there can be costs associated with use of evidence-based materials, over the years, we have been able to locate several free, evidence-based programs. There are several useful websites that can be used to find evidence-based school counseling classroom and small-group lessons. A few of our favorites are the *Substance Abuse and Mental Health Services Administration's (SAMHSA) National Registry for Evidence-Based Programs and Practices, The National Child Traumatic Stress Network, The California Evidence-Based Clearinghouse for Child Welfare: Information and Resources for Child Welfare Professionals, and Collaborative for Academic, Social, and Emotional Learning (CASEL).*

It is important to be a critical consumer by seeking the studies that include sample sizes and demographic information to substantiate claims by the intervention creators that a program is evidence based. We suggest asking for this information if it is not readily provided. While it may seem uncomfortable, researchers like to hear from potential consumers because they typically want to promote their work by providing access to users of the programming. Typically, without having access to academic journals, we have often found that journal websites that provide the abstract and/or a "fact sheet" include enough information to help school counselors determine whether the program is evidence based.

Closing the Gap

The use of a CSCP or a data-collection process is important because it can close opportunity and achievement gaps for students. Without utilizing assessments or data collection (e.g., attendance, discipline), school counselors would be unaware of the existing opportunity gaps within their school community. As mentioned earlier, being an active member of MTSS teams and the PBIS process through the use of universal screeners and data collection can help close these gaps.

Professional Development

With appropriate knowledge, training, and computer access, school counselors can find low-cost or no-cost, valid and reliable assessment tools. However, upon graduation, school counselors no longer have access to scholarly journals that are housed in university libraries, thereby limiting their access to valid and reliable assessment instruments. With limited access to scholarly journals where assessments are published, school counselors may not have a budget to purchase valid and reliable instruments. Due to access and financial barriers, school counselors will often create an informal assessment to gather information about the school counseling program. However, these self-created assessments are not empirically tested to ensure that they measure what they were created to measure (i.e., if the measure is internally valid). School counselors often claim that they must create their own assessments because of budget constraints. It would be nearly impossible to argue that budget deficits will be resolved in the near future. Thus, it is important for school counselors to seek out professional development opportunities to learn about low-cost or no-cost assessment tools that may be implemented within their CSCP.

These instruments are often structured around the following populations and needs: students, school counselors, school counseling programs, faculty and staff, and school climate. Low-cost or no-cost assessments for these audiences and their respective needs allow school counselors to facilitate data-driven, evidence-based programs that align with the standards outlined by ASCA. Astramovich (2016) found that skill, interest, training importance, and confidence were higher in school counselors who previously engaged in professional development related to program evaluation. Additionally, Astramovich proposed having mentorship focus on data because it could help school counselors feel more confident in their abilities and continue to develop their skills. It is our intention that as you move through the chapters of this book, we can support your professional development and efforts to implement data-driven CSCPs.

The low-cost or no-cost assessments available in this book use appropriate terminology, acknowledge the gaps in training, and assess and discuss the time needed to conduct the assessments. The assessments are focused on the practice and scope of school counselors. We know that school counselors are faced with large caseloads and limited budgets. Thus, school counselors might feel the pressure to create assessments themselves that have not been tested for validity and reliability. Further, time is often unavailable to school counselors, given the added demands of statewide testing and other expectations imposed by school administration. In all honesty, most school counselors have inadequate time to search for low-cost or no-cost assessments, which continues to leave gaps in the professional practice of implementing data-driven, evidence-based school counseling programs. We strived for a holistic approach to assessments and data collection throughout this book to help you further develop your CSCP with confidence.

It is important to note that a variety of valid and reliable instruments exist to address all domains of the school counselor role: academic, personal/social/emotional, and career. This book provides some basics on instrument selection, but the central focus is to highlight measures that support students. The following assessments were selected to inform school counselors of relevant and available low-cost or no-cost assessment options. Each of these measures covers a different domain within the ASCA National Model to strengthen the use of valid and reliable instruments by school counselors (ASCA, 2019a).

How to Use This Book to Support Your Own Development

This book is consistent with current school counseling literature and will be of interest to school counselors, school counselor trainees, and school counselor educators who wish to learn more about data-driven CSCPs. Several studies have concluded that school counselors value the importance of program evaluation (Astramovich, 2016; Maras et al., 2013; Young & Kaffenberger, 2015) and training associated with effective school counseling programs (Astramovich, 2016). The remaining chapters seek to meet the needs of school counselors, such as those aiming to improve their school counseling program in data-driven, comprehensive ways. Our intention is for this book to be used as a guide in supporting your assessment-focused, data-driven CSCPs. As highlighted within this chapter, we feel it is important for school counselors to have access to valid and reliable assessments.

While this chapter focused on providing the foundational knowledge about the school counseling profession and how the educational environment has become data driven, we hope that this is just the beginning of your data-driven journey. As you progress through the chapters of this book, we hope to shape your competence and confidence in making data-driven decisions as you create and implement your CSCPs.

Additional Readings

Goodman-Scott, E., Betters-Bubon, J., & Donohue, P. (Eds.). (2019). *The school counselor's guide to multi-tiered systems of support*. Routledge.

Hatch, T., Kruger, A., & Pablo, N. (2019a). *Hatching tier two and three interventions in your elementary school counseling program*. Corwin.

Hatch, T., Triplett, W., Duarte, D., & Gomez, V. (2019b). *Hatching results for secondary school counseling: Implementing core curriculum, individual student planning, and other tier one activities*. Corwin.

Key Points

- Valid and reliable assessments, school-wide screeners through MTSS, and school data (e.g., state report card, attendance, and discipline) enhance the advocacy efforts of school counselors and help ensure positive student outcomes.
- Valid and reliable assessments can help school counselors select appropriate classroom and small-group evidence-based curricula.
- Data collection can shape how to develop and implement a CSCP.
- School counselors play an important role in data collection through their involvement with MTSS, PBIS, and other collaborative partnerships.

Questions for Reflection

- How has the history of school counseling shaped our approach to data collection, assessments, and the practice of school counseling?
- As a school counselor, what is your role in the MTSS team in relation to data collection and assessment?
- How can school counselors use assessments to effectively select curriculum, support students, and shape advocacy work to meet student needs?
- What ethical considerations are involved in using valid and reliable assessments as part of your school counseling practice?

References

American Academy of Pediatrics. (2020, June 25). *COVID-19 planning considerations: Guidance for school re-entry* [Press release]. https://services.aap.org/en/pages/2019-novel-coronavirus-covid-19-infections/clinical-guidance/covid-19-planning-considerations-return-to-in-person-education-in-schools/

American School Counselor Association. (n.d.). School reentry: The school counselor's role. *School Counseling Standards in Practice,* 1–10. https://www.schoolcounselor.org/getmedia/0034bb80-bd49-418c-9e17-d5bfdb5521da/SIP-School-Reentry.pdf

American School Counselor Association. (2012). *ASCA national model: A framework for school counseling programs* (3rd ed.). American School Counselor Association.

American School Counselor Association. (2016). *ASCA ethical standards for school counselors.* https://www.schoolcounselor.org/getmedia/f041cbd0-7004-47a5-ba01-3a5d657c6743/Ethical-Standards.pdf

American School Counselor Association. (2017). *The school counselor and school counseling programs.* https://www.schoolcounselor.org/Standards-Positions/Position-Statements/ASCA-Position-Statements/The-School-Counselor-and-School-Counseling-Program

American School Counselor Association. (2018a). *ASCA school counselor professional standards and competencies.*

American School Counselor Association. (2018b). *The school counselor and multitiered system of supports.* https://www.schoolcounselor.org/Standards-Positions/Position-Statements/ASCA-Position-Statements/The-School-Counselor-and-Multitiered-System-of-Sup

American School Counselor Association. (2019a). *ASCA national model: A framework for school counseling programs* (4th ed.). American School Counselor Association.

American School Counselor Association. (2019b). *ASCA school counselor professional standards and competencies.* https://www.schoolcounselor.org/getmedia/a8d59c2c-51de-4ec3-a565-a3235f3b93c3/SC-Competencies.pdf

American School Counselor Association. (2019c). *The school counselor and safe schools and crisis response.* https://www.schoolcounselor.org/Standards-Positions/Position-Statements/ASCA-Position-Statements/The-School-Counselor-and-Safe-Schools-and-Crisis-R

American School Counselor Association. (2020a). *The school counselor and school counseling preparation programs.* https://www.schoolcounselor.org/Standards-Positions/Position-Statements/ASCA-Position-Statements/The-School-Counselor-and-School-Counseling-Prepara

American School Counselor Association. (2020b, July). *About ASCA*. https://www.schoolcounselor.org/About-ASCA/Vision,-Mission-Goals

American School Counselor Association. (2020c). *ASCA toolkit: Virtual elementary school counseling*. https://www.schoolcounselor.org/Publications-Research/Publications/Free-ASCA-Resources/COVID-19-Resources/Virtual-Elementary-School-Counseling

American School Counselor Association. (2020d). *The school counselor and suicide risk assessment*. https://www.schoolcounselor.org/Standards-Positions/Position-Statements/ASCA-Position-Statements/The-School-Counselor-and-Suicide-Risk-Assessment

American School Counselor Association, & National Association of School Psychologists. (n.d.). *School reentry considerations supporting student social and emotional learning and mental and behavioral health amidst COVID-19*. https://www.schoolcounselor.org/getmedia/44fe18dc-6a97-4644-950d-0799d94caaa1/School-Reentry.pdf

Appling, B. M., Tuttle, M., & May, V. S. (2019). The experiences of school counselors who collaborate with clinical mental health counselors. *Professional School Counseling*, *23*(1), 1–10. https://doi.org/10.1177/2156759X19882660

Astramovich, R. L. (2016). Program evaluation interest and skills of school counselors. *Professional School Counseling*, *20*(1), 54–64. https://doi.org/10.5330/1096-2409-20.1.54

Astramovich, R. L., Coker, J. K., & Hoskins, W. J. (2005). Training school counselors in program evaluation. *Professional School Counseling*, *9*(1), 49–54. https://doi.org/10.5330/prsc.9.1.80442r1q5n29x546

Clemens, E. V., Carey, J. C., & Harrington, K. M. (2010). The School Counseling Program Implementation survey: Initial instrument development and exploratory factor analysis. *Professional School Counseling*, *14*(2), 125–134. https://doi.org/10.1177/2156759X100140020

Collaborative for Academic, Social, and Emotional Learning. (2020). *Reunite, renew, and thrive: Social and emotional learning (SEL) roadmap for reopening school*. https://casel.org/wp-content/uploads/2020/12/SEL-ROADMAP.20.pdf

Council for Accreditation of Counseling and Related Educational Programs. (2015). *2016 CACREP standards*. https://www.cacrep.org/for-programs/2016-cacrep-standards/

Council for the Accreditation of Educator Preparation. (2020, July). *American school counselor association*. http://caepnet.org/accreditation/caep-accreditation/spa-standards-and-report-forms/asca

Davis, K. M., Chang, C. Y., & McGlothlin, J. M. (2005). Teaching assessment and appraisal: Humanistic strategies and activities for counselor educators. *Journal of Humanistic Counseling, Education and Development*, *44*(1), 94–101. https://doi.org/10.1002/j.2164-490x.2005.tb00059.x

Dollarhide, C. T., & Saginak, K. A. (2017). *Comprehensive school counseling programs: K-12 delivery systems in action* (3rd ed.). Pearson.

Erford, B. T. (2019). Becoming a professional school counselor: Current perspectives, historical roots, and future challenges. In B. T. Erford (Ed.), *Transforming the school counseling profession* (5th ed., pp. 1–25). Pearson.

Eschenauer, R., & Chen-Hayes, S. F. (2005). The transformative individual school counselor model: An accountability model for urban school counselors. *Professional School Counselor*, *8*(3), 244–248. https://www.jstor.org/stable/42732465

Goodman-Scott, E. (2014). Maximizing school counselors' efforts by implementing school-wide positive behavioral interventions and supports: A case study from the field. *Professional School Counselor*, *17*(1), 111–119. https://doi.org/10.1177/2156759X0001700106

Goodman-Scott E., Betters-Bubon, J., & Donohue, P. (Eds.). (2019). *The school counselor's guide to multi-tiered systems of support*. Routledge.

Goodrich, K. M., Kingsley, K. V., & Sands, H. C. (2020). Digitally responsive school counseling across the ASCA national model. *International Journal for the Advancement of Counseling*, *42*, 147–158. https://doi.org/10.1007/s10447-020-09396-9

Hatch, T. (2017, March 8). Multi-tiered, multi-domain system of supports. *Hatching Results*. https://www.hatchingresults.com/blog/2017/3/multi-tiered-multi-domain-system-of-supports-by-trish-hatch-phd

Hatch, T., Kruger, A., & Pablo, N. (2019a). *Hatching tier two and three interventions in your elementary school counseling program*. Corwin.

Hatch, T., Triplett, W., Duarte, D., & Gomez, V. (2019b). *Hatching results for secondary school counseling: Implementing core curriculum, individual student planning, and other tier one activities*. Corwin.

Lee, V. V., & Goodnough, G. E. (2019). Systemic, data-driven school counseling practice and programming for equity. In B. T. Erford (Ed.), *Transforming the school counseling profession* (5th ed., pp. 67–93). Pearson.

Maras, M. A., Coleman, S. L., Gysbers, N. C., Herman, K. C., & Stanley, B. (2013). Measuring evaluation competency among school counselors. *Counseling Outcome Research and Evaluation, 4*(2), 99–111. https://doi.org/10.1177/2150137813494765

Mariani, M., & Perhay-Kuba, S. (2019). Evidence-based practices across MTSS. In E. Goodman-Scott, J. Betters-Bubon, & P. Donohue (Eds.), *The school counselor's guide to multi-tiered systems of support* (pp. 267–297). Routledge.

Mariani, M., Villares, E., Sink, C. A., Colvin, K., & Kuba, S. P. (2015). Confirming the structural validity of the My Class Inventory—Short Form Revised. *Professional School Counseling, 19*(1), 92–102. https://doi.org/10.5330/1096-2409-19.1.92

Nelson, M. D., & Tarabochia, D. S. (2020). A primer on designing a school counseling curriculum. *Journal of School Counseling, 18*(6), 1–26. ERIC. https://eric.ed.gov/contentdelivery/servlet/ERICServlet?accno=EJ1241835

Neukrug, E., Peterson, C. H., Bonner, M., & Lomas, G. I. (2013). A national survey of assessment instruments taught by counselor educators. *Counselor Education & Supervision, 52*, 207–221. https://doi.org/10.1002/j.1556-6978.2013.00038.x

Ohio Department of Education. (2016, May). *Ohio school counselor evaluation model.* http://education.ohio.gov/getattachment/Topics/Career-Tech/Career-Connections/Resources-for-School-Counselors/School-Counselor-Standards-and-Evaluation/OSCES-Model.pdf.aspx

Ohio Department of Education. (2019a, June). *Trauma-informed schools and social emotional learning.* https://www.education.ohio.gov/getattachment/Topics/Learning-in-Ohio/Social-and-Emotional-Learning/Social-and-Emotional-Learning-Standards/Trauma-Informed-Schools-and-SEL.pdf.aspx?lang=en-US

Ohio Department of Education. (2019b, June). *Ohio's K-12 social and emotional learning standards.* http://www.education.ohio.gov/getattachment/Topics/Learning-in-Ohio/Social-and-Emotional-Learning/Social-and-Emotional-Learning-Standards/K-12-SEL-Standards-Full-Final.pdf.aspx?lang=en-US

Ohio Department of Education. (2019c, November). *Positive behavioral interventions and supports and social-emotional learning.* http://www.education.ohio.gov/getattachment/Topics/Learning-in-Ohio/Social-and-Emotional-Learning/District-and-Building-Social-Emotional-Learning/PBIS-and-SEL-Comm-Reviewed.pdf.aspx?lang=en-US

Olsen, J. (2019). Providing support for students with elevated needs. In E. Goodman-Scott, J. Betters-Bubon, & P. Donohue (Eds.). *The school counselor's guide to multi-tiered systems of support* (pp. 133–162). Routledge.

Perera-Diltz, D. M., & Mason, K. M. (2010). An exploration of accountability practices of school counselors: A national study. *Journal of Professional Counseling: Practice, Theory, and Research, 38*(1), 52–70. https://doi.org/10.1080/15566382.2010.12033866

Scarborough, J. L. (2005). The School Counselor Activity Rating: An instrument for gathering process data. *Professional School Counseling, 8*(3), 274–283. https://www.jstor.org/stable/42732469

Sink, C. A. (2009). School counselors as accountability leaders: Another call for action. *Professional School Counseling, 13*(2), 68–74. https://www.jstor.org/stable/23801087

Sink, C. A., & Spencer, L. R. (2005). My Class Inventory-Short Form as an accountability tool for elementary school counselors to measure classroom climate. *Professional School Counseling, 9*(1), 37–48. https://doi.org/10.1177/2156759X0500900112

Sink, C. A., & Spencer, L. R. (2007). Teacher version of the My Class Inventory-Short form: An accountability tool for elementary school counselors. *Professional School Counseling, 11*(2), 129–139. https://doi.org/10.5330/psc.n.2010-11.129

Strear, M., Duffy, H., & Sunde, A. (2021). *When schools go dark, school counselors shine: School counseling during a global pandemic.* American Institutes for Research. https://www.air.org/sites/default/files/When-Schools-Go-Dark-School-Counselors-Shine-Feb-2021.pdf

Sugai, G., La Salle, T. P., Everett, S., & Feinberg, A. B. (2019). Multi-Tiered systems of support: The what, why, and the how for school counselor. In E. Goodman-Scott, J. Betters-Bubon, & P. Donohue (Eds.), *The school counselor's guide to multi-tiered systems of support* (pp. 1–28). Routledge.

Tadlock-Marlo, R. L., Zyromski, B., Asner-Self, K. K., & Sheng, Y. (2013). One school, many differences: An assessment tool for school counselors and multicultural counseling. *International Journal for the Advancement of Counseling, 35*(3), 234–250. https://doi.org/10.1007/s10447-012-9179-z. ERIC. https://eric.ed.gov/?id=EJ1037313

Wong, K. (2018, March 27). *Re: ASCA/ACA relationship update* [electronic mailing list message].

Young, A., & Kaffenberger, C. (2015). School counseling professional development: Assessing the use of data to inform school counseling services. *Professional School Counseling, 19*(1), 46–56. https://doi.org/10.5330/1096-2409-19.1.46

Zyromski, B., Hudson, T. B., Baker, E., & Granello, D. H. (2019). Guidance counselors or school counselors: How the name of the profession influences perceptions of competence. *Professional School Counseling, 22*(1), 1–10. https://doi.org/10.1177/2156759X19855654

Zyromski, B., & Mariani, M. A. (2019). Connect the dots: Using a logic model to connect goals with interventions, evaluation strategies, and outcomes. *Professional School Counseling, 22*(1b), 1–11. https://doi.org/10.1177/2156759X19834445

2

THE PROCESS OF ASSESSMENT AND DATA COLLECTION

The Process of Assessment and Data Collection

The process of assessment and data collection has evolved over the years in the profession of school counseling. As school counselors, our caseloads and other responsibilities may make the entire process of administering assessments and collecting data feel daunting. However, assessments and data collection greatly support our efforts with students and can help when 80% of our time is spent directly with students and 20% is spent on indirect or administrative tasks. For example, needs assessments help inform how we will spend our time serving students in the classroom, in small groups, and individually. A needs assessment allows school counselors to gather various perspectives from students, staff, teachers, and parents. Needs assessments permit school counselors to collect and analyze data to determine the best pathways to use to meet the unique needs of their school. The latest edition of the *American School Counselor Association (ASCA) National Model (Fourth Edition)* (ASCA, 2019a) takes this into account because updates to the model include greater shifts to incorporating data within lesson plans. The lesson plan template of the National Model includes a section called *Data Collection Plan,* which prompts the school counselor to collect what are known as *participation data, mindsets & behaviors data,* and *outcome data* (American School Counselor Association [ASCA], 2019a). Additionally, the model has an undertone of administrative language. The administrative tone is not meant to take away from the school counselor's role, but our opinion is that the tone helps school counselors communicate with their school administration. In fact, the administrative tone helps us speak their language while still holding true to our identity as school counselors.

In this chapter, we further explore how assessments and data collection go hand-in-hand. We focus on general types of assessments and discuss the intent of assessments for student behaviors as they are connected to academic, career, social–emotional learning. Our goal is to provide examples in each of these categories to support your understanding of the purpose of assessments and how to incorporate assessments into your practice. Additionally, we discuss the process of data collection related to working with administration, as well as best practices for incorporating data collection into your comprehensive school counseling program (CSCP).

Further, we explore data analysis, data interpretation, and meaningful ways to share these data with key stakeholders. We continue to examine the ASCA ethical standards in relation to administering assessments, collecting data, and disseminating data with key stakeholders. As we continue to learn more about the relevance of assessments and data collection, it is important to examine our roles and responsibilities as they pertain to the ASCA Professional Standards

& Competencies. Chapter 2 focuses on providing readers with a pragmatic understanding of the importance of a school counselor's purpose for collecting, interpreting, and applying data.

Relevance of Assessment and Data Collection

School counselors are uniquely positioned to use data (e.g., data from the pandemic, data regarding racial injustices, or data on remote learning) to create or select programing that meets the needs of their students. As Dollarhide and Saginak (2017) stated, "Data is everywhere. This is great news for school counselors who use data to show effectiveness and impact within the school" (p. 177). Valid and reliable assessments help inform our school counseling practice in meaningful ways by providing us with additional data sets beyond the standard data sources of attendance, grades, state report cards, discipline, and graduation rates. Assessments can help us confirm "gut feelings" related to the social and emotional needs of students to provide us with critical information related to student safety, wellness, and gained knowledge or skills. There are two main categories of assessment: formal and informal. Both types of assessments have strengths and limitations. We explore these assessment types along with practical examples offered for school counselors.

Valid and reliable assessments help inform our school counseling practice in meaningful ways by providing us with additional data sets beyond the standard data sources of attendance, grades, state report cards, discipline, and graduation rates.

Formal Assessments

Formal assessments are validated instruments that are normed to a specific population and designed to provide us with specific information regarding what they were designed to measure. Typically, in the educational setting, formal assessments are based on particular subject areas or skills (e.g., reading, math, social studies, and science) and are related to student performance. Statewide achievement tests are one example of a formal school-based assessment. These assessments have questions that have been field tested and measured before being administered to the general population of students. For example, as a school counselor, I [Jenna] remember helping to support several pilot versions of the computer-based, state-wide assessments for third grade. My district and school were selected among others to pilot these new assessments. While it is common to immediately think standardized testing when you hear formal assessments, it is important to stress that there are different types of formal assessments. These assessments also include psychometrics and research to validate the instruments. Some focus on constructs that are more clinical in nature, behavioral, and career focused versus focusing on measuring academics. For example, the Student Risk Screening Scale—Internalizing & Externalizing Behaviors (SRSS-IE) is an assessment that identifies both externalizing and internalizing behaviors of students. The SRSS-IE is completed by teachers every 6 to 8 weeks throughout the school year (Lane & Menzies, 2009). Additionally, the My Class Inventory—Short Form Revised was designed to help school counselors at the elementary level support teachers in measuring classroom and school climate (Sink & Spencer, 2005). Furthermore, the researchers intended for this assessment to help support school counselors in making data-based decisions for their CSCP (Sink & Spencer, 2005). Next, we highlight the strengths and limitations of this type of instrument.

Strengths of Formal Assessments

Formal assessments are often tested and normed with several different groups of students. For example, Mariani et al. (2015) collected and analyzed data to confirm the validity of the My Class Inventory—Short Form Revised, which was originally developed by Sink and Spencer (2005). Sink and Spencer (2007) also created the My Class Inventory—Short Form and Villares et al. (2016) completed a multilevel confirmatory factor analysis (CFA) on the teacher version. Both of these studies were conducted by different researchers to validate the assessments. These formal assessments are very applicable to the practice of school counseling. Later in this book we continue to touch upon the My Class Inventory—Short Form Revised and the Teacher My Class Inventory—Short Form, as well as its application for school counselors.

In addition to formal assessments being normed and tested with large populations of students, formal assessments provide key stakeholders (e.g., teachers, parents, and administration) with objective, evidence-based results. Formal assessments can be delivered in a computer-based format or scored via a computer system, which helps eliminate a higher level of error that might occur with hand-scored formal or informal assessments. The Renaissance Star suite of assessments are commonly used formal assessments in elementary schools. These assessments cover subjects ranging from early literacy to math. These assessments are valid, reliable, and they provide schools with individualized student data reports. The Renaissance Star assessments measure and track growth (Renaissance, 2020a). Further, the Renaissance Star Reading assessment is a computer-based measure that is often used as a district-wide benchmark tool to track student reading growth across grading periods. The goal of this assessment is to gather data to help inform instruction for each individual student (Renaissance, 2019). Renaissance reports that over 100 studies have been conducted on the assessment's ability to predict performance on state tests and is widely used in North American schools (Renaissance, 2020a).

There are other formal assessments that are not solely focused on achievement testing that are important to highlight as they can help the Multi-Tiered Systems of Support (MTSS) team support the whole student (e.g., the health academics, behaviors, etc. of a child). For example, the *My Class Inventory—Short Form Revised* and the *Teacher My Class Inventory—Short Form* are climate-based formal assessments that can be used in combination to gain data regarding teachers' perception, in comparison to the students' perception, on the classroom environment. These findings can help the school counselor and the MTSS team when determining supports or interventions for groups or individual students when there is a discrepancy between academic and behavioral data. Later, we highlight how formal district-wide benchmark assessments, such as the Star Reading assessment, can be coupled with informal assessments to provide school counselors, teachers, and administrators with additional data related to student achievement and progress. Using multiple types of assessments helps teams, such as the MTSS team, review data on individual students to ensure progress is being made, as well as formulate plans when progress has stopped or a decline in progress has been flagged.

Limitations of Formal Assessments

While there are many strengths to formal assessments, there are also limitations. A major limitation of many formal assessments is the cost associated with the administration and scoring of the assessment. For example, the Renaissance Cost Sheet for Ohio Department of Education, highlights a $750 fee per school. Additional costs include an $11.95 per student annual subscription fee with additional individual subscription costs for three different programs, each costing $4.95 per student (Renaissance, 2020b). For example, Middle Town Elementary school has 600 students who use the Star reading program from Renaissance. This means they have a $750 school fee, $7,170 in total student annual subscription fees, and $2,970 in fees for the Star reading program. The total cost for one academic year would be $10,890. Often, the associated costs are due to the research and development of the instrument as it takes time and resources to develop.

Moreover, some formal assessments, like standardized tests, often minimize individual students to a number. Students must hit a certain benchmark score in order to show progress. Therefore, district and state academic achievement assessments, which are used to benchmark students, do not consider important social and emotional factors. If, for example, a student has test anxiety or attention deficit hyperactivity disorder (ADHD), formal achievement tests are not going to take this into account for lower or inconsistent scores. Other formal assessments focused on career or college readiness can also minimize or "box" a student into a certain career path, and do not consider the individual student and their experiences.

Another potential limitation associated with formal assessments is the demographic of the sample population used during the assessment's validity and reliability testing. It is important to take into consideration whether a formal assessment has been validated with a diverse sample population. For instance, there is a current debate about whether the American College Test (ACT), an example of a formal assessment for college admissions, is an actual predictor of success in college. Allensworth and Clark (2020) found that high school grade point average (GPA) was a stronger predictor of successful college completion than ACT scores. The researchers also noted that the location where students attended high school also impacted college completion (Allensworth & Clark, 2020). Recently, a surge of colleges and universities have eliminated the ACT as a requirement for admission. This quickly prompted the ACT organization to issue a statement regarding their relevance. Jaschik (2020) cited both Allensworth and Clark's study and the ACT spokesperson's statement to highlight the importance of including multiple data points when admitting students into college. As school counselors, it is important for us to look at all of the data and not rely on one piece of information. Multiple forms of data can help us make informed decisions and support overall student success.

Informal Assessments

Informal assessments differ from formal assessments as they are not research based nor validated. They are not always created from data that are collected, but rather are created to help gather additional information to better inform decisions made for individual students, small groups, and selection of classroom curriculum. Informal assessments are not normalized through a rigorous process. As their name implies, these assessments are an informal way of gathering information or assessing a situation. Although they are not always data driven, informal assessments are equally valuable in our practice of gathering information about individuals or groups of students. For example, school counselors create informal pre- and posttests to determine what students learned from their engagement in a classroom lesson unit or during a small group.

School counselors often resort to creating their own assessments, as it can be difficult to locate a formal assessment, such as a needs assessment, that is designed to assess the exact needs of their school community. A self-created needs assessment is considered an informal assessment because it is designed by the user to target specific information from stakeholders. When needs assessments are self-created by a practicing school counselor, they have not undergone the rigorous research and validation process. Surveys are another example of informal assessments that are created by school counselors to gauge information from members of the school community. A survey could be created to gather information on what parents want included in a college and career night or a survey could seek input from students on what social–emotional services they would like the school counselor to add to their CSCP.

When coupled with formal assessments, informal assessments can provide an additional layer of insight. As a hypothetical example, Sammy continues to fall below the appropriate grade level on the district-wide Star Reading assessment, which is used to benchmark grade-level progress. Sammy's teacher reports that Sammy is often off task and inattentive. The school counselor could complete a behavioral observation or record the frequency of her behavior via a running record assessment at different times during the week to collect data on the number of times Sammy is off task during a set amount of time.

These running logs could then be compared to Sammy's Star Reading assessment data. This informal assessment is especially helpful if there are inconsistencies in Sammy's scores during the Star Reading assessment. Specifically, if Sammy's scores continue to fluctuate, the informal assessment can help the intervention team determine further steps of support or intervention. This example demonstrates the value of informal assessments, especially in conjunction with formal assessment data.

Strengths of Informal Assessments

Two strengths of informal assessments include their accessibility and lower costs. Running records and behavioral observations are informal assessments that school counselors can either create or quickly locate a template to implement. This flexibility can be a strength for school counselors who have heavy caseloads and limited budgets available to purchase assessments. A portfolio, or a compilation of a student's work, is another type of informal assessment. Students often decide what work should be included in their portfolios. Some schools have students create a portfolio for parent–teacher conferences to facilitate a conversation with parents about their child's academic progress. Portfolios can also be used as informal assessments by school counselors as an option for students to gather information in a flexible and creative way. While informal assessments can be used in conjunction with formal assessments to provide additional information, informal assessments can be used alone to provide meaningful context to a multitude of student behaviors and skills.

Limitations of Informal Assessments

There are several limitations to informal assessments. For example, informal assessments are not always research based or validated. Additionally, not all informal assessments are scored. Informal assessments are often conducted to gather information about the student related to their growth and development outside of academics, whereas formal assessments are often used to benchmark student academic progress on a particular subject area. Informal assessments are often used to inform the selection of appropriate interventions or other data-driven approaches for individual student growth. Informal assessments rely heavily on the person conducting the assessment to properly interpret the observation, because informal assessments do not always have a scoring system associated with them. Additionally, many informal assessments rely on teachers or school counselors to complete them; thus, a higher level of human error may occur, as compared to the computer-based scoring of formal assessments. For example, behavioral observations are often used to gather more information on a student's behavior to help inform their Individualized Education Program (IEP) goals and objectives. Although informal assessments are not scored, or they do not provide normed information to benchmark student progress, informal assessments can provide context to situations that cannot be gathered from a formal assessment.

Purpose of Assessments

It is important for us to discuss the intent of using assessments in our role as school counselors in connection to the ASCA Mindsets and Behaviors for Student Success (ASCA, 2014). In addition to utilizing assessments that align with the ASCA National Model and documents, school counselors also focus on utilizing data to enhance their practice. School counselors need to consider different types of assessments, such as screeners, needs assessments, surveys, and other forms of progress-monitoring tools, when developing their CSCP. School counselors can use multiple forms of assessment and data-collection methods to gather the full picture of what each student, as well as the whole school, needs in order to continue to develop. As school counselors, the intent of implementing assessments into our practice is to inform our work using data to create programing that best supports our students.

Additionally, we assess our current programs for their effectiveness. We have included a flow chart within this section to expand on these ideas and to highlight the process of using assessments within your practice. As noted in the *ASCA National Model (Fourth Edition)*, our role as school counselors is to continually assess our programs to ensure they are working, to provide evidence of necessity of change, and to showcase student growth as a result of their participation in programs provided through a CSCP (ASCA, 2019a). In this section, we discuss the purpose of assessments related to three domains of school counseling: academic development, career development, and social and emotional development (see Figure 2.1).

Academic Development

The ASCA National Model defines academic development as, "Competencies guiding school counseling programs to implement strategies and activities to support and maximize each student's ability to learn" (ASCA, 2019a, p. 4). When we connect this domain and our practices as school counselors to the purpose of assessments, we typically rely on assessments that are already selected by the state or district. We should also use these data to inform our programming for students. Dollarhide and Saginak (2017) explained, "school counselors are experts in using data to identify achievement gaps and students who need additional services in order to succeed academically" (p. 37). As school counselors, it is essential that we, in collaboration with administrators and teachers, examine academic assessment data to determine how our CSCP can support the closing of achievement gaps.

For example, a school-wide universal screener shows that 60% of students in the second grade are struggling with reading comprehension. These data could then be used to search for an evidence-based classroom curriculum that supports students with developing reading comprehension strategies and reading comprehension test-taking skills. The school counselor at this elementary school could collaborate with other members of the school team to develop a plan for addressing this achievement gap. This would be a critical time for a reading comprehension assessment and intervention because many states have a third-grade reading guarantee that are connected to state reading tests. If a student does not pass the state reading test in the third grade, they would have to repeat third grade language arts curriculum. As this example shows, assessment and proper intervention are crucial to supporting student learning. Similarly, the domain of student career development also benefits from the implementation and interpretation of assessments.

Career Development

The career development domain is centered around supporting students at all stages of development with career awareness at the elementary level, to career exploration in middle school, and career planning in high school. At each developmental level, school counselors should help students with career competencies to build awareness and prepare them to make informed decisions. For example, the Sonoma County Office of Education (n.d.) has a document, the *Career Development Continuum: Preparing all Youth for Success in College, Career, and Life*, which outlines awareness, exploration, and preparation into developmentally appropriate activities within in the school, community, and at home. The National Model argues that students must also successfully make this transition from K-12 to the next steps in their educational or vocational pursuits (ASCA, 2019a). The goals for student postsecondary options can be accomplished by implementing formal and informal career assessments, which collectively provide a holistic understanding of students (Niles & Erford, 2019). Assessments for students related to career development reciprocally help school counselors shape their CSCP (Niles & Erford, 2019). Personality-based career inventories and career assessments can help students start the process toward self-discovery. Informal assessments that provide practical experience opportunities can help

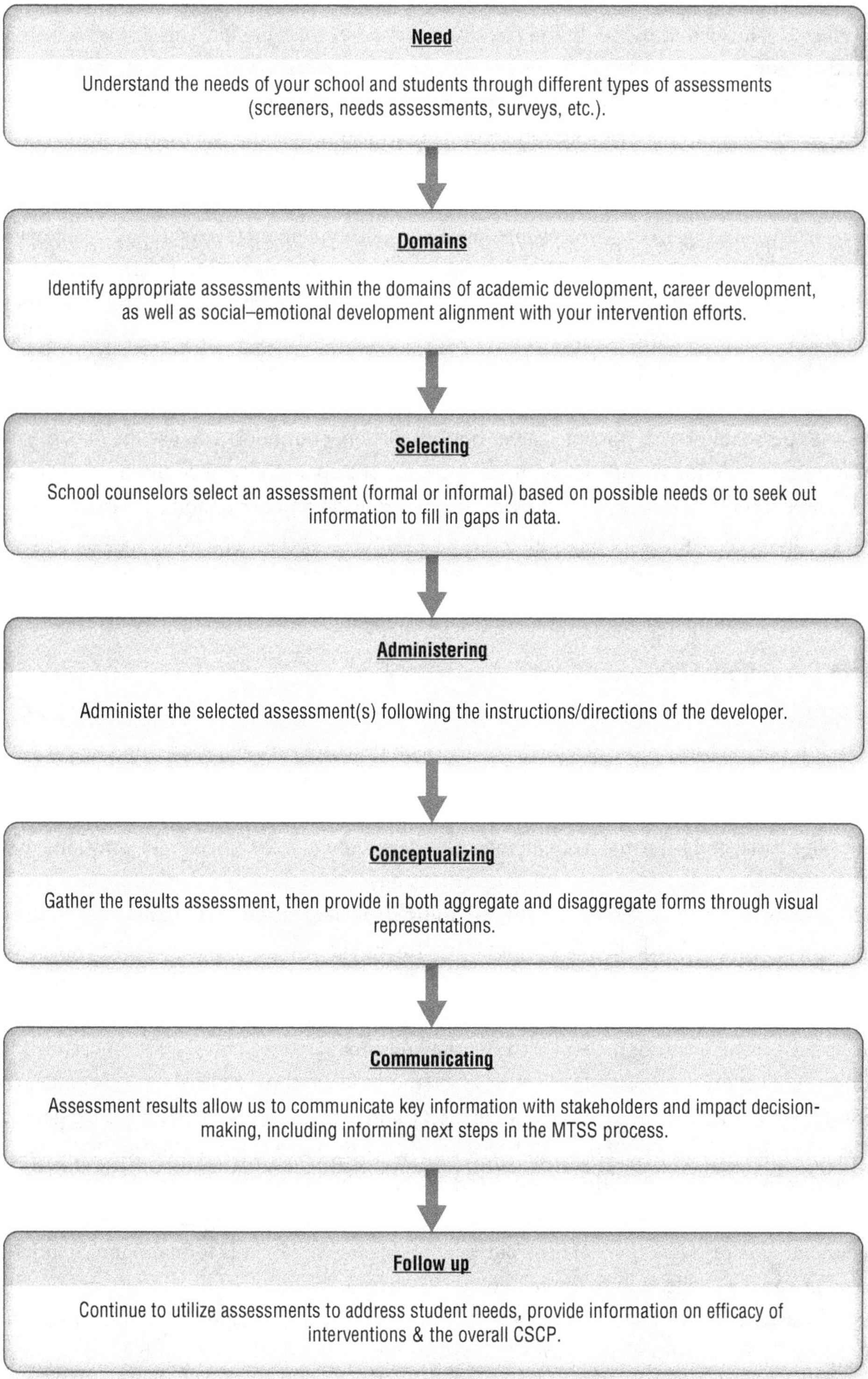

Figure 2.1 School counselor's approach to the process of assessment, which can be best visualized through these steps. CSCP, comprehensive school counseling program; MTSS, Multi-Tiered Systems of Support.

students confirm possible career avenues. For example, students can take a career test called Your Free Career Test (n.d.), located in the tools and resources section of this chapter. This test is an informal assessment that provides students with an opportunity to explore careers and work environments. Since this assessment is not validated, it is considered an informal assessment. Students could follow up a personality inventory with interviews of professionals or job-shadowing experiences in careers that are well suited for them based on the inventory results.

Dozens of career-related inventories will surface via a quick Google search. This information overload can be overwhelming, as the choices may seem endless. One popular personality inventory for the professional workforce is the Myers-Briggs. Another web-based assessment, mentioned by Niles and Erford (2019), is the Self-Directed Search (SDS). This assessment, which currently has a cost associated with it, which can be found within the tools and resources section of this chapter. The SDS is based on John Holland's RIASEC theory, which is based on six personality types: Realistic, Investigative, Artistic, Social, Enterprising, and Conventional (Niles & Erford, 2019; PAR, Inc., 2020). The idea of the SDS is to combine one's personality with possible career options. School counselors can use the SDS to guide career planning with individual students, with small groups of students, or as a component of a classroom lesson. As careers continuously evolve, the way we approach career curriculum and assessments needs to adjust. Furthermore, we should intentionally challenge our knowledge growth of career assessments. In addition to academic and career assessments, we also want to emphasize social and emotional development of assessments.

Social and Emotional Development

This section focuses on the intent of assessments connected to the social and emotional development domain in the ASCA National Model. Our professional organization, ASCA, defines social and emotional development as, "Competencies guiding school counseling programs to help students manage emotions and learn to apply interpersonal skills" (ASCA, 2019a, p. 4). School counselors should implement both formal and informal assessments to understand students' social and emotional development. Social and emotional development assessments have continued to grow within our profession, especially as many states have shifted toward providing social and emotional learning (SEL) standards.

The Collaborative for Academic, Social, and Emotional Learning (CASEL, n.d.) provides access to many evidence-based SEL tools and assessments. With the recent shift toward SEL, CASEL has emerged as a resource for showcasing different evidence-based curriculum. While there is not currently a recommended SEL assessment through CASEL (n.d.), they do provide access to *The SEL Assessment Guide,* which offers support on appropriately selecting assessments in relation to SEL data. This guide works in collaboration with other corporations, school districts, and universities (CASEL, n.d.). To get access to the guide, potential users must sign up and create an account. More information can be found within the tools and recourses section of this chapter. Once signed up, the assessment guide connects the user to plans for assessing SEL, selecting an appropriate assessment, and utilizing the data collected through the assessment. This resource drives home our goal of this book, which is to highlight the importance of assessment and data collection to implement a data-driven CSCP.

Informal assessments, such as observations of social and emotional responses of individual students, can help inform CSCPs. For example, informal assessments, such as the use of observations, can help inform small-group placements. Observations from teachers and other key stakeholders can provide information about placing students into the appropriate small groups for focused learning. For example, these data could be compared to formal SEL assessments of school-wide classroom curriculum. The informal assessment data could also be used to identify students who are not progressing with the SEL classroom curriculum. Such data helps school counselors identify students who need additional support via small groups. It is important that we carefully examine the types of assessments we plan to use to ensure they are being implemented as intended.

Process of Data Collection

The ASCA National Model sets standards for school counselors to be data informed and data responsive (ASCA, 2019a). It is important for us to explore what it means to be both a data-informed and data-responsive school counselor in terms of data collection. According to ASCA (2019a), "A data-informed school counselor consistently reviews school data to reveal trends across grades or years; inequities in student achievement, opportunity or attainment; and student needs revealed by changes such as school attendance, disciplinary problems and/or academic performance" (p. 32). This description implies that the process of data collection is not just a formality that happens at the start and end of each school year. Rather, the National Model argues that as a data-driven school counselor, your process of data collection should be ongoing throughout each academic year. Consistent review of data helps us continue to close the achievement gap and to address ongoing inequities. Further, ASCA (2019a) explains, "A data-responsive school counselor further uses data to determine if school counseling program strategies, interventions and activities are effective and to make decisions about future practice" (p. 32). As highlighted in these two explanations of data-driven and data-responsive practices, school counselors should use data to inform their approach and subsequently adjust their CSCPs accordingly. Data-driven decisions affect curriculum adjustments, intervention selection, and your overall programming.

Now that we have discussed data-driven and data-responsive actions related to school counseling practices, let's discuss the actual process of data collection. Several different approaches to data collection are available within our professional literature. When we look to our national organization, ASCA, they continue to respond to the increased demands on school counselors at the state and local level to continue to be data driven and responsive and adjusted the ASCA National Model as well as school counseling standards to match state and local demands. The newest edition of the *ASCA National Model (Fourth Edition)* provides a user-friendly approach that guides school counselors through the data-collection process. Additionally, ASCA provides a supplemental book to complement the ASCA National Model titled, *ASCA National Model Implementation Guide: Manage & Assess* (ASCA, 2019b). The supplemental book is intended to expand the management and assessment components of the ASCA National Model, while providing school counselors with applied examples. It is our intent to prepare school counselors for the Recognized ASCA Model Program (RAMP) process, which that recognizes schools and school counseling programs that have implemented an ASCA National Model-aligned CSCP (ASCA, 2019b).

Let's approach the data-collection process from the lens of a novice school counselor who has begun working in a new building. First, the school counselor should utilize the *School Data Summary Template,* which assists in identifying the building data expert. The data expert could be a school counseling colleague, principal, instructional coach, secretary, or MTSS team member. The data expert within the building should be informed and skilled at data interpretation (ASCA, 2019a). Next, the school counselor should locate the school improvement plan to identify where the CSCP could help support the school in reaching its established goals (ASCA, 2019a). Often, the building administration has formed a building improvement team. In such a situation, it may be helpful for the school counselor to consult with this team. Next, the school counselor should locate data reports from prior academic years. If the information is available, we recommend locating at least 5 years of data reports from prior academic years. Then, they should review these reports to identify trends in the data (ASCA, 2019a). The *School Data Summary Template* includes question prompts to support school counselors' data-exploration review and support for identifying trends in the data (ASCA, 2019a). Once school-level data have been gathered, it would be appropriate for the school counselor to consider district-level and state-level data. After identifying trends, the school counselor could compare these data to the overall district and state data (ASCA, 2019a). Then, the school counselor should decide whether any additional information is needed. For example, they may determine that a needs assessment would provide additional insight to discipline and attendance data trends. In this example, a needs assessment with questions related to mental health, peer relationships, and overall self-satisfaction with school performance could provide the school counselor with additional information on the social–emotional well-being of students and can lend greater insight regarding lower attendance or higher discipline referrals. Finally, the school counselor should determine their main data point(s) and how they plan to address these points through their CSCP within their goals, objectives, and curriculum (ASCA, 2019a).

Collaborative Efforts

The process of data collection is not an individual effort performed by the school counselor. Instead, this process involves collaboration with multiple stakeholders. Active collaboration with administration (e.g., principals, assistant principals, and district administration) could be approached in a variety of ways. Additionally, teachers and administration responsibilities within the schools provide school counselors with a great deal of assistance in collecting school-wide, classroom, or individual student data. These stakeholders are an asset to school counselors as gathering data is truly a collaborative effort. In our experience, administrators are often aware of micro-and macro-level student data trends before other stakeholders. Understanding that your administrators are aware of all levels of student data trends can help support your advocacy efforts for curriculum programming and implementation.

You should establish your role as both a data-informed and data-responsive school counselor with your administration team. Actively embracing this identity opens the lines of communication about data with your administrators. For example, as a school counselor, my [Jenna] principal had meetings with the district principals who would discuss discipline data trends. I had established myself with my principal to be a data-focused school counselor (*data informed* and *data responsive*). Our data analysis confirmed that the discipline referrals and suspension rates of African American male students were disproportionately higher than in other district schools. As a result, each school was charged with creating support systems and processes to address this inequity. I was able to realign my efforts as a part of my CSCP through this collaboration. Moreover, I worked with our Positive Behavioral Interventions and Supports (PBIS) team to form new initiatives to better support our students. This is an example of partnering with the administration to support students, which is also referred to as a *direct call to action* in the ASCA National Model (ASCA, 2019a). School counselors are able to support student behavioral outcome goals by collaborating with administration and decreasing the disciplinary gap (ASCA, 2019a).

Best Practices for Successful Data Collection

While data collection may seem like a daunting task, there are several best practices that school counselors can implement for successful data collection. The *School Data Summary* section of the ASCA National Model walks school counselors through six process questions to get started with data collection (ASCA, 2019a). For example, some of the questions pertain to identifying support personnel who have access to data and identifying different forms of data they need (ASCA, 2019a). The question prompts can help make the data-collection process feel manageable because they provide school counselors with to-do lists for data collection. The National Model also provides school counselors with an action prompt to create a *School Data Summary Template* as a way to start organizing the different types of data in connection with school improvement plan goals (ASCA, 2019a). This summary template prompts school counselors to gather achievement, attendance, and disciplinary data from school data reports (ASCA, 2019a) that are often readily available.

In addition to ASCA's suggested best practices for data collection, the professional literature provides other suggested best practices. For example, Zyromski and Mariani (2016) provide a three-step approach to gathering the necessary types of data in order to evolve your CSCP. The authors proposed that school counselors should gather school improvement data, teacher and student needs assessment data, and report card data (Zyromski & Mariani, 2016). It is recommended that the School Improvement Plan is a starting point for data collection (ASCA, 2019a). To illustrate how you would do this, Mrs. Apple at Country Middle School will gather the School Improvement Plan from the state or district office, run reports from the schools' databases on student attendance and grade reports to illustrate the percentage of students with Ds and Fs. Then, Mrs. Apple would work to gather additional stakeholder information from a needs assessment to inform her CSCP.

Making Sense of the Data

Once you have collected your data, it is time to make sense of it all, which can feel as overwhelming as locating your data. However, it is important to remember that while you might feel overwhelmed, there are many possibilities and opportunities that lay within the data to help you create a solid CSCP. The key is to take clear steps to make meaningful interpretations of your collected data. The goal is to either incorporate new interventions that meet the needs of your students or to make adjustments to existing programs that are aligned with what the data tell you the needs are for your students. In order to interpret your data, you must first understand the different types of data. In this section, we highlight ASCA's different categories of data and address ways to meaningfully interpret the data. We further address this in more extensive detail in Chapter 5. However, we have created a flow chart within this chapter for meaningful interpretation of your collected data related to your steps of data collection (Figure 2.2).

Meaningful Interpretation

As we discuss meaningful interpretation of data, it is important to also examine the different types of data. Indeed, ASCA (2019a) highlights several different types of data sets: *participation data*, *mindsets and behaviors data*, and *outcome data*. Participation data tell us who engaged in the intervention, as well as the type and time frame of the intervention (ASCA, 2019a). Participation data also explain the program delivery method, the number of students impacted by the intervention, and describe the intervention's details (ASCA, 2019a). The mindsets and behavior data outlines which of the ASCA Mindsets and Behavior standards were addressed along with student progress. Mindsets and behavior data show the intervention's impact on students and the evidence of meeting the mindsets and behaviors standards (ASCA, 2019a). Outcome data examine the results of a student's engagement in the CSCP activity or intervention in connection with the ASCA Mindsets and Behaviors (ASCA, 2019a). Outcome data may come from multiple sources, analyze overall student impact effects, and are not limited to the outcome associated with participation in the intervention (ASCA, 2019a). To illustrate how to do this, we provide the following example. When reviewing the eighth-grade end-of-course exam results, all percentage pass rates increased by 5% for all students, except those in Mrs. Jones classroom. This is to be expected as Mrs. Jones was a long-term substitute who was brought in after a teacher abruptly resigned. Here is another example used to illustrate data interpretation: according to the attendance data for this year, the school is at a 92% attendance rate, which is a marked decline compared to the last 3 years. However, this should be considered in light of the consecutive natural disasters that hit the region recently.

School counselors must examine school data, including state test results, attendance records, disciplinary reports, and other grade-level appropriate data (ASCA, 2019a). Each of these types of primary data sets are highlighted within the National Model. The primary data types provide us with information on the number of students who participated, the ASCA Mindsets and Behavior standards that were targeted within a lesson or group, and provide us with evidence of student results (ASCA, 2019a).

Meaningful Distribution and Dissemination

Data collection and interpretation are critical steps in the assessment process. However, distribution and dissemination of the information is just as critical. Zyromski and Mariani (2016) argued that as school counselors, we should be focused on serving our students. Further, the authors discussed that the process of self-promotion is not always second nature for many school counselors, but that sharing our results and interpretation with key stakeholders should be part of our advocacy process. For example, school counselors have created what they call "spotlight" presentations. Another, name for these presentations is *flashlights* (Hatch, 2014; Zyromski & Mariani, 2016). Hatch (2014) explained that the flashlight approach was adapted from a logic model for disseminating information. In these presentations, school counselors share key information related to their data-informed CSCP goals, action steps taken to help close any achievement gaps, details of the implemented interventions, and the results of these interventions. Hatch (2014) provides step-by-step instructions and a rubric for which key elements to include within these presentations. These PowerPoint presentations are often shared with teachers and administrators during staff meetings. Presentations help break down information into concise and clear chunks and use visual elements to aid in data dissemination. A similar presentation approach can be taken for data dissemination with parents and the general community. School counselors should use their leadership and advocacy skills to demonstrate their data-informed and data-responsive backgrounds. We recommend referencing Chapter 6, where we discuss in more detail how and where to present data, findings, and recommendations (Figure 2.2)

Legal and Ethical Considerations

When collecting assessment data, school counselors need to consult the ASCA Ethical Standards (2016) and the ASCA Professional Standards and Competencies (2019c) to ensure that they are staying within the scope of their school counseling practice. The ethical standards state that school counselors have an ethical obligation to implement a data-informed CSCP (ASCA, 2016). Thus, school counselors should use school data to make informed decisions to address inequities in the services provided through their CSCP (2016). Addressing inequities in services through a CSCP is not limited to programming, it also includes the school counselor's holistic role in advocating for change. Another key ethical standard is our duty to ensure that we share our data with administrators, teachers, students, parents, and the community (2016). Disseminating the data we have collected is as important of a task as collecting data, as our work needs to be able to demonstrate how students are impacted as a result of our efforts. Importantly, ASCA calls for school counselors to maintain confidentiality when utilizing various platforms or tools to aid in the practice of obtaining and storing data.

ASCA Professional Standards and Competencies

School counselors must ensure that student engagement with CSCPs is connected to the Mindsets and Behaviors standards (ASCA, 2016). School counselors collect assessment data in order to create yearly goals for student improvement, which are connected to the improvement goals set by the school

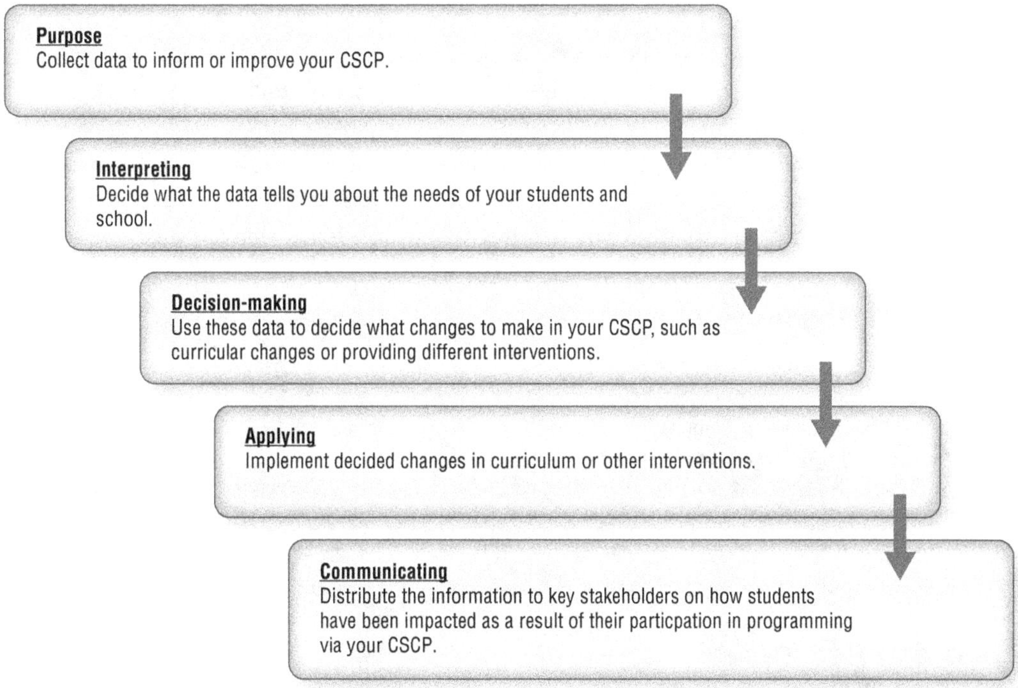

FIGURE 2.2 Data-collection purpose and process. This figure describes the steps in data collection for a comprehensive school counseling program. CSCP, comprehensive school counseling program.

district (2016). The ASCA professional standards and competencies confirm this point because school counselors are required to utilize assessments as the basis for their programming (ASCA, 2019c). The *ASCA School Counselor Professional Standards and Competencies* includes a set of behaviors that are directly connected to planning and assessment.

As an organization, ASCA (2019a) charges school counselors with developing goals that are based on student data, which are completed via the *Annual Student Outcome Goal Plan Template* within the ASCA National Model. Further, ASCA (2019a) recommends that school counselors complete this template using the specific, measurable, achievable, relevant, time-bound (SMART) goal format. Our professional organization, ASCA (2019a), provides the following definition for a SMART goal, "A well-established format used to plan and achieve a goal, which stands for specific, measurable, attainable, relevant, and time-bound" (p. 150). The format and structure of SMART goals effectively create and communicate goals (Doran, 1981).

As a hypothetical example, Happyville Elementary has noticed a 20% increase in office referrals for fighting in the fourth grade. The school just started its school-wide PBIS program in August. Over the summer, the school district implemented its redistricting plans, which created an increase in fourth-grade students enrolled at Happyville who originally spent four academic years at Sunny Elementary. Using the SMART goals format provided through the National Model, a goal could be, "By the end of May 2021, fourth-grade students referred for fighting will decrease by 20% from 20 referrals during the second trimester to 16 referrals for fighting in the fourth grade during the final grading period through a fourth-grade peer mediation program." Effectively communicating annual student outcome goals based on student data with school administration is important and helps foster a positive school culture. School counselors believe that SMART goals should be shared with all key stakeholders (ASCA, 2019c).

Conclusion

Chapter 2 focused on providing readers with a pragmatic understanding of the intent for collecting, interpreting, and using data. In order to effectively use data, we discussed the different types of assessments (informal and formal) that inform our work with students through interventions and advocacy. Further, we discussed our professional standards. We also reminded school counselors that disseminating the results of our data collection is vital to the assessment process. Assessments help us collect data that inform our CSCP goals in order to facilitate meaningful change for our students and within our schools.

Additional Reading

American School Counselor Association. (2019a). *The ASCA national model: A framework for school counseling programs* (4th ed.). American School Counselor Association.

American School Counselor Association. (2019b). *ASCA national model implementation guide: Manage and assess* (2nd ed.). American School Counselor Association.

Dollarhide, C. T., & Saginak, K. A. (2017). *Comprehensive school counseling programs: K-12 delivery systems in action* (3rd ed.). Pearson.

Hatch, T. (2014). *The use of data in school counseling: Hatching results for students, programs, and the profession.* Corwin.

Tools and Resources

- Collaborative for Academic, Social, and Emotional Learning offers access to resources to help support data collection and monitoring related to SEL. *CSI Resources: Assessment* (https://www.casel.org/csi-resources-assessment/).
- PAR, Inc. offers access to a formal career assessment and exploration tool that helps students explore aspirations, activities, and talents. *What Is the Self-Directed Search?* (https://self-directed-search.com/what-is-it/).
- Rethink Old School, Inc. offers a free career test: Your Free Career Test: Free Career Test for Students & Adults (https://www.yourfreecareertest.com/career-tests/free-career-test-for-students/).

Key Points

- School counselors are experts at collecting and analyzing data.
- Data-informed decision-making supports school counselors' efforts in closing achievement gaps.
- Using informal and formal assessments provides data, which serves as an opportunity to advocate on behalf of students for systemic change.
- School counselors are able to utilize data collected from assessments to inform their CSCP and appropriate services.

Questions for Reflection

- Identify at least two formal and informal assessments. How you can utilize them in your school?
- Why is it important to gather data from both informal and formal assessments?
- How can a school counselor utilize data to enhance their Comprehensive School Counseling Program (CSCP)?
- Why is it important to be both a *data-informed* and *data-responsive* school counselor?

References

Allensworth, E. M., & Clark, K. (2020). High school GPAs and ACT scores as predictors of college completion: Examining assumptions about consistency across high schools. *Educational Researcher, 49*(3), 198–211. https://doi.org/10.3102/0013189X20902110

American School Counselor Association. (2014). *Mindsets and behaviors for student Success: K-12 college-and career-readiness standards for every student.* https://www.schoolcounselor.org/getmedia/7428a787-a452-4abb-afec-d78ec77870cd/Mindsets-Behaviors.pdf

American School Counselor Association. (2016). *ASCA ethical standards for school counselors.* https://www.schoolcounselor.org/getmedia/f041cbd0-7004-47a5-ba01-3a5d657c6743/Ethical-Standards.pdf

American School Counselor Association. (2019a). *ASCA national model: A framework for school counseling programs* (4th ed.). American School Counselor Association.

American School Counselor Association. (2019b). *ASCA national model implementation guide: Manage and assess* (2nd ed.). American School Counselor Association.

American School Counselor Association. (2019c). *ASCA school counselor professional standards and competencies.* https://www.schoolcounselor.org/getmedia/a8d59c2c-51de-4ec3-a565-a3235f3b93c3/SC-Competencies.pdf

Collaborative for Academic, Social, and Emotional Learning. (n.d.). *CSI resources: Assessment.* https://www.casel.org/csi-resources-assessment/

Dollarhide, C. T., & Saginak, K. A. (2017). *Comprehensive school counseling programs: K-12delivery systems in action* (3rd ed.). Pearson.

Hatch, T. (2014). *The use of data in school counseling: Hatching results for students, programs, and the profession.* Corwin.

Jaschik, S. (2020, February 3). Study: Grades are 5 times stronger than ACT scores. *Inside Higher Ed.* https://www.insidehighered.com/admissions/article/2020/02/03/study-finds-grades-are-five-times-stronger-act-scores

Lane, K. L., & Menzies, H. M. (2009). *Student risk screening scale for internalizing and externalizing (SRSS-IE).* http://www.ci3t.org/screening

Mariani, M., Villares, E., Sink, C. A., Colvin, K., & Kuba, S. P. (2015). Confirming the structural validity of The My class inventory—Short form revised. *Professional School Counseling, 19*(1), 92–102. http://dx.doi.org.proxy.libraries.uc.edu/10.5330/1096-2409-19.1.92

Niles, S. G., & Erford, B. T. (2019). Promoting career and individual planning in schools. In B. T. Erford (Ed.), *Transforming the school counseling profession* (5th ed., pp. 250–268). Pearson.

PAR, Inc. (2020). *What is the self-directed search*? Self-Directed Search. https://self-directed-search.com/what-is-it/

Renaissance Learning, Inc. (2019). *Star reading: K-12 assessments for reading mastery.* Author. https://p.widencdn.net/yjhnaa/300804-Star-Reading-flyer

Renaissance Learning, Inc. (2020a). *Star assessments.* Author. https://p.widencdn.net/xoeysj/302820-Star-Gatefold_final

Renaissance Learning, Inc. (2020b). *Cost sheet for Ohio department of education: Approved assessments 2020–2021.* Author. https://doc.renlearn.com/KMNet/R61849.pdf

Rethink Old School, Inc. (n.d.). *Your free career test: Free career test for students & adults.* https://www.yourfreecareertest.com/career-tests/free-career-test-for-students/

Sink, C. A., & Spencer, L. R. (2005). My Class Inventory—Short form as an accountability tool for elementary school counselors to measure classroom climate. *Professional School Counseling, 9*(1), 37. https://doi.org/10.1177/2156759X0500900112

Sink, C. A., & Spencer, L. R. (2007). Teacher version of the My Class Inventory—Short form: An accountability tool for elementary school counselors. *Professional School Counseling, 11*(2), 129–139. https://doi.org/10.5330/psc.n.2010-11.129. http://www.schoolcounselor.org/content.asp?contentid=235

Sonoma County Office of Education. (n.d.). *Career development continuum: Preparing all youth for success in college, career, and life.* https://www.calcareercenter.org/Uploads/Categories/84/Files/338/SonomaCareerContinuum.pdf

Villares, E., Mariani, M., Sink, C.A., & Colvin, K. (2016). Multilevel confirmatory factor analysis of the Teacher My Class Inventory—Short form. *Measurement and Evaluation in Counseling and Development, 49*(4), 263–273. https://doi.org/10.1177/0748175616639107

Zyromski, B., & Mariani, M. A. (2016). *Facilitating evidence-based, data-driven school counseling: A manual for practice.* Corwin.

3

ASSESSING THE DEVELOPMENT, IMPLEMENTATION, AND MANAGEMENT OF YOUR COMPREHENSIVE SCHOOL COUNSELING PROGRAM

Introduction

In this chapter, we focus on the steps you can take to assess the development, implementation, and management of your comprehensive school counseling program (CSCP). Our goal is to highlight how assessment should be integrated into the creation and annual revision of your CSCP. Often, when you are building a school counseling program for the first time, regardless of the amount of experience you have as a school counselor, the process can feel overwhelming. We also discuss the history and the various approaches to conceptualize CSCPs that are found within the literature.

The current version of the American School Counselor Association (ASCA) National Model argues that school counselors should be action orientated and should utilize various assessments. Implementing several types of new assessments supports the existing data already found within your school. Further, ASCA (2019a) highlights that school counselors should use the National Model as a framework to connect the needs of the school with their already established CSCP. In doing so, school counselors create more data-responsive CSCPs. The revision to the fourth edition of the National Model was intended to streamline the process of becoming a data-driven and data-informed school counselor (ASCA, 2019a).

In addition to streamlining the National Model, ASCA released a revised companion guide, *ASCA National Model Implementation Guide: Manage and Assess*, which provides school counselors with ASCA-aligned information for the creation of a CSCP within their school (ASCA, 2019b). School counselors can utilize the guide to help build a data-driven CSCP by using the provided guidelines about pre- and postassessments that are aligned with the Mindsets and Behaviors standards of the ASCA National Model. The guide is also intended to help support school counselors throughout the application process of becoming a Recognized ASCA Model Program (RAMP; ASCA, 2019b). Our organization encourages professional school counselors who are interested in becoming a RAMP school to complete the assessment found within the ASCA National Model to gauge the current state of their CSCP (2019b). We recognize that each school counselor is uniquely positioned within different school environments. Some schools may not have the possibility of obtaining RAMP status; however, our goal is to equip school counselors with various assessments to assess the status of their CSCP.

Our goal throughout this chapter, and this book, is to emphasize various valid and reliable assessments to support you. In addition, we highlight various approaches to CSCPs. The process of connecting assessment and data collection when working towardsbuilding or revising a CSCP is rarely discussed within our profession. Our intention is to provide you with a wealth of information related to valid and reliable assessments that could fit within your CSCP. Additionally, many states have moved to specific school counseling frameworks and evaluation systems. These are typically aligned with the ASCA National Model and require school counselors to provide supporting evidence of how they are meeting students' needs. School counselors can supply adequate evidence to meet job requirements and serve all students through data collection and assessment. As previously discussed, school counselors often resort to creating assessments due to budgetary restrictions and lack of access to scholarly journals where a multitude of free, valid, and reliable assessments can be found.

Throughout this chapter, we explore various types of assessments that help school counselors define, manage, deliver, and assess their CSCP based on the four quadrants of the ASCA National Model. These four quadrants are: *Define*, *Manage*, *Deliver*, and *Assess*. We aim to demonstrate that school counselors can use assessments to create data-driven CSCPs that benefit all students. We elaborate on how to use these assessments within your practice by providing ample examples. This chapter demonstrates how assessments contribute to the development, implementation, and management of a CSCP, whereas Chapter 4 showcases assessments to consider in your direct counseling services.

Approaches to Comprehensive School Counseling Programs

The use of a CSCP or a data-collection process is important because it can close the opportunity and achievement gaps for students. Erford (2019) explained, "achievement gaps are the differences in academic performance among groups of K-12 students based on ethnicity/race, gender, social class, disability status, language status, and other variables" (pp. 176–177). Opportunity gaps refer to the lack of access and quality of resources available to the student that help prepare students for life after graduation (Erford, 2019). Being intentional with your data collection and how you approach your CSCP based on the data can help you combat other gaps such as attainment. Attainment gaps refer to the gaps associated with college completion based on a students' minority identity (2019). Without utilizing assessments or data collection (e.g., attendance, discipline), school counselors would be unaware of the existing opportunity gaps within their school community. As discussed in Chapter 1, being an active member of the Multi-Tiered Systems of Support (MTSS) team, the Positive Behavioral Interventions and Supports (PBIS) process, using universal screeners, and collecting data can help close this gap. Additionally, there are different approaches of CSCPs that school counselors can implement when developing their own methods of collecting data.

Being intentional with your data collection and how you approach your CSCP based on the data can help you combat other gaps such as attainment.

Without utilizing assessments or data collection (e.g., attendance, discipline), school counselors would be unaware of the existing opportunity gaps within their school community.

As Dahir and Stone (2006) noted, the ASCA National Model was born out of the work of many scholars and influences the changing landscape of our education system. For the purposes of this chapter, we focus on the work of Johnson and Johnson (2002) and Gysbers and Henderson (2001). While we focus on the aforementioned authors' work, it is important to note that Dr. Robert Myrick has published several editions of his original book on this subject matter, initially published in 1978 titled *Developmental Guidance and Counseling: A Practical Approach*. He is noted within the professional literature for his contributions and we have included his most current edition within our reference list (Myrick, 2011).

A common thread among these approaches is a focus on school counseling curriculum (Nelson & Tarabochia, 2020). Our interpretation for this commonality, is school counseling curriculum is widely accepted within the profession as a foundational direct service provided to all students. DuFour et al. (2002) proposed a collaborative approach for *learning organization* for collaborative data collection and assessment of school programs aligned with the ASCA domains of academic, career, and social–emotional (formerly personal–social) development (Johnson & Johnson, 2002). From our perspective, DuFour et al. were describing modern-day CSCPs working in tandem with PBIS and MTSS frameworks. Ironically, they project into the year 2021, stating that school counselors will utilize technology to service students in new ways, collect and track large amounts of data, and highlight the impact technology will have on collaborative relationships (DuFour et al., 2002). Furthermore, Gysbers and Henderson (2001) stressed the importance of having a clear operational system that allows school counselors to work from and provide services for students. Whether you are utilizing a state-created approach or a different approach to your CSCP, it is important to ensure you are working to collect data that informs the programs and services provided to students. For example, several states have created guides for CSCPs. The Missouri Comprehensive Guidance and Counseling Program provides school counselors with a process for creating, updating, and growing a CSCP (Gysbers et al., 2017). Additionally, the state of Ohio has made a comprehensive school counseling manual available to Ohio-based school counselors that is linked to the Ohio school counselor evaluation process (Ohio Department of Education [ODE], 2016a, 2016b).

It is important for us to discuss how we began the practice of CSCPs by exploring the history of the ASCA National Model. With collective changes in the educational system, changes to our profession have been warranted. Dahir and Stone (2006) discussed educational reform in connection to the professional responsibility of school counselors to ensure all students' needs are met. In order to do this, we needed to have a system that allows us to collect, assess, and manage data. Not only do we need a system that supports us in organizing our data, but we need a system that allows us to house our programming and monitor how students change after engaging in our program.

Since the inception of the ASCA National Model in 2003, several approaches to CSCPs and data collection have emerged, and some include a social justice focus. ASCA (2012) started the development of the first National Model by gathering a group of school counseling experts together for 2 years before releasing the first National Model. Bringing together individuals with school counseling knowledge and experience was done in response to the need for school counselors to incorporate data into their school counseling practice to demonstrate their ability and the value they bring to their schools (ASCA, 2012). Drs. Trish Hatch and Judy Bowers developed the first National Model and supported ASCA in the revisions to the third edition (2012). Next, we explore an approach connected to CSCPs that uses a social justice lens.

Dahir and Stone (2009) studied school counseling programs with a connection to social justice. This study reminded us of the Change-Agent-for-Equity (CAFE) Model, which connects social justice to CSCPs. Mason et al. (2013) developed the CAFE Model to build upon the ASCA National Model to provide school counselors with an additional framework rooted in social justice. The CAFE Model expands on what it means to be a change agent to provide school counselors with an action-oriented approach to delivering programs and services. School counselors are committed to CSCPs that are rooted in providing services at all levels that are inclusive while embracing their professional identity. Within this section, we continue to expand on the work of those who have influenced the creation and evolution of CSCPs while describing more recent approaches available to school counselors.

School counselors are committed to CSCPs that are rooted in providing services at all levels that are inclusive while embracing their professional identity.

The Use of Data in School Counseling (Hatch, 2014) connects the CAFE Model to our work and our commitment to grow as social justice advocates who use data to close the opportunity gap for students. Hatch (2014) outlined data collection for school counselors in a way that bridged the gap between ideal school counseling data-collection methods and the reality of the day-to-day school counseling career. In Hatch's book, the approach to school counseling programming is rooted in manageable steps and interconnecting data. For example, Hatch highlights the importance of data and data dissemination through systems in your school, such as Multi-Tiered, Multi-Domain Systems of Support (MTMDSS), MTSS, and PBIS teams. It is important for school counselors to understand the multiple systems at play within a school system and how many of these systems are directly connected to our work as school counselors. To highlight this point, Goodman-Scott and Ockerman (2019), clearly highlight the working relationship between MTSS and CSCP as well as the empirically based research that has been conducted on the alignment of CSCP, MTSS, and PBIS. We have referenced Goodman-Scott et al.'s (2019) edited book, *The School Counselor's Guide to Multi-Tiered Systems of Support,* in Chapter 1 as well as this chapter as we feel it provides our readers with additional information on the connection of MTSS within the practice of school counseling. Goodman-Scott and Ockerman (2019) suggested incorporating MTSS team members into the Advisory Council as a way to connect the two systems with intentionality. Additionally, they recommend that school counselors include foundational MTSS components within the annual agreement, mission, vision, and other core tenants of the CSCP. Connecting these systems helps to clearly depict the integral role the school counselor and the CSCP can have within a school.

As discussed in Chapter 1, Hatch takes similar approaches within her work. Specifically, in *The Use of Data in School Counseling,* Hatch (2014) introduces, "While guidance is often provided for every student, the concept behind *intentional guidance* is some kids need more" (p. 37). We want to recognize that as a profession we are moving away from the word guidance to discuss any of our work as professionals. However, it is extremely important to highlight the meaning behind the quote cited here. To us, Hatch (2014) was stressing the importance of using data, the ASCA National Model, MTSS, and PBIS in connection with evidence-based practices to be *intentional* in everything we do as school counselors. This is why operating within a data-driven CSCP is critical. Why? Because data give voice and evidence to our gut feelings as school counselors. Data allow us to be better advocates, leaders, and agents of change.

Data allow us to be better advocates, leaders, and agents of change.

Zyromski and Mariani (2016) wrote *Facilitating Evidence-Based, Data-Driven School Counseling: A Manual for Practice* which can work in tandem with the ASCA National Model. The authors highlighted that data collection and evidence-based school counseling programming can be a process rather than a model for school counseling. Through their book, they discuss the purpose of setting goals and using data-driven decision-making to help school counselors prioritize their time. Zyromski and Mariani expand on the Logic Model, which they adapted from Dimmitt et al.'s (2007) book, *Evidence-Based School*

Counseling: Making a Difference with Data-Driven Practices. The Evidence-Based School Counseling Logic Model includes the following seven items: assess, data indicators, data goals, interventions, logistics, evaluation, and evolution. These elements are integrated throughout their book as they walk readers through how to incorporate the Logic Model within the practice of school counseling by first starting with the data indicators. They explain that school counselors can use the model to pinpoint important data and "drill down" into the data to dissect and describe how students are being impacted (Zyromski & Mariani, 2016). This can be done to narrow in on the gaps for populations of students and allow the school counselor to locate the most appropriate interventions, ideally evidence based, to support student growth within a CSCP. Also, the school counselor can use the model to highlight logistics of their programming, the evaluation, and the evolution of the services (2016).

Similar to Hatch's approach, Zyromski and Mariani walk school counselors through the process of connecting data to their CSCP while highlighting Dr. Hatch's Flashlight approach to disseminating information. The Flashlight approach was adapted from Weiss's Logic Model as a way to visually describe the results of your CSCP in relation to data as a way to demonstrate to key stakeholders the results of your program (Hatch, 2014). Utilizing this approach is typically done through a structured digital presentation, for example, PowerPoint, while encompassing the ASCA National Model. For example, Zyromski and Mariani, highlighted that the Flashlight presentation should include ASCA Mindsets and Behaviors that were addressed withing the selected lessons or programs utilized within your CSCP. They continue to expand on Hatch's original idea to encourage school counselors to use school data coupled with intentional graphics (Zyromski & Mariani, 2016). Hatch (2014) includes a Flashlight Rating Scale Rubric to help school counselors evaluate their presentation. We encourage our readers to review the examples and in-depth details of this approach in Hatch's (2014) book as well as Zyromski and Marinai's (2016) book.

Just as our colleagues, Zyromski and Mariani (2016) mentioned in their book, the ideas around data collection and CSCP are not our own, but rather a collection of all the great work that has been disseminated related to how to organize and communicate your CSCP. We hope to add to these concepts by offering the importance of assessment in the development and implementation of your CSCP and as a way to continue to enhance our profession. We encourage our readers to explore the approaches discussed within this section to see how they can fit within your practice. Next, we explore the importance of engaging in self-assessment as a school counselor. As we have mentioned throughout Chapters 1 and 3, our goals are to provide you with ways to integrate assessments into your CSCP to help you continue to build upon the approaches to CSCPs.

Self-Assessment

It is important to engage in self-assessment regarding your attitudes, skills, and knowledge related to your school counseling program in order to understand their influences on your CSCP. This allows you to best meet the current needs of students and establish, or further enhance, your school counseling program. It can be overwhelming to build or restructure school counseling services. Thus, we recommend the practice of self-assessment as it provides you with direction and action steps to support the process.

Conducting self-assessments aligned with our professional standards, both the ASCA standards and applicable state standards, is a great place to start. Upon our review, we found a comprehensive assessment within the National Model is the ASCA School Counselor Professional Standards & Competencies Assessment (ASCA, 2019a). School counselors can use this assessment to measure the effectiveness of their CSCP on the Mindsets and Behaviors standard of the National Model.

The assessment can also be used to create an action plan for implementing or revising a CSCP (ASCA, 2019a). Another self-assessment aligned to the ASCA National Model is the School Counseling Program Implementation Survey (SCPIS). The goal of the SCPIS is to help school counselors understand how their CSCP is being implemented to align with the ASCA National Model (Clemens et al., 2010). The assessment is based on the existence of essential components of CSCPs, which include, but are not limited to, a mission statement, goals and objectives, and data. Another related self-assessment is the School Counselor Activity Rating Scale (SCARS), which was designed to measure any discrepancies between a school counselor's goals for their work activities and their actual work activities (Scarborough, 2005a). In Chapter 4, we discuss additional assessments and how to incorporate each into a school counselor's work practice.

Assessment Related to the ASCA National Model

The process of creating a CSCP that is informed by assessment data helps to support school counselors' efforts in creating CSCPs that meet the needs of all students. School counselors learn the needs of their students and key stakeholders through the use of assessments. What follows is a discussion of how assessments directly connect to the *Define*, *Manage*, *Deliver*, and *Assess* quadrants of the ASCA National Model. In addition to briefly describing the goal of each quadrant, we connect each quadrant to specific assessments that align with the purpose of each respective quadrant.

Define

The Define quadrant of the ASCA National Model opens by explaining the importance of using the foundational documents to inform our practice as school counselors (ASCA, 2019a). For example, both the *ASCA Mindsets & Behaviors for Student Success: K-12 College-and Career-Readiness for Every Student* and the *ASCA School Counselor Professional Standards and Competencies* are explicitly explained within this section to highlight the intentionality of their design that connects to the other quadrants within the National Model (2019a). Our focus within this book is to continue to connect the importance of data and assessment to the meaningful work you do as a school counselor. We can see this shift throughout our profession and within ASCA. Indeed, ASCA (2019a) explains that the ASCA Mindsets and Behaviors standards were conceptualized and informed by college and career documents created by various organizations. This exemplifies how our profession continues to shift toward being more data driven and research informed. Additionally, ASCA summarizes the use of a noncognitive factors framework for the ASCA Mindsets and Behaviors standards and provides key literature supporting the rationale related to the organizational design and the final product.

The overarching goal of the Define quadrant is to show the significance of these ASCA documents and how they intersect with the formation of a CSCP. The second goal is to provide implementation steps for school counselors. The key documents include student standards of the *ASCA Mindsets & Behaviors for Student Success: K-12 College-and Career-Readiness Standards for Every Student* (2014), the *ASCA Ethical Standards for School Counselors* (2016), and the *ASCA School Counselor Professional Standards and Competencies* (2019c). In addition, the goal of the Define quadrant is to provide these key documents in one place for school counselors to utilize as they work through the National Model. Our professional organization makes these documents readily available in portable document format (PDF) on its website for free and in books available for purchase published by ASCA. We have intentionally cited these stand-alone key documents throughout this book to support accessibility for our readers. Now, let's explore the use of the SCPIS.

School Counseling Program Implementation Survey

Elsner and Carey (2005) initially developed the SCPIS as an unpublished instrument that was cited by Clemens et al. (2010). As originally developed, the goal of the survey was to use clear language that was both observable and measurable (Clemens et al., 2010). The survey began with 25 questions. After conducting an internal consistency reliability analysis of the questions, the SCPIS was reduced to 20 questions (2010). The researchers took the remaining questions and conducted two separate studies. During the first study, the survey was sent to several states to better understand and evaluate the possible outcomes related to the professional relationship between school counselors and school administrators (Clemens et al., 2009). Clemens and colleagues worked with the Center for School Counseling Outcome Research, located at the University of Massachusetts Amherst, to conduct a statewide study. The SCPIS aims to assess the current level of a school counseling program's utilization of the ASCA National Model through the school counselor's self-examination of what they currently have in place in their CSCP (2010). Each question on the SCPIS asks participants to respond on a 4-point scale, ranging from "not present" to "fully implemented." Our readers can find a copy of the SCPIS within the Clemens et al. (2010) article. We recognize that many of our readers have limited access to journal articles, however, ASCA members have access to this article with their ASCA membership.

It is important to note that there have been updates to the ASCA National Model since Elsner and Carey (2005) originally developed the scale and since Clemens et al. (2010) conducted an exploratory factor analysis (EFA). Nevertheless, the survey items still align with the foundational structure of the National Model. Despite the updated National Model, we feel the SCPIS can be a valuable tool for school counselors. Let us examine the first checklist item of the survey, "a written mission statement exists and is used as a foundation by all counselors" (Clemens et al., 2010, p. 134). The rationale for having this be the first question is to ensure that all school counselors have adopted their own personal or a collective mission statement developed by a team of school counselors and are using this statement as a working definition for their CSCP. The Define quadrant provides a foundation of important documents related to the professional identity of a school counselor in order to help the school counselor develop a well-informed and intentional mission statement. In the Manage section, we cover assessments that continue to help school counselors build and assess their CSCP. The SCPIS is an effective tool to use to determine where your school counseling program is before moving to the Manage section of the ASCA National Model.

The additional questions in the SCPIS assessment cover relevant and current school counseling practices. The second question within the SCPIS addresses the overall delivery of school counseling services to ensure all students are served through a CSCP. The third question continues to build upon the foundations by addressing fairness and equity by assessing whether the school counselor has action plans associated with the achievement gap or what is also referred to as the *opportunity gap* within educational literature. The SCPIS includes a question on utilizing needs assessment regularly, but does not address whether the needs assessments, and others like it, are reliable and valid. As we previously indicated, self-created assessments are considered informal assessments, which we address in Chapter 5.

After completing all 20 questions, our recommendation is to highlight or color-code your answers to indicate items that are absent from your program as well as items that are completely present. We suggest making a column that includes all items in your CSCP that are data informed and then creating a running list of elements that require your attention. Focusing on the aspects missing from your CSCP, let us say that it is five out of the 20 presented questions, we recommend starting with two or three items to avoid getting overwhelmed. For example, if your CSCP is missing a mission statement along with goals and objectives, it is important to first develop these items as they are the foundation of your program.

As emphasized by ASCA (2019a), the mission statement helps to focus the school counseling program, provide it with direction that aligns with the vision, and helps to shape the goals and objectives. It is recommended to use the specific, measurable, attainable, results-oriented and time-bond (SMART) goal format to form goals and objectives, as described in Chapter 2. When initially developing your CSCP, we recommend starting with the SCPIS within the Define section to help ease any feelings of being overwhelmed. We continue to build upon understanding the Manage section as well as connecting other assessments that align with it.

Manage

The Manage quadrant provides school counselors with a system to keep their CSCP organized (ASCA, 2019a). The idea is to provide a structured system that allows school counselors to manage the multiple hats they wear within their professional role and to carry out effective school counseling programs. School counselors can use this framework to find tools and assessments to manage their CSCP. Indeed, as ASCA (2019a) highlighted, "The assessments and tools help school counselors develop, implement and assess their school counseling program based on clearly defined priorities reflecting student needs" (p. 29). Establishing these priorities in connection with student needs demonstrates the efforts school counselors take to map out the various types of data, from multiple data sources, that they need and use within their CSCP to support the exact needs of their students. Documenting the CSCP with the ASCA-provided templates is a large focus of the Manage quadrant. Throughout the Manage quadrant, ASCA clarifies how to connect each template with data, which creates a building-block structure between each template.

The goal of the Manage quadrant is to combine the standards and initial data from the Define quadrant to develop and monitor programming within a CSCP by using action-oriented templates (ASCA, 2019a.) The Manage quadrant intentionally builds upon the Define quadrant to help school counselors clarify the focus of their CSCP. This is achieved by creating a vision and mission statement that is later connected to assessment data. The goal of a strong connection to data is to drive home the importance of how powerful data are in informing CSCPs.

Needs Assessments

As discussed in Chapter 2, needs assessments are often informal assessments created by school counselors to gain feedback regarding the unique needs of their school. While our focus is to highlight the importance of using valid and reliable assessments, we recognize that school counselors will need to use informal assessments, such as needs assessments, to gather input from key stakeholders. Throughout this section, we discuss some self-assessments that school counselors can use to support their school counseling program to gain additional information from stakeholders.

In the Manage section, ASCA (2019a) highlights that, "supplemental methods solicit additional information from students and relevant stakeholders about the need identified in school data" (p. 37). This is where a needs assessment can support school counselors in selecting, building, and creating materials for their CSCP. To do so, ASCA (2019a) recommends the following pathways for gathering additional information, "methods include conversation, interviews, needs assessments, climate survey, and opinion surveys" (p. 37). Using other pathways to gather data can provide you with additional information and context that can be applied to your school counseling program.

As noted in the ASCA National Model, and similar to what we have mentioned throughout this book, it is important not to rely on one form of data, but rather use formal and informal assessments together. The following sections highlight other assessments that can support your CSCP program and provide examples of how to incorporate these into practice. These self-assessments are focused on your role as a school counselor and understanding your job functions.

School Counselor Activity Rating Scale

The School Counselor Activity Rating Scale (SCARS) is a self-assessment tool that is designed to measure how professional school counselors spend their time in comparison to how they would actually prefer to spend their work-related time. If school counselors are interested in a copy of the SCARS, Scarborough (2005a) highlighted in her 2005 article titled *The School Counselor Activity Rating Scale: An Instrument for Gathering Process Data*, that school counselors can access a copy of the SCARS by directly emailing her. Additionally, a copy of the SCARS can be located though the *UMass Amherst School Counselor Resources* web page (UMass Amherst College of Education, 2019); the link is located within the tools and resources section of this chapter. This self-assessment can help support school counselors in collecting self-reflective data. The SCARS assessment and its components (i.e., actual and prefer scale) connect to the ASCA National Model Manage section pertaining to constructing a school counseling program that is connected to role-appropriate duties. Some of the questions found within the SCARS are considered to acknowledge role-inappropriate duties. For example, if a school counselor prefers the job functions of a test coordinator, then this would be a point of evaluation for the school counselor or school counseling team as the job function could be taking away from providing direct services to students.

Scarborough (2005b) outlines her stages of development of the SCARS as two phases; the first phase focused on the creation of the assessment including layout, question format, and scaling structure. Then, in phase two, the product of phase one was pretested (Scarborough, 2005a). To develop the statements that are found within the SCARS, *Scarborough (2005)* used the ASCA's working definitions of how services are delivered; this includes what we now refer to as direct (individual, small group, and classroom lessons) and indirect services (other services, such as consultation and collaboration, that are focused on supporting students and the school counseling program). The SCARS includes what Scarborough referred to as *clerical duties,* which are now commonly referred to as *role-inappropriate duties* in the ASCA National Model.

Though dated, the SCARS can still be used in a variety of ways. School counselors can use this to advocate for role-appropriate duties with administrators. Additionally, a school counseling team could use the SCARS as a way to determine each team member's preferences. Then the team could collaborate together to establish preferred tasks within a CSCP. In the next section, we focus on a tool that helps school counselors better understand their time. This connects more to the data-collection focus of this book and how assessments also connect to one another.

School Counselor Use of Time Analysis

While the School Counselor Use of Time Analysis (SCUTA) is not an assessment, but rather a tool, it is important to highlight its functions as it supports the development of a CSCP that is connected to the ASCA National Model. This interactive computer-based tool helps school counselors keep track of their time and document information to build a data-informed CSCP (SCUTA, 2020). While there is a free trial available, SCUTA has costs associated with purchasing a license, depending on the version: Lite, Pro, Max, R, SD, or University. One of the main functions of the SCUTA is that it allows school counselor to run analyses of how they are using their time. In addition, school counselors can keep detailed notes on their daily, weekly, and monthly activities through a secure login. This process can be especially helpful for school counselors during annual evaluations with administrators. We discuss this tool and its utility in greater detail in Chapter 6.

Deliver

The Deliver quadrant of the ASCA National Model explains how school counselors' time should be spent. Two major categories—*direct student services* and *indirect student services*—divide a school counselor's time (ASCA, 2019a). Under the direct student services umbrella, ASCA uses the categories of instruction, appraisal, advisement, and counseling to dissect how school counselors directly serve students. Therefore, ASCA (2019a) clearly connects to the *ASCA Mindsets & Behaviors for Student Success: K-12 College and Career Readiness Standards for Every Student* by emphasizing the importance of intentionality of services. The indirect student services a school counselor provides are achieved through an advocacy lens to help support the educational experience of each student. ASCA (2019a) defines *indirect student services* as the school counselor's work that involves consultation, collaboration, and referrals on behalf of the student. The two overarching categories of student services (i.e., direct and indirect) are divided by the 80/20 rule, respectively. As we have discussed in Chapters 1 and 2, the 80/20 rule means that 80% of a school counselor's time should be spent working directly with students (e.g., classroom lessons, small groups, one-on-one). The remaining 20% of a school counselor's time should be spent advocating for students through indirect service as a collaborator, consultant, and by completing referrals for additional services for students that are beyond the scope of the school counselor (ASCA, 2019a). For example, a school counselor can be a collaborator and consultant through membership on the MTSS or PBIS team. As a member of these teams, the school counselor can collaborate with other team members to make decisions on school-wide programming and provide consultation or support services for individual students.

The goal of the Deliver quadrant is to explain the school counselor's role for direct work with students and the indirect services that are provided on behalf of the students. To reiterate, ASCA clearly explains what ratio of time should be spent on each type of service. To make a clear connection as to how assessments can be connected within this quadrant, we are going to first expand on the direct student services categories of instruction, appraisal, advisement, and counseling. ASCA (2019a) states that, "instruction includes teaching the school counseling curriculum to students focused through the lens of selected student standards from the ASCA Mindsets & Behaviors" (p. 78). This includes school counselors working with students in whole or small groups to deliver content to support student development related to academic, career, and social and emotional learning. These lessons are intentional and are connected to the school counselor's CSCP.

The Deliver quadrant continues to expand on other services, including appraisal and advisement. Indeed, ASCA defines this as two-steps to support students in their development and is connected back to the *ASCA Mindsets & Behaviors* through direct services (ASCA, 2019a). According to ASCA (2019a), "appraisal is the process where school counselors work with students to analyze and assess their abilities, interests, skills and achievements" (p. 80). The appraisal process occurs by using preexisting data and gathering new data via assessments (2019a). This step of the process is where valid and reliable assessments can help support school counselors through the appraisal process. School counselors can use inventories, surveys, and assessments that provide information about a student's performance. This could be in relation to executive functioning, organization, peer relations, or career planning. However, career is a common topic of conversation with students within the appraisal process—particularly with students in grades 7th to 12th. The appraisal process may be more focused on needs associated with being successful within the classroom for younger students. Advising builds on appraisal by taking the information learned and working with students to create an action plan (2019a).

School counselors can support students' social and emotional needs in the form of individual, small-group, and core curricular classroom lessons (ASCA, 2019a). While school counselors do not provide long-term counseling, they do work with students to help support their development as it relates to the academic, career, and social–emotional domains (2019a). In our role of supporting students within our scope and practice, valid and reliable assessments can provide additional data to enhance our practices. Various assessments can be used to gather information on where a student is, and in turn can be used to advocate for a student's needs with key stakeholders.

Strengths and Difficulties Questionnaire

Goodman (1997) created the Strengths and Difficulties Questionnaire (SDQ), which comes in multiple versions, including a parent, teacher, and student report. Since the creation of the SDQ, it has become a popular tool to use to gain more insight into children's mental health wellness (Goodman et al., 2010). The parent report is intended to be used to record information on children between the ages of 4 and 16. The teacher report is divided into two reports: one for ages 4 through 11 and another for ages 11 through 16. The student self-report is intended for students between the ages of 11 and 16. Originally reported by Goodman (1997) and Goodman et al. (1998), the SDQ was intended for ages 4 through 16. However, the website where the SDQ versions are housed, in multiple languages, includes age ranges from 2 to 18 years and older. School counselors can access copies of the SDQ as a downloadable PDF for free. The link can be found within the tools and resources section of this chapter.

As a whole, the various versions of the SDQ are behaviorally based screeners intended to measure both internalizing and externalizing behaviors that lead to an overall Total Difficulties Score (Goodman, 1997; Goodman et al., 2010). In addition to this total score, the screeners are broken into five subscales: Emotional Symptoms, Conduct Problems, Hyperactivity/Inattention, Relationship Problems, and Prosocial Behavior, which include five questions for each of the subscales (Goodman et al., 1998). The SDQ was measured against another similar valid and reliable questionnaire and found that it performed as well as the other questionnaire (Goodman, 1997). Additionally, a pilot study was conducted on the SDQ self-report version to demonstrate promising validity, but concluded more research was needed (Goodman et al., 1998).

While the SDQ has been wildly popular in clinical settings related to better understanding children and adolescent mental health (Goodman et al., 2010), the SDQ can have a wide application to your school counseling practice and can be a valuable tool for collecting data. Through consultation and collaboration, the SDQ can be used to gather more information from the teacher, parent, and the student (if age appropriate) on the child's behavior. This information can be used within your MTSS team to discuss and determine the best services for your student(s). Additionally, through your CSCP, this information can be used as a discussion point with parents during conferences to discuss the referral of community-based counseling services. It is important to remember that our role is to advocate for students using data. As we discussed in Chapter 2, it is important to have multiple forms of data when determining program and services for students. Now we explore how to evaluate your CSCP through application of the Assess quadrant of the ASCA National Model.

Assess

The Assess quadrant focuses on the results of the school counselor's CSCP. School counselors confirm student learning within CSCPs by analyzing data. Indeed, ASCA (2019a) states, "School counselors engage in assessment to inform potential improvements to school counseling program design and delivery and to show how students are different as a result of the school counseling program" (p. 85). Assessments provide additional data regarding student learning and growth through participation in CSCPs.

The Assess section highlights how to engage in program assessment by using the School Counseling Program Assessment, which includes standards for CSCP programs that are aligned with the ASCA National Model (ASCA, 2019a). We were unable to find any information on the validity and reliability of this assessment; however, as we pointed out in Chapter 2, informal assessments also provide school counselors with valuable information. Furthermore, ASCA guides school counselors to review their responses after completing the self-assessment to determine the areas of strength, the potential for growth, and their plans to improve their CSCP (2019a). While engaging in your own assessment for professional growth, it is important to assess your program for student growth.

Other components of the Assess section include an explanation of annual results reports as well as how to use these reporting methods to support a CSCP. Again, ASCA (2019a) explains that results reports should be data-informed. To accomplish this, ASCA (2019a) provides school counselors with two types of annual results reports: Classroom and Group Mindsets & Behaviors Results Report and Closing-the-Gap Action Plan/Results Report. School counselors enhance their programming by collecting data from these reports and by collecting Participation, Mindsets & Behaviors and Outcome data (ASCA, 2019a). These three types of data are discussed in detail in the forthcoming chapters.

The analysis of the *Classroom and Group Mindsets & Behaviors Results Report* is an ASCA-provided template that helps school counselors collect and organize all of the information and data from both whole-group and small-group lessons (ASCA, 2019a). The assessment template is structured around Participation, Mindsets & Behaviors, and Outcome data. The template provides school counselors to determine three data-focused questions in the Implications section, which probe the school counselor to determine ways to use the data to inform their ongoing practice (2019a). Additionally, other questions help school counselors analyze their classroom- and small-group services-specific data. The Closing-the-Gap Action Plan/Results Report, which is also highlighted in the Manage section, describes how to analyze the results (2019a).

The ASCA School Counselor Professional Standards & Competencies Assessment is provided within the Assess quadrant, which is intended as a self-assessment for the school counselor to inform their assessment of their professional practice (ASCA, 2019a). Further, ASCA (2019a) states, "the assessment is a self-report of the acquisition of the mindsets and behaviors school counselors need to meet the school counseling profession's rigorous demands and pre-K–12 students' needs" (p. 94). School counselors can use the ASCA School Counselor Professional Standards & Competencies Assessment to create a professional development plan (2019a) or use it in conjunction with their state-mandated school counselor's evaluation.

The Assess quadrant provides additional guidance and direction regarding how to share information about the school counseling program. Some ideas include sharing information via the school counselor webpage, through the creation of graphics or digital presentations, as well as other means of communication as highlighted by the ASCA National Model (ASCA, 2019a, p. 93). We have seen school counselors post informative information through their "School Counselor's Corner" webpage that is housed within the school's website. The key takeaway is to refrain from keeping information related to a program's success in a locked file. Rather, the goal is to disseminate this information in the community to show the value that the CSCP and the school counselor as a whole bring to the student body and subsequent student growth (2019a). Additionally, school counselors can use Dr. Hatch's Flashlight approach to disseminating information that was discussed earlier within this chapter. For more ways to highlight and promote your CSCP, refer to Chapter 6.

While one of the goals of the Assess quadrant is to help school counselors organize their data, ultimately, we are gathering this information to show how students were impacted by participation. This organization is achieved by providing school counselors with guiding questions to organize the reporting process of their data. The overarching idea is to ensure that school counselors can effectively communicate their student success program accomplishments to inform key stakeholders.

School Counselor Evaluation

It is important for us to address your role as a school counselor, where you are employed, and how you are evaluated by your district. We do so by showcasing a few state evaluations. Some state evaluations require you to provide evidence of how you serve students through your CSCP. For example, several states have adopted their own statewide school counselor evaluation systems. In this section, we highlight a few state examples as well as the ASCA National Model School Counselor Performance Appraisal Template, which administrators use to evaluate school counselors' performance (ASCA, 2019a). The following sections will highlight the various school counselor evaluations.

Ohio School Counselor Evaluation Model

The Ohio Department of Education (ODE) has a state-specific evaluation process and standards for school counselors. In 2015, the state adopted school counseling standards in response to changes in Ohio law regarding how educators are evaluated to better support school counselors in their professional role (ODE, 2020). As outlined in the *Ohio Standards for School Counselors*, developing the evaluation included support from the Ohio School Counselor Association (OSCA), which saw the need to create a set of Ohio-based standards to support both school counselors and evaluators through the new Ohio evaluation system (ODE, 2015). What is unique about the development of the Ohio school counselor evaluation process is the external documents that were considered in the creation of the system. The ODE (2015) formed a writing team that reviewed the ASCA National Model, the National Board School Counseling Standards, and training standard issued by Council for Accreditation of Counseling and Related Educational Programs (CACREP) for counselor preparation programs (2015).

The Ohio standards are to be used by school counselors to provide an overview of what is expected of them as a school counselor while providing opportunities to continue to grow (ODE, 2015). Additionally, adopting statewide school counseling standards helps to support professional continuity among districts regarding the professional role of the school counselor (2015). Having a state standard that outlines a CSCP as a role-appropriate function is critical. This allows school counselors to advocate for time and space to evaluate data and develop a CSCP, as it is tied to their state standards. Other standards include a focus of direct services, data, leadership, advocacy, and continued professional development.

The evaluation framework, as highlighted by the ODE (2016a), was designed to incorporate the newly created Ohio School Counseling standards into an evaluation model. This allows administrators the opportunity to evaluate school counselors in relation to their professional role rather than using a standard teacher evaluation. The standards-based model works to support school counselors in their growth while considering all areas of performance and their continued commitment to student outcomes (2016a). The model is composed of four ratings, including ineffective, developing, skilled, and accomplished. Each of these rating areas is later addressed for each of the standards (2016a).

The *Ohio School Counselor Evaluation Model* manual provides a complete overview of the framework and process for evaluating school counselors (ODE, 2016b). The manual includes guidelines and examples for the observation process for both formal and informal observations. Additionally, it outlines the expectations for both the school counselor and the evaluator during the review process. The Ohio school counseling standards, framework, and evaluation model appear to be most in line with the ASCA National Model and ASCA's School Counselor Mindsets & Behaviors. The Ohio documents are representative resources for other states wanting to adopt statewide standards or an evaluation process for school counselors.

Colorado Special Services Providers: School Counselors

The Colorado Department of Education (CDE; 2016) has its own manual regarding school counselors' practice—*Colorado State Model Evaluation System for Specialized Service Professionals: Practical Ideas Guide for Evaluating School Counselors*. The manual was developed in 2016 after a pilot study was conducted. During the 2013 to 2014 school year, the CDE (2015) conducted a pilot study on their state school counselor evaluation system. The CDE has a specific scoring rubric called, *Rubric for Evaluating Colorado Special Services Providers: School Counselors,* that is used to evaluate school counselors (CDE, n.d.). It is important to note that an updated evaluation model could not be located in connection to the recently updated ASCA National Model.

The CDE manual outlines the passage of Colorado's Senate Bill 10-191, which mandates all licensed individuals working within Colorado schools must be evaluated annually and details the improvements that have been made to the evaluation process for school counselors. To address the unique roles and services provided by school counselors, the CDE completed a pilot study of the school counseling specific evaluation and found that 96% of all school counselors were at least proficient within their professional role on a 5-point rating scale within 12 school districts (CDE, 2015). The study stated, "school counselors performed the best on Standard 1 (Professional Expertise) and Standard 4 (Reflect on Practice). Standard 3 (High Quality Delivery) was the standard with the most school counselors below the level of proficient" (2015, p. 1). Additionally, a positive shift was reported in all areas of the state model evaluation system in comparison to the former system (2015). The CDE (2016) highlights within the manual that it recognizes that not all school counselors will be working within or from a CSCP. However, school counseling programs should be student centered, data driven, sustainable, evaluated, regularly and focused on student needs, which is in line with the ASCA National Model *when this document was published* (CDE, 2016).

Other ASCA recommendations of percentage of time and school counselor to student ratio were highlighted. However, the CDE included its own breakdown of services by percentage and grade level. Other items from the third edition of the *ASCA National Model* were referenced or included as graphics within the model (ASCA, 2012). The purpose of the manual was to provide samples of the evaluation process for both school counselors and administrators. Samples highlighted a demonstration of implementations of a CSCP that was geared toward the needs of the students. A complete chart was included to guide ratings with artifacts submitted to support school administrators in the appropriate evaluation of school counselors. The scoring rubric addresses different levels of practice among various elements with respect to the core functions of what the state has defined as the school counselor's roles (CDE, n.d.). While the rubric lacks core ASCA language, it does address ethical practice, evidence-based programming, and alignment with laws and policies at all levels.

ASCA National Model School Counselor Performance Appraisal Template

The School Counselor Performance Appraisal within the National Model is intended to be used as a template that can be connected to other frameworks used by the school district or the state department of education (ASCA, 2019a). School counselors are encouraged to have a qualified individual, such as a building administrator, complete the evaluation. The language within this template should be used to create a district or state version of a school counselor evaluation. Ultimately, ASCA states that the evaluation should assess the fundamental elements of a CSCP that includes data-informed goals and services.

We encourage our readers to reference the current edition of the ASCA National Model for a complete list of the core items that can be included in a school counselor's performance evaluation. With ASCA's recommendation to have a statewide performance evaluation, the preceding sections highlighted state-specific examples of evaluations that are designed to measure school counselors' performance within that state. This is not an exhaustive list of all states that have incorporated an evaluation system for school counselors. In the past, school counselors have been evaluated using the same state standard evaluations as teachers.

Conclusions

The goal of Chapter 3 is to help you understand how assessment intersects with each of the quadrants of the ASCA National Model. We covered how assessments provide a starting point for school counselors when building or restructuring a CSCP. The assessments covered within this chapter are valid and reliable in helping school counselors make informed decisions regarding their CSCP. While some of the assessments are dated in comparison to the recently updated fourth edition of the ASCA National Model, each assessment discussed is still relevant to current school counseling practices. Importantly, each assessment demonstrates how school counselors can incorporate various assessments into the development, implementation, and management of a CSCP.

Additional Readings

American School Counselor Association. (2019a). *ASCA national model: A framework for school counseling programs* (4th ed.). American School Counselor Association.

American School Counselor Association. *(2019b). ASCA national model implementation guide: Manage and assess* (2nd ed.). American School Counselor Association.

Goodman-Scott, E., Betters-Bubon, J., & Donohue, P. (Eds.). (2019). *The school counselor's guide to multi-tiered systems of support.* Routledge.

Hatch, T. (2014). *The use of data in school counseling: Hatching results for students, programs, and the profession.* Corwin.

Zyromski, B. & Mariani, M.A. (2016). *Facilitating evidence-based, data-driven school counseling: A manual for practice.* Corwin.

Tools and Resources

- A copy of the SCARS can be located through the *UMass Amherst School Counselor Resources* (https://www.cscoreumass.org/sc-resources)
- A copy of the Strengths & Difficulties Questionnaire and related items be accessed through the developer's website (https://www.sdqinfo.org/py/sdqinfo/b0.py)

Key Points

- The use of assessments can be incorporated into each of the four quadrants of the ASCA National Model.
- Valid and reliable assessments can help school counselors assess the current state of their CSCP.
- School counselors can use valid and reliable assessments to inform both their direct and indirect service delivery.
- Assessments shape the direction of all school counseling services and provide school counselors with data to enhance their service efficacy and advocacy efforts.

Questions for Reflection

- How can a school counselor use the SCPIS to shape their practice?
- How are assessments utilized in the Manage quadrant of the ASCA National Model?
- Which assessments are connected to direct student services and how can these assessments be used by school counselors who are working directly with students?

References

American School Counselor Association. (2012). *ASCA national model: A framework for school counseling programs* (3rd ed.). American School Counselor Association.

American School Counselor Association. (2014). *ASCA mindsets & behaviors for student success K-12 college-and career-readiness standards for every student.* https://www.schoolcounselor.org/getmedia/7428a787-a452-4abb-afec-d78ec77870cd/Mindsets-Behaviors.pdf

American School Counselor Association. (2016). *ASCA ethical standards for school counselors.* https://www.schoolcounselor.org/getmedia/f041cbd0-7004-47a5-ba01-3a5d657c6743/Ethical-Standards.pdf

American School Counselor Association. (2019a). *ASCA national model: A framework for school counseling programs* (4th ed.). American School Counselor Association.

American School Counselor Association. (2019b). *ASCA national model implementation guide: Manage and assess* (2nd ed.). American School Counselor Association.

American School Counselor Association. (2019c). *ASCA school counselor professional standards and competencies.* https://www.schoolcounselor.org/getmedia/a8d59c2c-51de-4ec3-a565-a3235f3b93c3/SC-Competencies.pdf

Clemens, E., Milsom, A., & Cashwell, C. (2009). Using leader-member exchange theory to examine principal–school counselor relationships, school counselors' roles, job satisfaction, and turnover intentions.*Professional School Counseling, 13*(2), 75–85. https://doi.org/10.5330/PSC.N.2010-13.75

Clemens, E. V., Carey, J. C., & Harrington, K. M. (2010). The School Counseling Program Implementation Survey: Initial instrument development and exploratory factor analysis. *Professional School Counseling, 14*(2), 125–134. https://doi.org/10.1177/2156759X100140020

Colorado Department of Education & Practitioners Across Colorado. (2016). *Colorado state model evaluation system for specialized service professionals: Practical ideas guide for evaluating school counselors.* https://www.cde.state.co.us/educatoreffectiveness/practical_ideas_guide_schoolcounselors

Colorado Department of Education. (n.d.). *Rubric for evaluating Colorado special services providers: School counselors.* https://www.cde.state.co.us/educatoreffectiveness/sspcounselorrubric

Colorado Department of Education. (2015). *Colorado state model evaluation system for school counselors: 2013–2014 pilot report.* https://www.cde.state.co.us/educatoreffectiveness/ssppilotreportcounselor

Dahir, C. A., & Stone, C. B. (2006). *Preparing the next generation: Implementing new paradigms for school counseling preservice and practice.* In Ideas and Research You Can Use: VISTAS 2006. https://www.counseling.org/docs/default-source/vistas/preparing-the-next-generation-implementing-new-paradigms-for-school-counseling-preservice-and-practce.pdf?sfvrsn=2dd7e2c_10

Dahir, C. A., & Stone, C. B. (2009). School counselor accountability: The path to social justice and systemic change. *Journal of Counseling & Development, 87*(1), 12–20. https://doi.org/10.1002/j.1556-6678.2009.tb00544.x

Dimmitt, C., Carey, J. C., & Hatch, T. (2007). Evidence-based school counseling: Making a difference with data-driven practices. Corwin.

DuFour, R., Guidice, A., Magee, D., Martin, P., & Zivovic, B. (2002). The student support team as a professional learning community. In C. D. Johnson & S. K. Johnson (Eds.), *Building stronger school counseling programs: Bringing futuristic approaches into the present* (pp. 19–36). CAPS.

Elsner, D., & Carey, J. (2005). *School counseling program implementation survey.* Unpublished assessment instrument.

Erford, B. T. (2019). Culturally competent school counselors: Affirming diversity by challenging oppression. In B. T. Erford (Ed.), *Transforming the school counseling profession* (5th ed., pp. 172–189). Pearson.

Goodman, A., Lamping, D. L., & Ploubidis, G. B. (2010). When to use broader internalising and externalising subscales instead of the hypothesized five subscales on the Strengths and Difficulties Questionnaire (SDQ): Data from British parents, teachers and children. *Journal of Abnormal Child Psychology, 38*(8), 1179–1191. https://doi.org/10.1007/s10802-010-9434-x

Goodman, R. (1997). The Strengths and Difficulties Questionnaire: A research note. *Child Psychology & Psychiatry & Allied Disciplines, 38*(5), 581–586. https://doi.org/10.1111/j.1469-7610.1997.tb01545.x

Goodman, R., Meltzer, H., & Bailey, V. (1998). The Strengths and Difficulties Questionnaire: A pilot study on the validity of the self-report version. *European Child & Adolescent Psychiatry, 7*(3), 125–130. https://doi.org/10.1007/s007870050057

Goodman-Scott, E., Betters-Bubon, J., & Donohue, P. (Eds.). (2019). *The school counselor's guide to multi-tiered systems of support.* Routledge.

Goodman-Scott, E., & Ockerman, M. S. (2019). Integrating school counseling and MTSS. In E. Goodman-Scott, J. Betters-Bubon, & P. Donohue (Eds.), *The school counselor's guide to multi-tiered systems of support* (pp. 29–61). Routledge.

Gysbers, N. C. & Henderson, P. (2001). Comprehensive guidance and counseling programs: A rich history and bright future. *Professional School Counseling, 4*(4), 246–256.

Gysbers, N. C., Stanley, J. B., Kosteck-Bunch, L., Magnuson, C. S., & Starr, M. F. (2017). *Missouri comprehensive school counseling program: A manual for program development, implementation, evaluation, and enhancement.* http://www.missouricareereducation.org/doc/guidemanual/Manual.pdf

Hatch, T. (2014). *The use of data in school counseling: Hatching results for students, programs, and the profession.* Corwin.

Johnson, C. D., & Johnson, S. K. (2002). *Building stronger school counseling programs: Bringing futuristic approaches into the present.* CAPS.

Mason, E. C. M., Ockerman, M. S., & Chen-Hayes, S. F. (2013). Change-Agent-for-Equity (CAFE) model: A framework for school counselor identity. *Journal of School Counseling, 11*(4), 1–25. http://www.jsc.montana.edu/articles/v11n4.pdf

Myrick, R. D. (2011). *Developmental guidance and counseling: A practical approach* (5th ed.). Educational Media Corporation.

Nelson, M. D., & Tarabochia, D. S. (2020). A primer on designing a school counseling curriculum. *Journal of School Counseling, 18*(6), 1–26. http:/www.jsc.montana.edu/articles/v18n6.pdf

Ohio Department of Education. (2015). *Ohio standards for school counselors.* http://education.ohio.gov/getattachment/Topics/Career-Tech/Career-Connections/School-Counselors/School-Counselor-Standards-and-Evaluation/SchoolCounselorStandards.pdf.aspx

Ohio Department of Education. (2016a). *Evaluation framework for school counselors.* http://education.ohio.gov/getattachment/Topics/Career-Tech/Career-Connections/School-Counselors/School-Counselor-Standards-and-Evaluation/School-Counselor-Evaluation-Framework-04-15-2016.pdf.aspx

Ohio Department of Education. (2016b). *Ohio school counselor evaluation model.* http://education.ohio.gov/getattachment/Topics/Career-Tech/Career-Connections/Resources-for-School-Counselors/School-Counselor-Standards-and-Evaluation/OSCES-Model.pdf.aspx

Ohio Department of Education. (2020). *School counselor standards and evaluation.* http://education.ohio.gov/Topics/Teaching/Educator-Evaluation-System/School-Counselor-Standards-and-Evaluation

Scarborough, J. L. (2005a). The School Counselor Activity rating Scale: An instrument for gathering process data. *Professional School Counseling, 8*(3), 274–283. https://www.jstor.org/stable/42732469

Scarborough, J. L. (2005b). *The School Counselor Activity Rating Scale.* https://85366e73-a5db-4b8c-a573-ed2d99e88528.filesusr.com/ugd/b96ded_c73e4fd77d814fc1903f452b3ad314f4.pdf

SCUTA. (2020). *What is SCUTA?* https://www.myscuta.com/

UMass Amherst College of Education. (2019). *School counselor resources: Instruments.* https://www.cscoreumass.org/sc-resources

Youth in Mind. (2015a, January, 1). *What is the SDQ?.* https://www.sdqinfo.org/ao.htm

Youth in Mind. (2015b, December, 9). *Downloadable SDQs and related items.* https://www.sdqinfo.org/py/sdqinfo/b0.py

Zyromski, B., & Mariani, M. A. (2016). Facilitating evidence-based, data-driven school counseling: A manual for practice. Corwin.

4

ASSESSMENTS TO SUPPORT DATA-DRIVEN DIRECT SERVICES

Assessments to Support Data-Driven Direct Services

The current climate of our educational system, as well as society, emphasizes the importance of accountability and student success. Regardless of one's specific career or job responsibilities, being able to measure change, growth, or success is critical, especially for the data-driven school counselor. Thus, formal and informal assessments can and should be used to inform the work counselors perform as well as measure student progress. This chapter focuses on describing instruments for school counselors to utilize when providing direct services to students, whether it be during individual counseling, group counseling, whole-class lessons, or school-wide activities.

Often, when educators hear the word *assessment*, a common thought process is to consider assessment for the purpose of determining eligibility for special education services or further intervention. Although this is correct, the reality is that whether someone is a teacher, nurse, administrator, or school counselor, they are utilizing assessments and their associated data as a part of their role. For instance, teachers rely heavily on numerous measures to assess their student's content knowledge and skills, whereas administrators rely on measures to evaluate teacher performance. For school counselors, assessments, whether formal or informal, offer the opportunity to make data-driven decisions that are in the best interest of students.

The Influence of Assessment on Delivery of Services

As mentioned in Chapter 1, the findings of Neukrug et al. (2013) highlighted that very few assessments that are included in counselor preparation program assessment courses are of relevance or significance to the work of school counselors. The notion that school counselors are not being adequately introduced to appropriate assessments to inform their work is of great concern. We are doing a disservice to school counselors and students alike when they are not provided with opportunities to develop competence in this area. So you are probably left wondering, "Why don't school counselors-in-training have knowledge and competence in using assessment as a critical part of their role?"

Addressing the Research-to-Practice Gap

The reality of the research–practice gap really hit me [Sandra] during my doctoral studies. While I was consistently researching and writing, I was also being exposed to the breadth of literature that exists on this subject, including scholarly articles about various counseling assessments. At the time, I was also providing clinical supervision to school counselors-in-training. Vividly, I remember conducting weekly individual supervision sessions with students and was excited to share information about instruments that I thought might be helpful to their practice. Often, they were excited about the potential of using them, but were often met with equal disappointment because they did not know the instruments existed. Sometimes my supervisees were so enthusiastic that they would return to their practicum or internship site and share the instrument with their site supervisor. This continued to happen for consecutive semesters. It was then I realized the research-to-practice gap is real.

As you are reading this, you might be thinking to yourself, "Yes, I would not even know where to begin, when it comes to looking for assessments that I can or should use!" If so, you are not alone. This very notion really was the impetus that led us to write this book. We wanted to create an easier and more accessible way to develop the attitudes, knowledge, and skills to be a data-driven school counselor who is competent in assessment and data collection.

Use of Valid and Reliable Instruments

When I (Sandra) utter the phrase *valid and reliable* to school counselors or those in training, it is often met with an eye roll or an audible sigh. Often, what people think of is their lack of confidence or competence in research and assessment, which is often attributed to not learning the necessary skills in their counselor preparation program. But the good news is that you don't have to be an expert in this area, as you are simply a consumer of a researcher's work. Rather than being responsible for creating and testing an instrument's utility, you get to reap the benefits of a researcher's investment in developing such a valid and reliable measure. As a practicing school counselor, it is important that you approach your work from the framework of evidence-based practice. Bardhoshi et al. (2019) emphasize that "selecting appropriate tools to demonstrate positive outcomes on key emotional and behavior concerns is an essential component of establishing evidence-based practice" (p. 89). We encourage you to review this article, as the researchers provide an excellent introduction to free, valid, and reliable instruments that are appropriate for school counselors focused on evidence-based outcomes for students who exhibit common internalized emotional and externalized behavioral concerns. Reviewing this information will help you understand the connection of the evidence, or rather data, that you collect on your students and how it directly influences your school counseling practice and implementation of your comprehensive school counseling program (CSCP).

Also, we wanted to encourage you to seek out the information that you need. Feel free to contact authors/researchers to request use of their instrument and share with them how you are interested in using it in your practice; Trust me, they appreciate it. Nonetheless, we are excited to be able to offer you this unique opportunity to learn more about a variety of assessments, many of which are free, valid, and reliable, and online platforms that address the academic, career, and social–emotional domains of the critical work we do as school counselors.

Databases and Compendiums Available for Your Use

We know firsthand the demands and struggles that you all face on a daily basis. One of the aspects in utilizing assessment begins with knowing what is available and accessible. For some of you, exploring online databases might be a great starting place. Getting to know what exists can help inform which instruments you decide to collect. There are two key databases that we want to encourage you to utilize. First, *RAND Education Assessment Finder* is an online database that allows you to explore instruments that are designed to measure social, emotional, and academic competencies, all of which align well with our American School Counselor Association (ASCA) National Model. The second is Measuring SEL: Assessment Guide from the Collaborative for Academic, Social, and Emotional Learning (CASEL). This online database allows you to review assessments and make decisions about which instrument may be best for your intended goals and audience. Additional resource guides are available to assist you in the decision-making aspects of your planned assessment process.

Finally, there are a number of organizations that have created compendiums of a variety of assessments that are relevant to school counselors. For instance, the U.S. Department of Education has created a suite of survey instruments known as *ED School Climate Surveys (EDSCLS)*. CASEL also has a variety of resources to support school assessment practices, including a *Compendium of Preschool through Elementary School Social–Emotional Learning and Associated Assessment Measures.* In addition to these organizations, Zyromski and Mariani (2016) also provide a sample list of instruments that are valid and reliable that may be used in assessing school-based curricula, programs, and interventions. If you don't immediately have time to search the databases or feel like that is not enough structure for you, in this chapter, we describe numerous assessments that you may consider utilizing, organized by the ASCA domains of academic, career, and social–emotional development and with respect to desired outcome areas. But first, let's begin by considering what may already be available at your school or district.

In-House Data

While much of this chapter is focused on formal assessment, it's important to realize that sources of data already exist at the school, district, and state levels. For instance, every school counselor should have access to running reports in their school's student information system (SIS). Of course, these vary from district to district, but most should be able to provide reports that can provide helpful data. For instance, you might want to know, after the first 9 weeks of the term, how many ninth-grade students have earned three or more Ds or Fs. Your data-collection efforts are actually quite simple for this: Run a query/report from your system and there you go. You have data. This is directly tied to academic achievement, so yes this is appropriate to consider within this domain. But the same also holds true for aspects like attendance. Thus, we could focus on data-collection efforts that pinpoint attendance concerns or patterns. For instance, you might want to know how many and which students are excessively tardy to the first class of the day. By reviewing such a query, you may then be able to determine which students you want to check in with and see how you can support them making it to school on time. Speaking to each of these students, you may be able to identify resources or other supports that can improve their ability to attend school and thereby be more academically successful.

In addition to looking for data about your own students, you might want to know how your data compares to other schools in your district. We highly recommend using the SchoolDigger website, where you can search any school in the United States, public or private, and get instant access to school demographics and performance. According to their website (www.schooldigger.com), the database contains more than 20 years of enrollment data, test scores, free/reduced lunch rates, and educator statistics that come from national education reporting agencies like the U.S. Department of Education. Further, we recommend that you monitor your school's data on this website, in conjunction with your district and state portals in order to be aware of the current or emerging trends.

Consider that you are entering the new academic school year at a new school. Perhaps one of your very first steps is to review the existing school data: school improvement plan, school report card, and annual and grading period reports that show nonpassing grades, truancy issues, and enrollment patterns. While it is important that school counselors create their own sources of data, we also need to work

TABLE 4.1 SOURCES OF DATA EXISTING IN SCHOOLS

ATTENDANCES RATES (ABSENCES, TARDY, TRUANCY)	ACHIEVEMENT-RELATED TEST SCORES
School Climate Survey data	Needs assessment data
Demographic data (i.e., free/reduced lunch status, race, ethnicity, English language learner, special education eligibility)	Health surveys
Completion rates (i.e., FAFSA, 4- or 6-year academic plans, homework)	Grade point averages
College acceptance rates	PSAT, SAT, ACT, AP test scores
Retention data	End-of-course exams
Parental engagement/involvement rates	Graduation and dropout rates
Comparison data with school district or state level	Course enrollment patterns
Grade reports of Ds/Fs	Discipline, suspension, & expulsion data
School rank	Student-to-counselor ratio

ACT, American College Test; AP, advanced placement; PSAT, Preliminary Scholastic Aptitude Test; SAT, Scholastic Aptitude Test.

smarter, not harder, and that includes starting with the data that you have available. From there, you can decide what further data you need or want to collect to inform your work.

Assessments to Address the Academic Domain

As one would expect, schools are organizational systems that heavily focus on academic assessment, and specifically focus on standardized testing approaches that aim to measure student learning outcomes. Yet, a critical thing to understand is that one's academics success is not simply about achievement; it is also about the learning environment. Thus, we believe it is important to highlight instruments that address school climate within this domain. Now, let's dive into discussing both formal and informal assessments that are easily accessible and that you may find helpful for your school counseling practice. Remember that *formal assessment* simply refers to those instruments are designed and then validated by researchers for an intended audience (i.e., not a pre–posttest that you created based on your small-group counseling intervention).

Social, Academic, and Emotional Behavior Risk Screener

The Social, Academic, and Emotional Behavior Risk Screener (SAEBRS; Kilgus et al., 2013) is a great comprehensive tool that can be used in grades K-12 as a universal screener. While this instrument could also be categorized under other types of assessments that we discuss, we know that academic performance does not function independently of one's social and emotional behavior; in fact, it is important to recognize the intersectionality of these three areas that represent the subscales of the instrument, and directly influence academic performance and success. Perhaps this is why this is one of our favorite assessments to share with you. Moreover, it has strong psychometrics and is easy to administer. It contains a rating scale that uses a simple 4-point Likert scale from 0=never to 3=almost always. We appreciate that the scale does not include *always* as it is not typical for a student to always perform the identified behaviors during the previous month. It is recommended that this screener be utilized on a consistent basis, perhaps quarterly or following a report card-type schedule. Using this screener across all grades could be managed by creating a Google form, wherein the classroom teachers complete one for each of their students at a given interval, or a pencil-paper version given its brevity.

Since the tool does not have formal cutoff scores, you can determine how the scores want to be used for further intervention. For instance, the summative scores (or subscales for that matter) at one school may highlight that cooperation with peers is a pervasive issue. Thus, the school counselor decided to implement core curricular lessons that address this challenge across all classroom. In comparison, another school may find that cooperation with peers is an issue in two particular classrooms with a subset of students. Here, the school counselors' time and efforts may be best spent in delivering small-group counseling to those identified students. So this assessment is both comprehensive in addressing three different areas of student behavior and also flexible in terms of scoring and subsequent interventions.

My Class Inventory (MCI) Measures

The My Class Inventory (MCI) instruments intend to measure school climate, specifically, classroom climate in upper elementary: fourth through sixth grade. There are multiple versions of this instrument, each with fewer than 30 items, that allow perspectives from various stakeholders, including self (student version), teacher version, and parent/caregiver version. Sink and Spencer created and validated both instruments, My Class Inventory–Short Form Revised (MCI-SFR; Sink & Spencer, 2005) and My Class Inventory–Short Form for Teachers (TMCI-SF; 2007), for use among elementary school students and teachers. More recently, the parent version, My Child's Classroom Inventory-Short Form (MCCI-SF; Sink, 2017) was designed to provide school counselors with further perspective about students' classroom environment. One of the benefits of this assessment is that you are able to gather data about a particular aspect from various perspectives or stakeholders. With scoring being a relatively simple process, the results can easily help the school counselor better understand the current satisfaction, friction, competition, and cohesiveness within a classroom from all three perspectives. Such information can help shed light on which services are best for the counselor to provide. These instruments are free and publicly accessible (Exhibits 4.1–4.3).

The Community and Youth Collaborative Institute—School Experience Surveys

The Community and Youth Collaborative Institute—School Experience Surveys (CAYCI-SES; Anderson-Butcher et al., 2013) is a collection of assessment tools designed to support schools in understanding a broad range of aspects from multiple stakeholders. Perhaps one of the more comprehensive assessments that we highlight in this book, this instrument can help school counselors and administrators best understand their school's culture and performance. The available versions are for elementary school students, middle/high school students, teacher/staff, and parent/caregiver. In the elementary and middle/high versions, students are asked to respond to a variety of domains, including academic motivation, career and college readiness, family & community connections, parental involvement internalizing and externalizing behaviors, peer relationships, perceived school climate and safety, and school connectedness. In the school employee version, individuals are asked about the school environment and study body, specifically on how the school and local community help to support student achievement, through domains such as family support for learning, school support for parent/caregiver engagement, community services, diversity, perceived school climate, student psychological well-being, and teacher/staff commitment. Lastly, the parent/caregiver version focuses on capturing the perspective they have on their own children's learning, including career and college readiness, experiences of teacher and school support, family engagement efficacy, parent/caregiver support and involvement in activities. Due to the comprehensive nature of the CAYCI-SES, school counselors will have ample opportunity to engage in disaggregating the data to uncover the areas of improvement or concern. Therefore, you can engage in data-driven decision-making that will inform the implementation of your comprehensive

My Class Inventory (2005)

Student Actual Short Form—Revised[1] (Sink & Spencer, 2005)

Name: ______________________ Teacher: ______________________

Grade level: 4th 5th 6th (circle one) I am a GIRL or a BOY (circle one)

Directions:

This is not a test. The questions are to find out what your class is really like.

Each sentence asks you to think about what your classroom is like right now. Draw a circle around

YES if you agree with the sentence.
NO if you do not agree with the sentence.

EXAMPLE

27. Most students in our class are good friends.

If you agree that most students in the class are actually good friends, you circle YES like this:
(Yes) No

If you do NOT agree that most students in the class are actually good friends, you circle NO like this: Yes (No)

Please answer all questions. If you change your mind about an answer, just cross it out and circle the new answer. Example: ~~Yes~~ (No)

Remember, you are describing your actual classroom as you see it right now.	Circle your answer here	Scorers Use Only
1. Students in my class enjoy their schoolwork.	Yes No	
2. Students are always fighting with each other.	Yes No	
3. Students often race to see who can finish first.	Yes No	
4. In my class everyone is my friend.	Yes No	
5. Some students are not happy in my class.	Yes No	R

EXHIBIT 4.1 Partial representation of My Class Inventory (Student Version). Used with permission.

school counseling program. Importantly, all of these instruments are free, publicly accessible on the researcher's website.

While school counselors typically have more readily available academically focused data, it is nonetheless important for school counselors to recognize how factors, such as school and classroom climate, can impact students' academic success. Given the extensive amount of achievement-focused testing that occurs in classrooms, we chose to highlight assessments that are related to aspects, such as school climate and culture, rather than academic achievement specifically. Now, let's move on to discussing assessments that address the career domain.

My Class Inventory—Short Form for Teachers[c]

Please answer all questions. If you change your mind about an answer, just cross it out and circle the new answer.

Remember, you are describing your actual classroom as you currently see it.	Circle your answer here
1. The students enjoy their schoolwork in the class. (S)	1 strongly disagree 2 disagree 3 neutral 4 agree 5 strongly agree
2. Students never fight with each other. (PR-RC)	1 strongly disagree 2 disagree 3 neutral 4 agree 5 strongly agree
3. Students often race to see who can finish their work first. (C)	1 strongly disagree 2 disagree 3 neutral 4 agree 5 strongly agree
4. In the class, the work is hard to complete. (D)	1 strongly disagree 2 disagree 3 neutral 4 agree 5 strongly agree
5. In the class, everyone is friends. (PR)	1 strongly disagree 2 disagree 3 neutral 4 agree 5 strongly agree
6. Students are happy with the class.	1 strongly disagree 2 disagree 3 neutral 4 agree 5 strongly agree
7. Some students in the class are mean.	1 strongly disagree 2 disagree 3 neutral 4 agree 5 strongly agree
8. Most students want their work to be better than their friend's work.	1 strongly disagree 2 disagree 3 neutral 4 agree 5 strongly agree
9. Most students cannot complete their assignments without a lot of help.	1 strongly disagree 2 disagree 3 neutral 4 agree 5 strongly agree
10. The school counselor aids with building classroom cohesion.	1 strongly disagree 2 disagree 3 neutral 4 agree 5 strongly agree
11. Students in the class have good buddies.	1 strongly disagree 2 disagree 3 neutral 4 agree 5 strongly agree
12. Students seem to like the class.	1 strongly disagree 2 disagree 3 neutral 4 agree 5 strongly agree
13. Many students in the class provoke tension.	1 strongly disagree 2 disagree 3 neutral 4 agree 5 strongly agree
14. Some students feel bad when they do not do as well as others.	1 strongly disagree 2 disagree 3 neutral 4 agree 5 strongly agree

EXHIBIT 4.2 Partial representation of My Class Inventory (Teacher Version). Used with permission.

Assessments to Address the Career Domain

One aspect that I (Sandra) have encountered is that there seems to be a widely held belief among many adults that addressing career development is only important once students are in high school. In reality, school counselors have a responsibility to address every domain (academic, career, and social-emotional) across the grade levels. Thus, addressing this domain should follow the *Career Development Continuum* developed by the Sonoma County Office of Education. In the elementary years, the focus is on *career awareness*, providing opportunities for all students to be exposed to the world of work,

My Child's Classroom Inventory - Short Form (Parent/Caregiver)

Directions: This questionnaire asks for your perceptions of your child's present classroom experience. There are no correct responses. To indicate your opinion, please circle **one** of the following options that BEST reflects your view right now. Please respond to all statements. If you want to change your answer, just cross it out and circle a new answer.

To better understand your responses below, please indicate:

- Your relationship to child (circle one): Mother Father Grandmother Grandfather Other caregiver: ____________
- Your child's current grade level (circle one): K 1st 2nd 3rd 4th 5th 6th Mixed Grades: ________
- If relevant, your child's participates in a special program: ELL ESE Gifted Special Education
- Your child's age: _____
- Your child's ethnicity (circle all that apply): Asian Black Hispanic/Latino Native American White Other: ____________
- Your ethnicity: Asian Black Hispanic/Latino Native American White Other: ____________

Statements	Circle one answer for each statement				
1. My child benefits from the classroom learning activities.	Strongly disagree	Disagree	Unsure	Agree	Strongly agree
2. My child rarely has conflicts with classmates.	Strongly disagree	Disagree	Unsure	Agree	Strongly agree
3. My child often competes with classmates to see who can finish their assignments first.	Strongly disagree	Disagree	Unsure	Agree	Strongly agree
4. My child sees the classroom work as challenging to finish.	Strongly disagree	Disagree	Unsure	Agree	Strongly agree
5. My child is good friends with most classmates.	Strongly disagree	Disagree	Unsure	Agree	Strongly agree
6. My child is happy with his/her classroom experience.	Strongly disagree	Disagree	Unsure	Agree	Strongly agree
7. My child says some classmates are mean.	Strongly disagree	Disagree	Unsure	Agree	Strongly agree
8. My child wants to do better on his/her assignments than classmates.	Strongly disagree	Disagree	Unsure	Agree	Strongly agree
9. My child can easily complete most of the class assignments.	Strongly disagree	Disagree	Unsure	Agree	Strongly agree
10. My child likes her/his classmates.	Strongly disagree	Disagree	Unsure	Agree	Strongly agree
11. My child values the learning experience in the classroom.	Strongly disagree	Disagree	Unsure	Agree	Strongly agree
12. My child says several classmates cause tension.	Strongly disagree	Disagree	Unsure	Agree	Strongly agree
13. My child feels bad when classmates get better grades.	Strongly disagree	Disagree	Unsure	Agree	Strongly agree

EXHIBIT 4.3 Partial representation of My Class Inventory (Parent Version). Used with permission.

and developing skills that will benefit students in the future. Envision elementary students becoming familiar with the many careers that exist and broadly learning how people earn a living with a job or career through your core curricular classroom lessons. Another way to is have some community engagement at your school and invite individuals to a career day or speaker series on jobs in the community and emphasize awareness of all of the possibilities that exist, rather than just exposing students to traditional jobs and careers.

During the middle school years, the focus is on *career exploration* and teaching students about what preparation and training are necessary for specific jobs and careers. In some states, there may be requirements for students at the secondary level to complete a career exploration and planning course or to complete specific activities such as creating a 4- or 6-year academic plan. During the middle school years, students can learn about jobs and careers by researching what the pathways are to specific careers. Many state departments of education or workforce development offices often have career exploration activities or curriculum developed and ready for school counselors to use. For instance, Kuder Career Planning System has *Direct Your Future*, an 11 module curriculum (Exhibit 4.4) that is intended to offer career exploration. The content of these core curricular lessons includes career exploration activities that require self-reflection, online research, and use of the Kuder system.

During my time as a middle school counselor (Sandra), while the school did not have a required course in career exploration, I was able to work with one teacher, with whom I had a strong collaborative relationship, who agreed to take on a career exploration elective with my assistance.

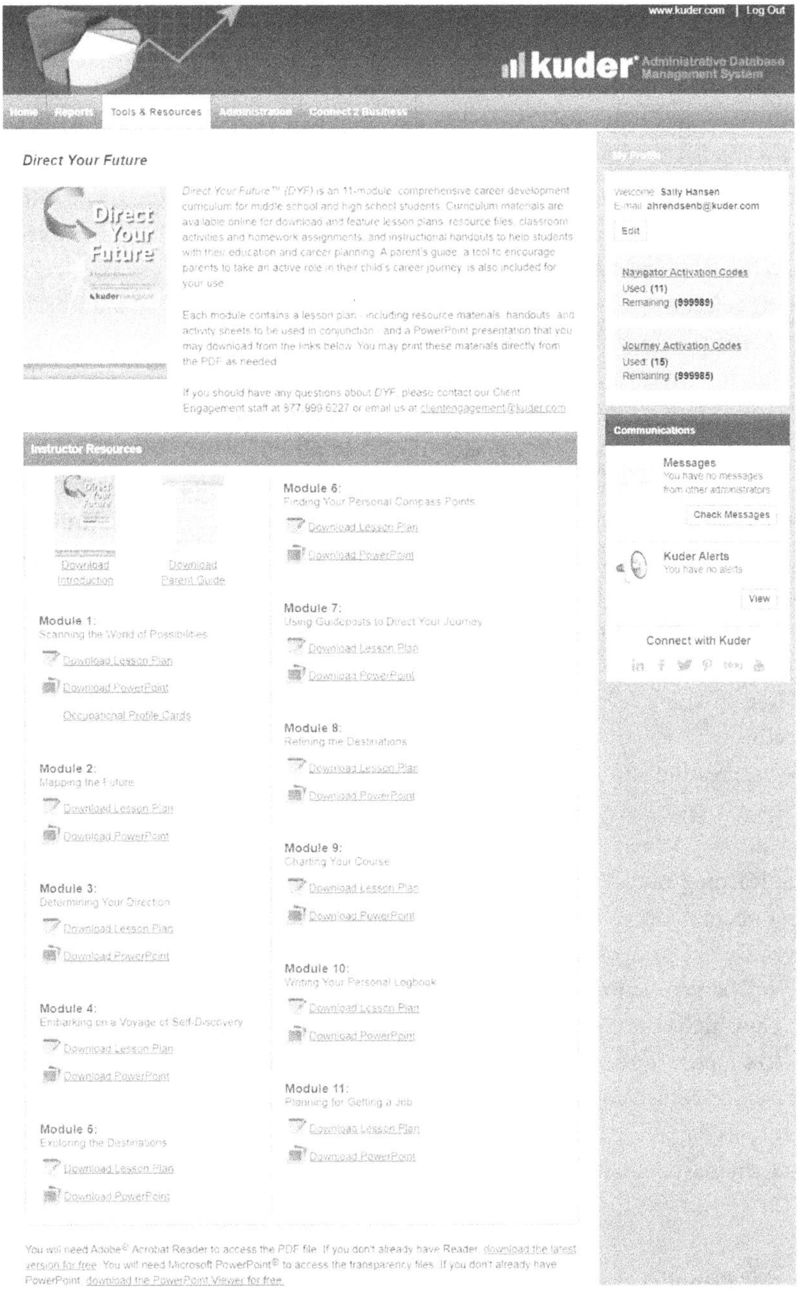

EXHIBIT 4.4 Kuder classroom curricula for grades 6–12. Used with permission.

Through funds from our Parent-Teacher Association (PTA), we were able to purchase The Real Game (California), which was a curriculum that spanned an entire trimester through a simulation of students assuming the role of an adult with an assigned work role. The four units of simulation are: Making a Living, Quality of Life, Changes and Choices, and The Personal Journey. The overall intent is that students' experience what it is like to be an adult, make decisions, and manage a job or career. As the school counselor, I even visited the class and distributed layoff notices to some participants and they had to learn what decision they would make next.

At the high school level, school counselors should focus on the *career preparation* of all students for postsecondary success. Developmentally, this may be a time that some students take on their first job, so it is important that school counselors can assist them with writing a résumé, practicing their interviewing skills, and opportunities for learning and evaluating their future goals and interests. One recommendation is for you to learn about RoadTrip Nation, an excellent comprehensive resource for students to use to focus on experiences and career development. They have a free interactive career interest survey that connects students with casual interviews conducted by young adults who wanted to learn more about work and life in perspective of various careers. Additionally, these resources offer career-related experiences and project-based learning curriculum that addresses key career and workforce standards.

There are a number of organizations that provide learning opportunities for students. For instance, WorkForce Solutions partners with the Texas Workforce Commission to provide free, state standards-aligned curriculum for their *When I Grow Up* campaign, which includes career education lessons for K-12th grades. This is an excellent collaboration example and we encourage you to seek out what collaborations you can make with your state-level career-focused organizations. But if you don't know where to start, we suggest CareerOneStop, which is sponsored by the U.S. Department of Labor. Here you can find a wealth of resources, including career inventories and assessments to support students' college and career readiness and exploration.

In the spirit of collaboration, we encourage you to reach out to your local colleges and universities. You may be surprised to know just how many resources and opportunities may exist, whether it be sending college pennants, creating summer bridge programs, or even providing a part-time college counselor for your school or district. When you are deciding what other resources may be of interest to you, consider what the learning outcomes are for your students. Do you want them to learn about college entrance requirements? Do you want them to experience what it is like to have a job? Regardless of the school level, we encourage you to think creatively about how you can collaborate with others to infuse college and career readiness throughout the curriculum for all students.

Regardless of the school level, we encourage you to think creatively about how you can collaborate with others to infuse college and career readiness throughout the curriculum for all students.

Currently, many high schools and even complete districts have chosen to utilize comprehensive online platforms to support students and school counselors alike in the career domain. A few of the most popular are Naviance, Kuder, and Xello. While we could discuss these platforms in Chapter 6, where we discuss various tools for you to use to be a data-driven school counselor, each of these systems also has inventories and other assessments integrated in it, so we decided to discuss them here.

Kuder

The Kuder Career Planning System is a popular online platform that has products to support all developmental levels: Galaxy for elementary students, Navigator for secondary students, and Journey for postsecondary students and adults. Importantly, there are extensive resources and curricula also available. For instance, as mentioned earlier, school counselors could use the *Direct Your Future* curriculum as the core curricular lessons that are distributed to middle and/or high school students to address the career domain. Similarly, you may find that using the curriculum during targeted small groups could work best for you. We encourage you to check with your state department of education and workforce development offices to see whether this resource is available to you. For example, according to their website, MyCareerShines, the Florida version of Kuder's career planning system is fully funded for all Florida residents through the Florida legislature.

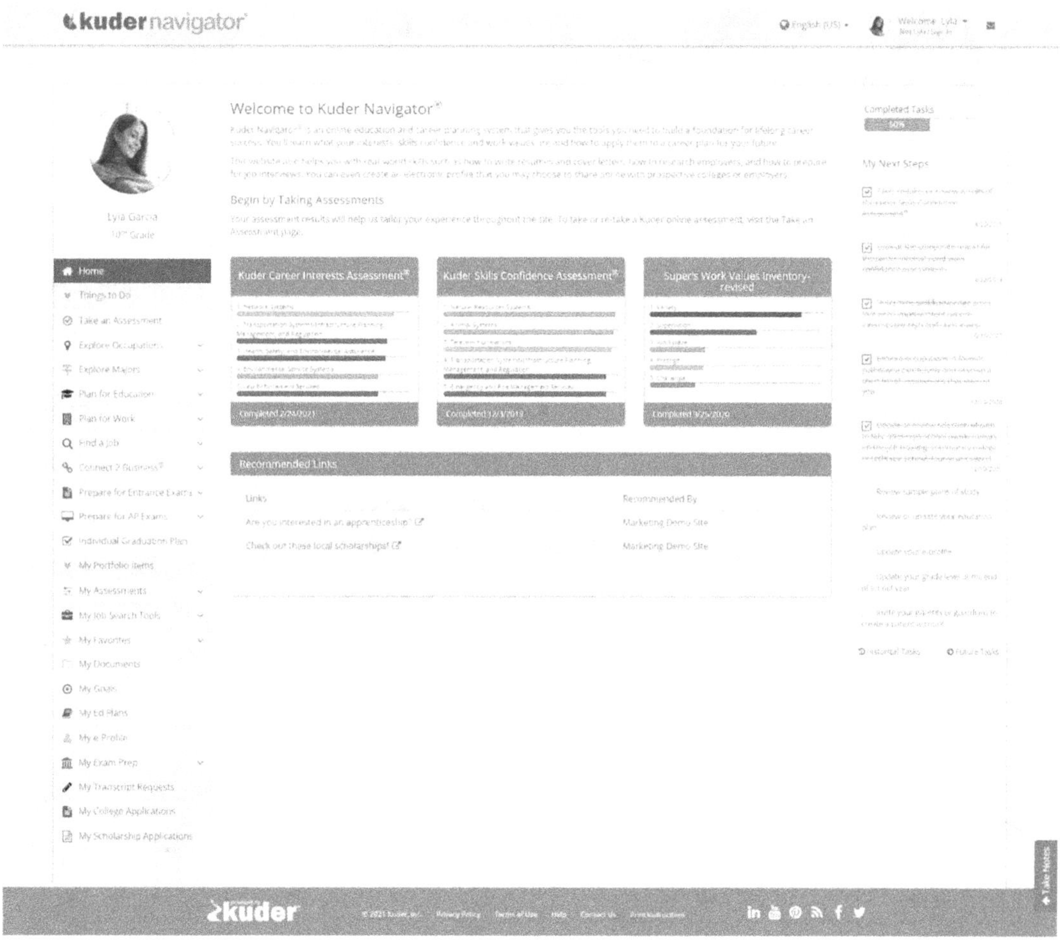

EXHIBIT 4.5 Kuder Navigator dashboard illustrates a variety of functions and tasks for students to complete. Used with permission.

From the Navigator dashboard (Exhibit 4.5), you can navigate to a variety of tasks on the left-hand column, while the right-hand column manages a student's to-do list in terms of tasks. Three assessments are offered to all users of the platform: Kuder Career Interests Assessment®, Kuder Skills Confidence Assessment®, and Super's Work Values Inventory—Revised. As illustrated in Exhibit 4.6, upon completion of the Kuder Career Interests Assessment®, the system will show the top five career pathways, as well as additional tabs to address further occupations to explore, majors to consider, and sample educational plans or pathways. Exhibit 4.7 provides a visual explanation of how students' assessment results align in terms of interests, skills, and values, and relevant occupations.

In addition to a variety of features for the user, Kuder also has extensive administration features that are extremely helpful for school counselors in providing appropriate individual student planning and advisement, small groups, and delivering core curricular classroom lessons. School counselors who are coordinating the platform also have the ability the manage activation codes and utilize various reporting functions for assessments and other student produced tasks as illustrated in Exhibit 4.8. Importantly, those who serve as administrators, such as school counselors, have the ability to run summative student assessment reports, which are helpful for providing individual student planning and career development (Exhibit 4.9). For instance, assessment results may indicate that the student's top two clusters

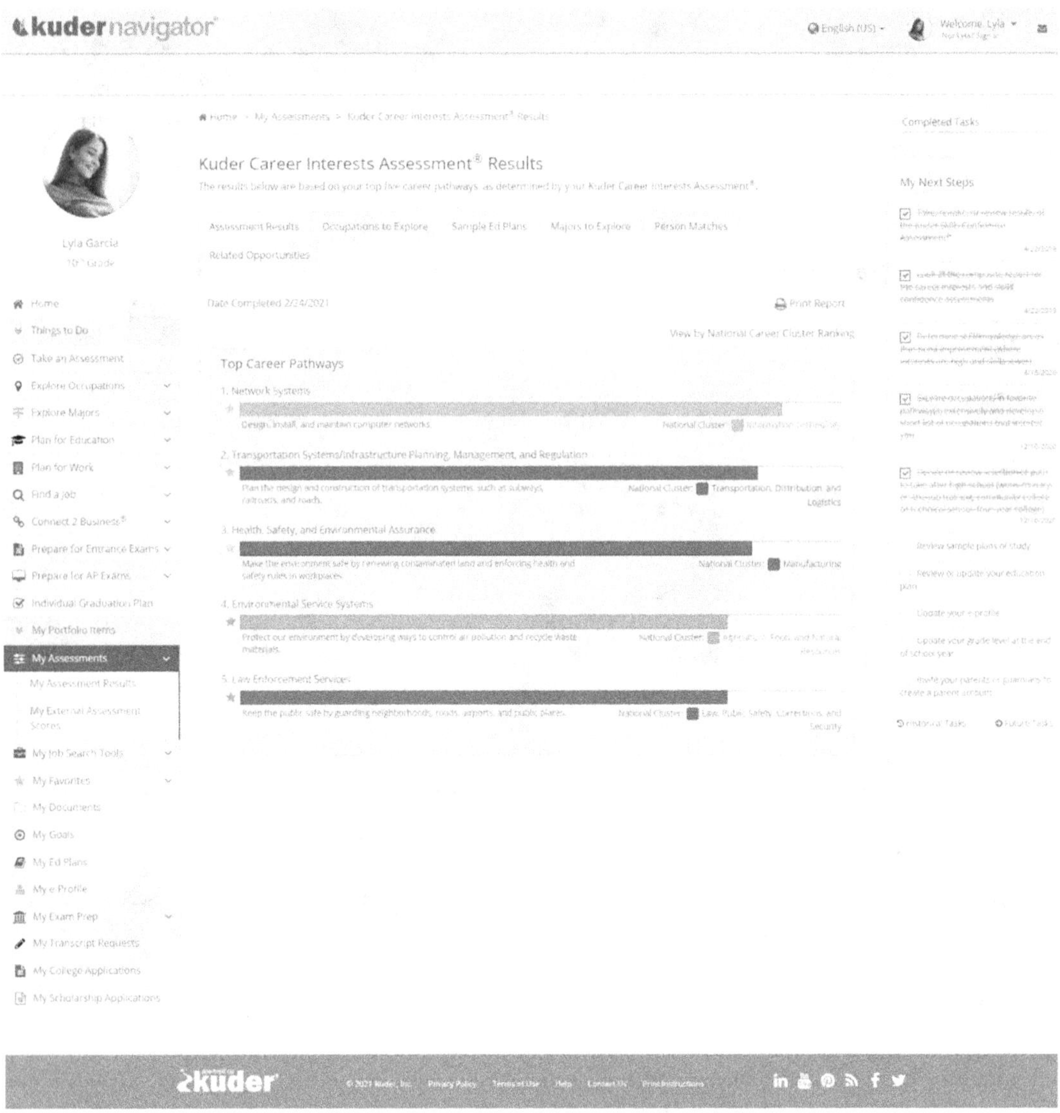

EXHIBIT 4.6 Kuder Career Interest Assessment results and additional information to explore. Used with permission.

are: Education and Training and Human Services. This information can alert the school counselor to provide further direction to the student in these areas.

Naviance

Naviance is a widely popular online platform designed to support postsecondary success through its research-based College, Career, and Life Readiness (CCLR) Framework. Informed by national standards, including those from ASCA, the framework focuses on six key core competencies that all secondary students need to experience to be college, career, and life ready:

1. Instill social emotional learning skills.
2. Expand interpersonal skills.
3. Develop academic skills.

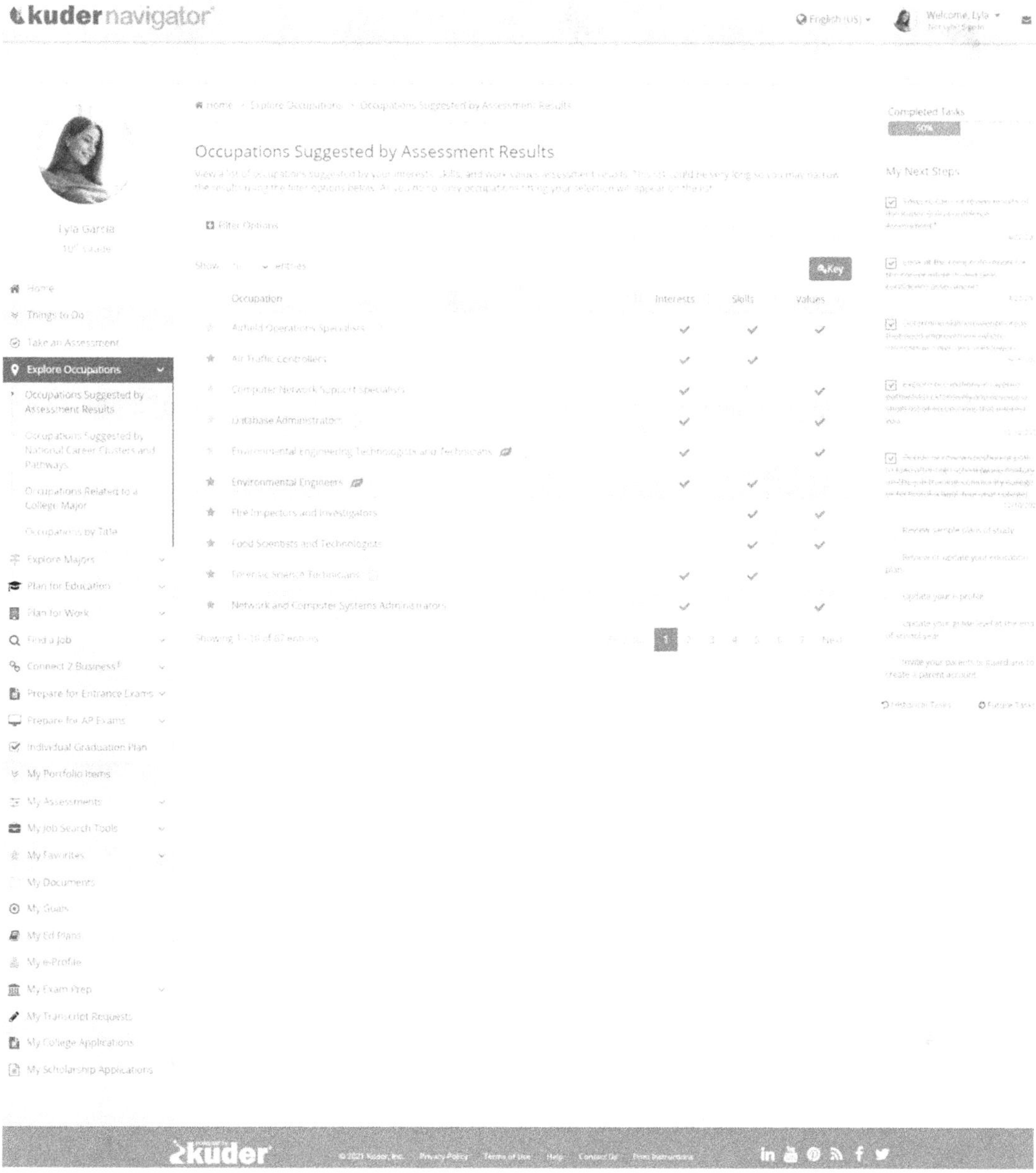

EXHIBIT 4.7 Occupations suggested by assessment results and their alignment to interests, skills, and values. Used with permission.

4. Cultivate career knowledge.
5. Grow college knowledge.
6. Promote transition skills.

Within the platform, you can navigate to the following tabs: Courses, Colleges, Careers, About Me, and My Planner. These areas allow students to review information about colleges and their admissions requirements, make notes about those of interest, manage scholarships and letters of recommendation, and complete interest inventories and personality assessments. In fact, there are many informal

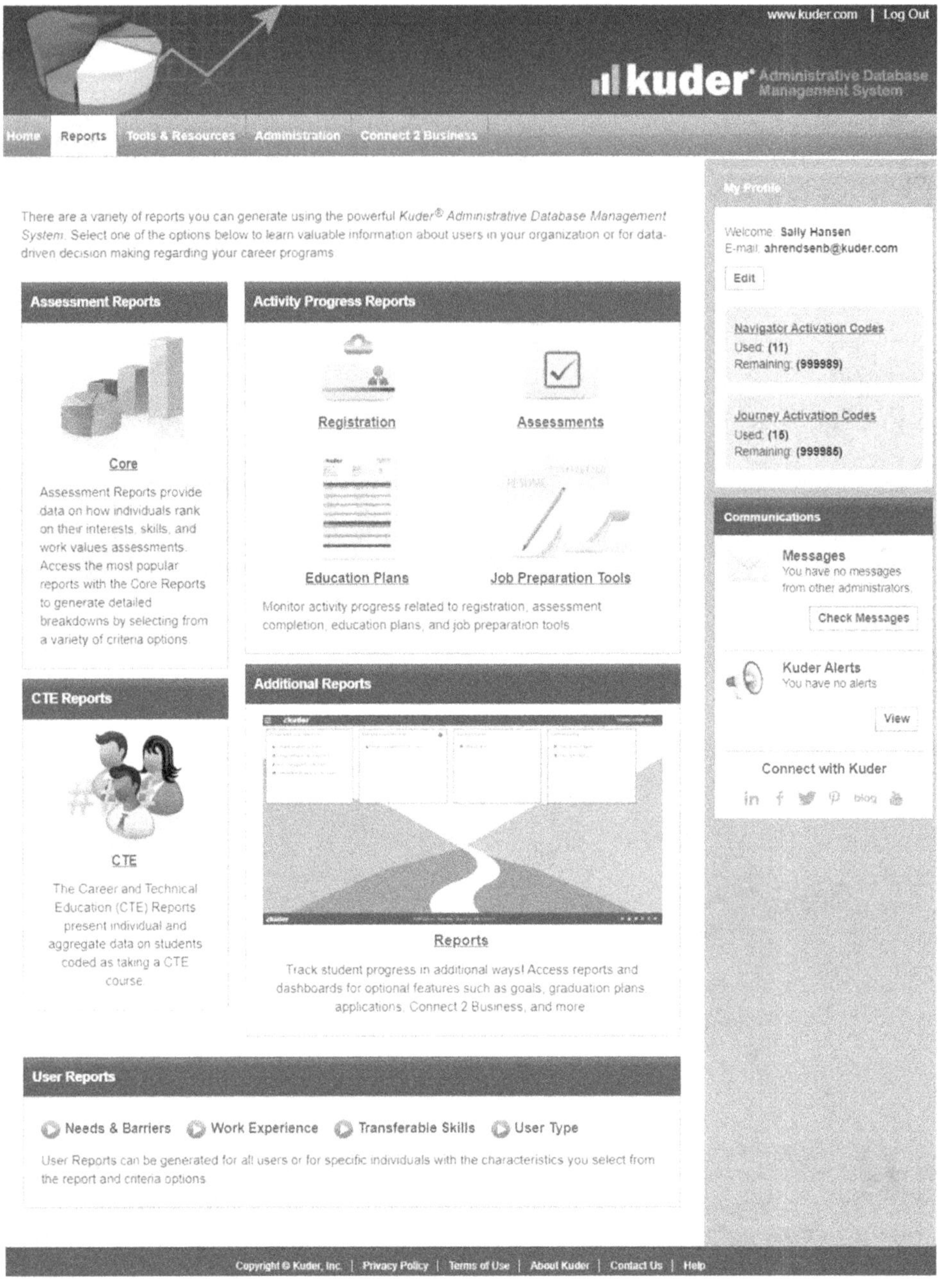

EXHIBIT 4.8 Kuder Administration dashboard, where school counselors can manage key functions, including student account management and reporting features. Used with permission.

assessments available on this platform: Do What You Are, Learning Style Inventory, MI Advantage, Career Cluster Finder, Career Interest Profiler, and Strengths Explorer. Each of these provides helpful information for both the student and the school counselor. Additionally, a valuable tool available with this system is Family Connection, which offers parents and other caregivers the opportunity to be aware of their teens' progress and interests.

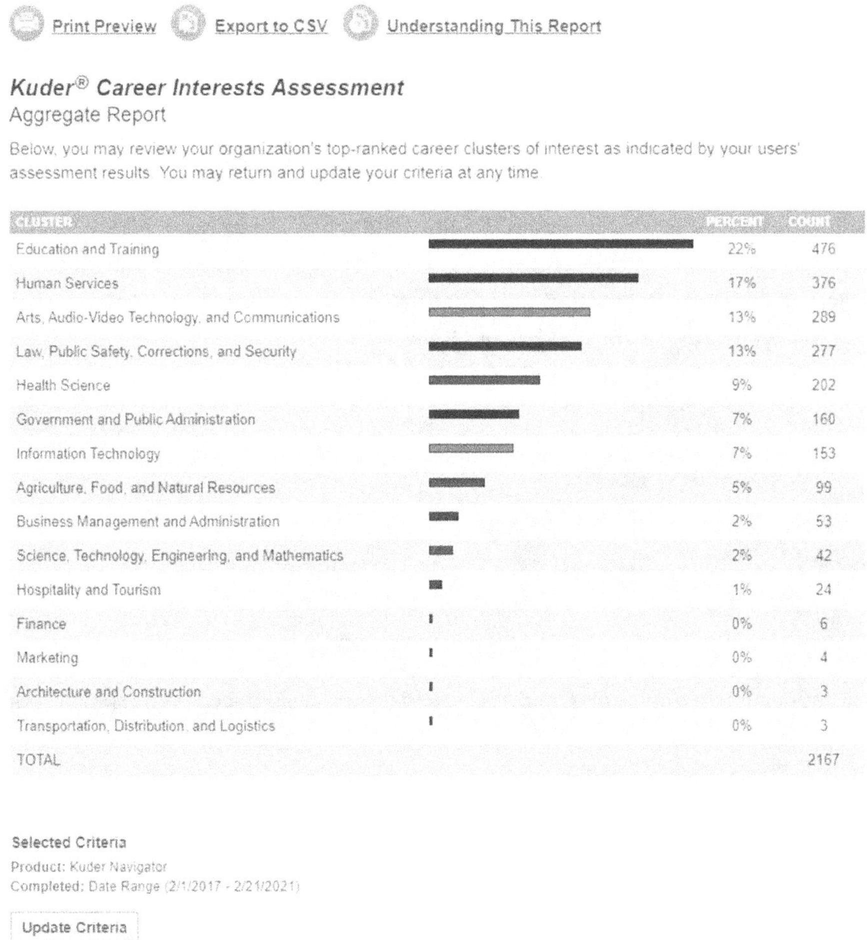

Print Preview Export to CSV Understanding This Report

Kuder® Career Interests Assessment

Aggregate Report

Below, you may review your organization's top-ranked career clusters of interest as indicated by your users' assessment results. You may return and update your criteria at any time.

CLUSTER	PERCENT	COUNT
Education and Training	22%	476
Human Services	17%	376
Arts, Audio-Video Technology, and Communications	13%	289
Law, Public Safety, Corrections, and Security	13%	277
Health Science	9%	202
Government and Public Administration	7%	160
Information Technology	7%	153
Agriculture, Food, and Natural Resources	5%	99
Business Management and Administration	2%	53
Science, Technology, Engineering, and Mathematics	2%	42
Hospitality and Tourism	1%	24
Finance	0%	6
Marketing	0%	4
Architecture and Construction	0%	3
Transportation, Distribution, and Logistics	0%	3
TOTAL		2167

Selected Criteria

Product: Kuder Navigator

Completed: Date Range (2/1/2017 - 2/21/2021)

Update Criteria

EXHIBIT 4.9 Kuder Administration report of a student's summative assessment results, which can be used for advising and planning purposes. Used with permission.

Xello

Another college and career-planning platform that may work for your school is Xello (formerly known as *Career Cruising*, which also managed The Real Game-California), an online program that helps K-12 students build knowledge, skills, and plans for future success. Through interactive activities and tasks focused on self-knowledge, exploration, and planning, counselors can help support students in these three areas. Many of the tasks and activities can be completed virtually and independently. Impressively, Xello has a variety of activities, lesson plans, and tasks that all come with educator guides for implementation, extensive support and tutorials, and better yet, they are organized by developmental levels: K-2, 3–5, and 6–12. Within Xello, there are a number of informal assessments that can yield helpful information, including a personality style assessment, a matchmaker assessment, and a skills assessment. In addition to utilizing comprehensive systems, like those discussed here, school counselors also have formal assessments available to support students' career awareness, exploration, and development.

College Admissions Knowledge Evaluation

The College Admissions Knowledge Evaluation (CAKE; Poynton et al., 2019) was developed to measure the knowledge of both high school students and their families with regard to making informed college decisions. These researchers' scholarly agenda includes the development of instruments that can be offered to school counseling professionals, free and publicly accessible. To this end, his website, College Sanity, houses the CAKE in an easy-to-navigate and interactive format, along with the College and Career Readiness Counseling Support Scales (CCRCS). Both of these instruments are designed to provide feedback to students and families about their knowledge regarding college admissions and working with counselors so that they can take the next steps toward being informed and prepared for the college admissions process. Example items from two of the subscales of the CAKE follow.

Examples of *Knowledge of College Life* subscale items:

In high school, you spend about 25 hours each week in academic classes with your teachers. As a full-time student in college, you will spend about hours each week in academic classes with your professors.

a. 10–12
b. 12–15
c. 20–25
d. 30–35
e. Not sure

In college, the document used to describe the course schedule, assignments, and expectations is called a:

a. Syllabus
b. Contract
c. Outline
d. Course Calendar
e. Not Sure

If you are accepted to a college, you are guaranteed to have a spot in the major you desire.

a. True
b. False
c. Not Sure

Examples of *Admissions Procedures & Financial Aid* subscale items:

When you apply to a college as an Early Action applicant, it means:

a. If you are accepted to the college, you will attend—it is a "binding" agreement
b. If you are accepted to the college, you can still choose another college—it is a "nonbinding" agreement
c. If you are accepted to the college, you are making a promise to attend the college
d. You can only apply to colleges early decision
e. Not sure

What does it mean if a college you have applied to "defers" making an admission decision?

a. A rejection from the college
b. You've been accepted, but will be starting at a later time than the semester you applied for
c. Your application will be reconsidered and a decision made at a later date
d. It is the same as being wait-listed
e. Not sure

The key difference between a loan and a scholarship is that:

a. There is no difference, they're just two names for the same thing
b. Loans need to be repaid, whereas scholarships do not

c. Scholarships are only offered by your school and loans are only offered by banks
d. Loans and scholarships both need to be repaid, but scholarships have more detailed applications
e. Not Sure

Sample instrument items used with permission.

MyNextMove/O*NET Interest Profiler

Perhaps one of the most well-known career resources is the O*NET Resource Center, sponsored by the U.S. Department of Labor. While many of its resources are intended for adults, they are still quite appropriate for adolescents. The O*NET Interest Profiler (IP) is a free self-assessment (30–60 questions, depending upon version) that can be administered online through MyNextMove or via paper/pencil, and focuses on career exploration, allowing students to discover the occupations and types of work that are of interest and align with their skills. Importantly, the IP is aligned with John Holland's R-I-A-S-E-C interest structure composed of: realistic, investigative, artistic, social, enterprising, and conventional. The assessment results are also integrated with other informational components that allow you to browse categories of careers or simply search key terms that are relevant to the student's results. This resource is especially helpful to those of you who have specific mandates for providing career exploration activities or lessons.

My Career Story

High school counselors who are seeking to complete specific career-focused activities may want to consider utilizing the My Career Story (MCS; Savickas & Hartung, 2012) workbook with their students. According to researchers, the MCS is intended to increase students' ability develop and share their emerging life-career stories and enact those stories in their school and work decision-making. Students construct their own career story in three parts: (a) Telling My Story, (b) Hearing My Story, and (c) Enacting My Story. Given the workbook format, this could be completed as a part of your core curricular classroom lessons across multiple sessions, so you may consider partnering with a teacher colleague. Part one focuses on students reflecting upon their preferences in a variety of aspects of their lives, from heroes to television shows to favorite catch phrases or sayings. In part two, students are instructed to take advantage of other free resources, such as O'Net, to explore specific careers and their education and experience requirements. For part three, students are to reflect upon the elements of their story and then craft their own unique, desirable, and believable story. Importantly, students must also perform some action that has them interacting with their developed story, such as talking to someone working in the desired occupation or volunteering in relation to the desired occupation. This workbook is free and publicly available in two versions in multiple languages (English, French, German, Italian, and Portuguese): one for the general population of individuals, and Form U for individuals with disabilities.

Student Career Construction Inventory

The Student Career Construction Inventory (SCCI; Savickas et al., 2018) is a relatively simple and brief instrument that school counselors may consider administering during the high school years as means for assessing where students are in their career exploration and planning process. Using a 5-point Likert scale, students are asked to identify how much thinking or planning they have done about each statement. For ease of scoring and analysis, we encourage school counselors to consider creating an online version of this instrument with Google Forms or a similar technological tool. The results can illuminate what areas students have and have not considered or started planning for, and this can be the very data that you can use to inform your counseling interventions and grade-level activities. These final two instruments, the MCS and SCCI, are available for free online.

Assessments to Address the Social–Emotional Domain

While all three domains of service are important, the social–emotional domain is by far the broadest. When we consider addressing the social–emotional needs of students, what exactly are we referring to? Well, the truth is, there are many aspects that comprise this domain, including behavioral challenges, depression, self-esteem, motivation, and many more. As school counselors, it is important to remember that we must work within our scope of practice. Following the guidelines on appropriate roles as outlined in the *ASCA National Model* (2019) and the *ASCA Ethical Standards* (2016), while we are not responsible for providing long-term therapeutic counseling, we are responsible for providing time-limited counseling services that are specific to supporting student success and well-being.

Motivational Assessment Scale

In order to better understand the motivations behind certain student behaviors, we must consider elements of motivation. The Motivational Assessment Scale (MAS; Durand & Crimmins, 1992) is a 16-item survey that utilizes a 6-point Likert scale response of 0 = never to 6 = always, wherein the respondent is given specific situations in which they are asked to rate how likely the target behavior is to occur (Exhibit 4.10). Ultimately, the items are categorized according to the four subscales: sensory, escape, attention, and tangible. Utilizing this instrument can be especially helpful when school counselors are collaborating with other stakeholders by providing them with information about a students' underlying motivations. By administering the MAS, stakeholders can learn about motivating factors for the student, which is particularly helpful during student intervention team meetings and when ultimately deciding what interventions are best for a particular student. While you can access parts of the assessment online, you do need to purchase the assessment in order to administer it to students.

Adolescent Domain Screening Inventory

The Adolescent Domain Screening Inventory (ADSI; Corrigan et al., 2007) is a valuable tool that school counselors can use to screen students who are at a high risk of substance abuse and identifies potential areas of life that may be the most problematic: community, family, individual/peers, and school (Exhibit 4.11). This free and accessible assessment is quite simple to administer and score with only 33 questions. The results can yield a total score that illustrates high-risk status or the need to seek further assessment for substance abuse as a primary condition. Additionally, the subscale scores can be used as an intervention guide, helping school counselors identify how to best support the student in the various areas of their lives. For example, this assessment could be distributed to all ninth graders toward the beginning of the year. The findings could help you identify the areas of greatest need for that specific student population. Alternatively, this assessment could be used during your individual or small-group counseling to get specific data or further details on the contributing factors that may be inhibiting a student's success.

Car, Relax, Alone, Forget, Friends, Trouble

Similar to the ADSI, the Car, Relax, Alone, Forget, Friends, Trouble instrument (CRAAFT; Knight, 2018) can be used to better understand potential substance use or other risky behavior considerations (Exhibit 4.12). Based upon the responses to this brief, four- to nine-item questionnaire, an adolescent can be categorized at

Motivation Assessment Scale

By V. Mark Durand and Daniel Crimmens

Name Johnathan Today's Date 8/29/20

Rater Karen

Behavior Description Throwing or dropping desk contents to the floor

Setting Description During one-to-one teaching sessions

ITEM	RESPONSE						
	Never	Almost Never	Seldom	Half the Time	Usually	Almost Always	Always
1. Would the behavior occur continuously, over and over, if this person was left alone for long periods of time? (For example, several hours.)	(0)	1	2	3	4	5	6
2. Does the behavior occur following a request to perform a difficult task?	0	1	2	3	4	5	(6)
⋮							
15. Does this person seem to do the behavior to get you to spend some time with him or her?	0	1	(2)	3	4	5	6
16. Does this behavior seem to occur when this person has been told that he or she can't do something he or she had wanted to do?	0	1	2	3	4	(5)	6

SCORING

	Sensory	Escape	Attention	Tangible
Total Score =	2	22	6	10
Mean Score =	0.5	5.5	1.5	2.5
Relative Ranking =	4	1	3	2

Monaco & Associates Incorporated

EXHIBIT 4.10 Partial representation of the Motivation Assessment Scale. Used with permission.

low, moderate, or high risk. While both a clinical and a self-administered version are available, from a developmental standpoint, adolescents are likely to be more forthcoming in the self-administered version. While this instrument is designed for a more clinical setting, it can absolutely be utilized by school counselors. Consider that you have a 10th grader who has made some significant declines in attendance at school and overall academic performance. You may be able to uncover more about the student's current functioning by having them complete the CRAAFT simply as an information-gathering exercise. This data could then be used to further discuss goal setting and decision-making that can lead to more successful outcomes.

Adolescent Domain Screening Inventory

Instructions:
1. This is not a test, so there are no "right or wrong" answers.
2. All of the questions should be answered by marking one of the answer spaces. If you don't find one that fits exactly, use the one that comes closest.

These questions ask about the neighborhood and community where you live.	**NO!**	**no**	**yes**	**YES!**
1. If a kid smoked marijuana in your neighborhood would he or she be caught by the police?	O	O	O	O
2. I like my neighborhood	O	O	O	O
3. There are people in neighborhood who are proud of me when I do something well.	O	O	O	O
4. How much does the following statement describe your neighborhood: crime and/or drug selling.	O	O	O	O
5. Are service clubs available in your community for people your age?	O	O	O	O
	Very Wrong	**Wrong**	**A little Bit Wrong**	**Not Wrong At All**
6. How wrong would most adults in your neighborhood think it was for kids your age to use marijuana?	O	O	O	O
	Very Hard	**Sort Of Hard**	**Sort Of Easy**	**Very Easy**
7. If you wanted to get some marijuana, how easy would it be for you to get some?	O	O	O	O
	Never	**1-2 times**	**3-6 times**	**7 or more times**
8. How many times have you changed homes since kindergarten?	O	O	O	O
The next few questions ask about your family.	**NO!**	**no**	**yes**	**YES!**
9. My parents ask me if I've gotten my homework done.	O	O	O	O
10. People in my family often insult or yell at each other.	O	O	O	O
11. If you drank some beer or wine or liquor (for example, vodka, whiskey, or gin) without your parents' permission, would you be caught by your parents?	O	O	O	O
12. My parents give me lots of chances to do fun things with them.				
	Very Wrong	**Wrong**	**A Little Bit Wrong**	**Not Wrong At All**
13. How wrong do your parents feel it would be for <u>you</u> to smoke marijuana?	O	O	O	O
	None	**1**	**2-4**	**5 or more**
14. About how many adults have you known personally who in the past year have used marijuana, crack, cocaine, or other drugs?	O	O	O	O
Have any of your brothers or sisters ever:		**NO or I have no brothers or sisters**	**YES**	
15. Smoked marijuana?		O	O	
16. Taken a handgun to school?		O	O	

EXHIBIT 4.11 Adolescent Domain Screening Inventory. Used with permission.

These questions ask about your feelings and experiences in other parts of your life.

How old were you when you first:	11 or less	12-15	16 or more	Never
17. Smoked marijuana?	O	O	O	O
18. Attacked someone with the idea of seriously hurting them?	O	O	O	O

How wrong do you think it is for someone your age to:	Very Wrong	Wrong	A Little Bit Wrong	Not Wrong At All
19. Drink beer, wine or hard liquor (for example, vodka, whiskey, or gin) regularly?	O	O	O	O
20. Smoke marijuana?	O	O	O	O
21. Use LSD, cocaine, amphetamines or another illegal drug?	O	O	O	O

	No Risk	Slight Risk	Moderate Risk	Great Risk
22. How much do you think people risk harming themselves (physically or in other ways) if they smoke marijuana regularly?	O	O	O	O

	Never	Rarely	1-2 Times A Month	About Once a Week or More
23. How often do you attend religious services or activities?	O	O	O	O

	None	1	2	3+
24. Think about your four best friends (the friends you feel closest to). In the past year (12 months), how many of your best friends have sold illegal drugs?	O	O	O	O

	NO!	no	yes	YES!
25. I do the opposite of what people tell me just to get them mad.	O	O	O	O

	No or Very Little Chance	Some Chance	Pretty Good Chance	Very Good Chance
26. What are the chances you would be seen as cool if you smoked marijuana?	O	O	O	O

	Grab a CD and leave the store	Ignore her	Act like it's a joke, and ask her to put the CD back.	Tell her to put the CD back
27. You're looking at CD's in a music store with a friend. You look up and see her slip a CD under her coat. She smiles and says "Which one do you want? Go ahead, take it while nobody's around." There is nobody in sight, no employees and no other customers. What would you do now?	O	O	O	O

	Never	I've done, but not in the past year	About once a month	Once a week or more
28. How many times have you done crazy things even if they are a little dangerous?	O	O	O	O

This section asks about your experiences at school.	NO!	no	yes	YES!
29. My teacher praises me when I work hard in school.	O	O	O	O
30. There are lots of chances for students in my school to get involved in sports, clubs, and other school activities outside of class.	O	O	O	O

Now, thinking back over the past year in school, how often did you…	Never	Seldom	Often	Almost Always
31. Enjoy being in school?	O	O	O	O
32. Try to do your best work in school	O	O	O	O

	None	1-2	3-5	6 or more
33. During the LAST FOUR WEEKS how many whole days have you missed because you skipped or "cut"?	O	O	O	O

EXHIBIT 4.11 (*continued*)

The CRAFFT Questionnaire (version 2.1)

To be completed by patient

Please answer all questions **honestly**; your answers will be kept **confidential**.

During the PAST 12 MONTHS, on how many days did you:

1. Drink more than a few sips of beer, wine, or any drink containing **alcohol**? Put "0" if none.	☐ # of days
2. Use any **marijuana** (weed, oil, or hash by smoking, vaping, or in food) or **"synthetic marijuana"** (like "K2," "Spice")? Put "0" if none.	☐ # of days
3. Use **anything else to get high** (like other illegal drugs, prescription or over-the-counter medications, and things that you sniff, huff, or vape)? Put "0" if none.	☐ # of days

READ THESE INSTRUCTIONS BEFORE CONTINUING:

- **If you put "0" in ALL of the boxes above, ANSWER QUESTION 4, THEN STOP.**
- **If you put "1" or higher in ANY of the boxes above, ANSWER QUESTIONS 4-9.**

	No	Yes
4. Have you ever ridden in a **CAR** driven by someone (including yourself) who was "high" or had been using alcohol or drugs?	☐	☐
5. Do you ever use alcohol or drugs to **RELAX**, feel better about yourself, or fit in?	☐	☐
6. Do you ever use alcohol or drugs while you are by yourself, or **ALONE**?	☐	☐
7. Do you ever **FORGET** things you did while using alcohol or drugs?	☐	☐
8. Do your **FAMILY** or **FRIENDS** ever tell you that you should cut down on your drinking or drug use?	☐	☐
9. Have you ever gotten into **TROUBLE** while you were using alcohol or drugs?	☐	☐

NOTICE TO CLINIC STAFF AND MEDICAL RECORDS:
The information on this page is protected by special federal confidentiality rules (42 CFR Part 2), which prohibit disclosure of this information unless authorized by specific written consent. A general authorization for release of medical information is NOT sufficient.

For more information and versions in other languages, see **www.crafft.org**

EXHIBIT 4.12 CRAFFT 2.1, self-administered questionnaire. Used with permission.

COLUMBIA-SUICIDE SEVERITY RATING SCALE
Screen with Triage Points for Schools

	Past month	
Ask questions that are in bold and underlined.	**YES**	**NO**
Ask Questions 1 and 2		
1) ***Have you wished you were dead or wished you could go to sleep and not wake up?***		
2) ***Have you had any actual thoughts of killing yourself?***		
If YES to 2, ask questions 3, 4, 5, and 6. If NO to 2, go directly to question 6.		
3) ***Have you been thinking about how you might do this?*** e.g. *"I thought about taking an overdose but I never made a specific plan as to when where or how I would actually do it....and I would never go through with it."*		
4) ***Have you had these thoughts and had some intention of acting on them?*** as opposed to *"I have the thoughts but I definitely will not do anything about them."*		
5) ***Have you started to work out or worked out the details of how to kill yourself? Do you intend to carry out this plan?***		
6) ***Have you ever done anything, started to do anything, or prepared to do anything to end your life?***	**Lifetime**	
Examples: Collected pills, obtained a gun, gave away valuables, wrote a will or suicide note, took out pills but didn't swallow any, held a gun but changed your mind or it was grabbed from your hand, went to the roof but didn't jump; or actually took pills, tried to shoot yourself, cut yourself, tried to hang yourself, etc.		
	Past 3 Months	
If YES, ask: ***Was this within the past 3 months?***		

Response Protocol to C-SSRS Screening

Item 1 Behavioral Health Referral
Item 2 Behavioral Health Referral
Item 3 Behavioral Health Referral and Consider Consultation (Psychologist/Social Worker) and Student Safety Precautions
Item 4 Student Safety Precautions and psychiatric evaluation by crisis team/EMT/Emergency room
Item 5 Student Safety Precautions and psychiatric evaluation by crisis team/EMT/Emergency room
Item 6 Behavioral Health Referral and Consider Consultation (Psychologist/Social Worker) and Student Safety Precautions
Item 6 3 months ago or less: Student Safety Precautions and psychiatric evaluation by crisis team/EMT/Emergency room

EXHIBIT 4.13 Columbia-Suicide Severity Rating Scale—Screen with Triage Points for Schools. Used with permission.

Importantly, the CRAAFT is available in a variety of languages and is accompanied by a provider manual that explains how to offer support at any risk level. Moreover, it contains some sample scenarios to illustrate how you can use the results of the assessment and provide the next steps of counseling and other supports that may be necessary including referral. This instrument and the manual are free and publicly available on the CRAAFT website.

Columbia-Suicide Severity Rating Scale

Perhaps one of the most well-known assessments that we discuss in this book is the Columbia-Suicide Severity Rating Scale (C-SSRS; Posner, n.d.) developed by The Columbia Lighthouse Project (Exhibit 4.13). This instrument is used as measure of suicidal ideation, intent, or plan, and past suicidal behavior. As a result of school tragedies and subsequent legislative changes, many schools and districts

COLUMBIA-SUICIDE SEVERITY RATING SCALE
Screening Version – Since Last Contact – for Schools

SUICIDE IDEATION DEFINITIONS AND PROMPTS	Since Last Contact	
Ask questions that are bold and underlined	**YES**	**NO**
Ask Questions 1 and 2		
1) *Have you wished you were dead or wished you could go to sleep and not wake up?*		
2) *Have you actually had any thoughts of killing yourself?*		
If YES to 2, ask questions 3, 4, 5, and 6. If NO to 2, go directly to question 6		
3) *Have you been thinking about how you might do this?* E.g. "*I thought about taking an overdose but I never made a specific plan as to when where or how I would actually do it....and I would never go through with it.*"		
4) *Have you had these thoughts and had some intention of acting on them?* As opposed to "*I have the thoughts but I definitely will not do anything about them.*"		
5) *Have you started to work out or worked out the details of how to kill yourself? Do you intend to carry out this plan?*		
6) *Have you done anything, started to do anything, or prepared to do anything to end your life?* Examples: Collected pills, obtained a gun, gave away valuables, wrote a will or suicide note, took out pills but didn't swallow any, held a gun but changed your mind or it was grabbed from your hand, went to the roof but didn't jump; or actually took pills, tried to shoot yourself, cut yourself, tried to hang yourself, etc.		

Recommended Response Protocol to C-SSRS Screening

Item 1 Behavioral Health Referral
Item 2 Behavioral Health Referral
Item 3 Behavioral Health Referral and Consider Consultation (Psychologist/Social Worker) and Student Safety Precautions
Item 4 Student Safety Precautions and psychiatric evaluation by crisis team/EMT/Emergency room
Item 5 Student Safety Precautions and psychiatric evaluation by crisis team/EMT/Emergency room
Item 6 Student Safety Precautions and psychiatric evaluation by crisis team/EMT/Emergency room

EXHIBIT 4.14 Columbia-Suicide Severity Rating Scale—Since Last Contact for Schools. Used with permission.

have formulated mandated crisis plans and protocols, which include the administration of the C-SSRS. Given that a school intervention or crisis team is composed of a variety of school personnel, it is imperative that all team members understand how to assess for suicide. A few of the most noteworthy aspects of the C-SSRS are its easy administration, no advanced training is required, it is free of charge and widely accessible on the website. Importantly, it has strong psychometrics and extensive research validating the instrument. There are multiple versions of the assessment, including those specific to the school setting.

For instance, you may utilize the *Screen With Triage Points for Schools* when a student is initially referred to the crisis team, as this version is formatted to ask about thoughts and feeling in the past month, past 3 months, and lifetime. In comparison, you may want to utilize the *Screening Version—Since Last Contact—for Schools* version during a subsequent, perhaps follow-up interaction with a student who has previously interacted with school personnel (Exhibit 4.14). While school counselors will not necessarily

6-ITEM Kutcher Adolescent Depression Scale: KADS

NAME :________________ DATE :________________

OVER THE LAST WEEK, HOW HAVE YOU BEEN "ON AVERAGE" OR "USUALLY" REGARDING THE FOLLOWING

1. Low mood, sadness, feeling blah or down, depressed, just can't be bothered.

☐ a) Hardly Ever ☐ b) Much of the time ☐ c) Most of the time ☐ d) All of the time

2. Feelings of worthlessness, hopelessness, letting people down, not being a good person.

☐ a) Hardly Ever ☐ b) Much of the time ☐ c) Most of the time ☐ d) All of the time

3. Feeling tired, feeling fatigued, low in energy, hard to get motivated, have to push to get things done, want to rest or lie down a lot

☐ a) Hardly Ever ☐ b) Much of the time ☐ c) Most of the time ☐ d) All of the time

4. Feeling that life is not very much fun, not feeling good when usually would feel good, not getting as much pleasure from fun things as usual.

☐ a) Hardly Ever ☐ b) Much of the time ☐ c) Most of the time ☐ d) All of the time

5. Feeling worried, nervous, panicky, tense, keyed up, anxious

☐ a) Hardly Ever ☐ b) Much of the time ☐ c) Most of the time ☐ d) All of the time

6. Thoughts, plans or actions about suicide or self-harm.

☐ a) Hardly Ever ☐ b) Much of the time ☐ c) Most of the time ☐ d) All of the time

TOTAL SCORE: ________________

EXHIBIT 4.15 Kutcher Adolescent Depression Scale (KADS-6). Used with permission.

be providing long-term clinical services to students, they are, in fact, responsible for the safety of all students and that includes suicide prevention and education.

Kutcher Adolescent Depression Scale

School counselors can benefit from administering the Kutcher Adolescent Depression Scale (KADS-6; Kutcher, 2008) when there is concern or suspicion about a student being depressed (Exhibit 4.15). Through this free, brief, six-item assessment, determination can be made as to indicate "possible depression" and a need for more thorough assessment or to ascertain whether depression may not exist. It is important to note the prompt for this instrument is "over the last week, how have you been 'on average' or 'usually' regarding the following . . ." So it is possible that a student has had elevated risk more than 1 week ago, so timing is an important consideration. Utilization of this assessment would be best when there is potential, current concern. In this event, the school counselor can help with referring to appropriate community mental health services. Additionally, this instrument could be used as a progress-monitoring tool as a follow-up with a student who you have previously supported.

Spence Children's Anxiety Scale

While the school counselors' role does not include providing long-term therapy, it is helpful to be able to utilize instruments that can screen or measure children's anxiety as a pre/posttest. The Spence Children's Anxiety Scale (SCAS; Spence, 1998) is an excellent assessment to consider when working with individual students or in small groups to produce outcomes data. The measure consists of 44 items that are rated on a 4-point Likert scale of never, sometimes, often, always, across the six domains of generalized anxiety, panic/agoraphobia, social phobia, separation anxiety, obsessive-compulsive disorder, and physical injury fears. Just like any other clinical assessment that a school counselor may use, the SCAS should not be used to make a clinical diagnosis, but rather to collect data for decision-making and intervention. The SCAS has a child version as well as a parent version, both of which are free on the researcher's website, along with a variety of other relevant resources.

Strengths and Difficulties Questionnaire

One instrument that may help identify students who might need additional support is the Strengths and Difficulties Questionnaire (Goodman, 1997). The instrument has a variety of versions focused on children, adolescents, and adults and allows for three forms: self-report, parent/caregiver, and teacher. The instrument provides a Prosocial Score that identifies strengths, whereas a number of subscales comprise the Difficulties Score (Emotional Symptoms, Conduct Problem, Hyperactivity, Peer Problem). There are extensive materials available on the researcher's website pertaining to the instrument itself and another website that houses advanced tools for data collection, analysis, and visualization, both of which are free and publically accessible. I (Sandra) have used the SDQ as a screener during my time as a middle school counselor. By administering this assessment on a periodic basis, I was able to have a quick snapshot of students who may be experiencing challenges through the lens of three different stakeholders. This data allowed me to make data-driven decisions and provide intervention that directly supported student needs.

Student Risk Screening Scale for Internalizing and Externalizing Behaviors

The Student Risk Screening Scale for Internalizing and Externalizing Behaviors (SRSS-IE; Lane & Menzies, 2009) instrument is one that we *highly* recommend school counselors consider incorporating into their universal screening of students as a part of their CSCP. Typically, screening would occur three times per year with administration and completion of the SRSS-IE by teachers, who simply rate students on a 0-to-3 Likert scale, based on their observations of how often a target behavior is displayed by each student. Overall, the intent is to identify general risks that may be contributing to a students' ability to be successful, from the perspective of both internalizing and externalizing behaviors. A strength of this assessment is that there are electronic templates that you can simply provide to teachers to complete, perhaps giving them a 1-week window to complete the SRSS-IE on behalf of all of their current students. Additionally, there is an elementary version as well as a middle/high school version which allows this instrument to be used school/district-wide. There is a wealth of supporting materials and a website dedicated to the training and implementation of this instrument. Again, we cannot emphasize enough how valuable this instrument can be for screening and determining appropriate counseling interventions across all school settings. In fact, this may be of interest for Tier I district-wide implementation as areas throughout the country consider how to best implement Response to Intervention (RTI) and Multi-Tiered Systems of Support (MTSS) efforts.

As you are considering how you might best utilize this instrument in your school setting, we encourage you to consider the following questions: What is the current level of buy-in to support students' social, academic, and emotional needs? What can I do to support or improve the level of buy-in? How can I facilitate an easy and brief assessment process, for all stakeholders, while still being helpful in collecting important data? Here is one example that may help get the wheels turning:

> At Beachwalk Elementary School, the sole school counselor, Mrs. Parsons, found that she has not been able to keep up with all of the referrals coming from teachers across grade levels. Desiring to have a more intentional way of understanding the student needs, Mrs. Parsons decides to administer the SRSS-IE in a structured and consistent manner. As the school functions on a trimester system, she schedules the administration of the SRSS-IE by each classroom teacher halfway through each grading period, which is when progress reports are sent home. This allows the teacher and the counselor to identify students who may be struggling in time for growth or improvement to be made before the next grading period.

Buy-in from both administration and teachers is critical to your success in utilizing the SRSS-IE.

To garner support for this strategy, we encourage you to get administrative support and buy-in. Buy-in from both administration and teachers is critical to your success in utilizing the SRSS-IE. Additionally, we encourage you to make this as simple as possible for the teachers, so perhaps you send an email with a 1-week deadline asking teachers to complete the SRSS spreadsheet and then return it to you for review of the data. Having a completed spreadsheet is also helpful for record-keeping purposes and looking at data more longitudinally. Another way to facilitate the process is to make an electronic version of the document as a form for teachers to complete. This may be especially helpful for schools that already have strong technology integration with Microsoft or Google. While there are no cut scores, we do recommend reading the information on cut scores for data-informed decision-making by Lane et al. (2015) for elementary-level scores and Lane et al. (2016) for secondary-level scores.

Youth Risk Behavior Survey

The Youth Risk Behavior Survey (YRBS) offers a robust survey system that is nationally recognized and was developed by the Centers for Disease Control and Prevention (CDC) in the 1990s to monitor health behaviors that contribute to personal and societal challenges (CDC, n.d.). Intended for middle school and high school students, each version asks a comprehensive set of questions aimed at measuring the following behaviors:

- Inadequate physical activity, including obesity;
- Unhealthy dietary behaviors;
- Alcohol, tobacco, and other drug (ATOD) use;
- Sexual identity, behaviors, and activity, including pregnancy and sexually transmitted diseases.

Ultimately, the categories included in this survey often contribute to school challenges; thus, these also serve as important data elements for school counselors to use when designing targeted interventions and in their development and implementation of their CSCP. Given the widespread use of this system across the United States, both national data and state-level data are available online, as is the entire battery of YRBS instruments.

WellCheq

One informal assessment tool that may be a great option for you to consider using is WellCheq. While many teachers and school counselors have an informal, unstructured way of simply checking in with students who may need such attention, this tool provides some structure for this activity. It is a web-based platform that serves as a daily check-in tool to gauge how students are doing, by responding to two simple questions. As you will see in Exhibit 4.16, students are asked to respond to (a) How are you feeling today? and (b) Overall, how are you doing? Additionally, students who would like to express concerns with school personnel can select the *Cheq on Me* box, which alerts the teacher and another designated individual, such as the school counselor, that they would like someone to check in with them.

Figure 4.1 illustrates how you can specify a certain period of time for reporting the class average score on question 2 (Overall, how are you doing?), which can help identify trends related to classroom environment, instructional strategies, or even classroom management. For instance, looking at the

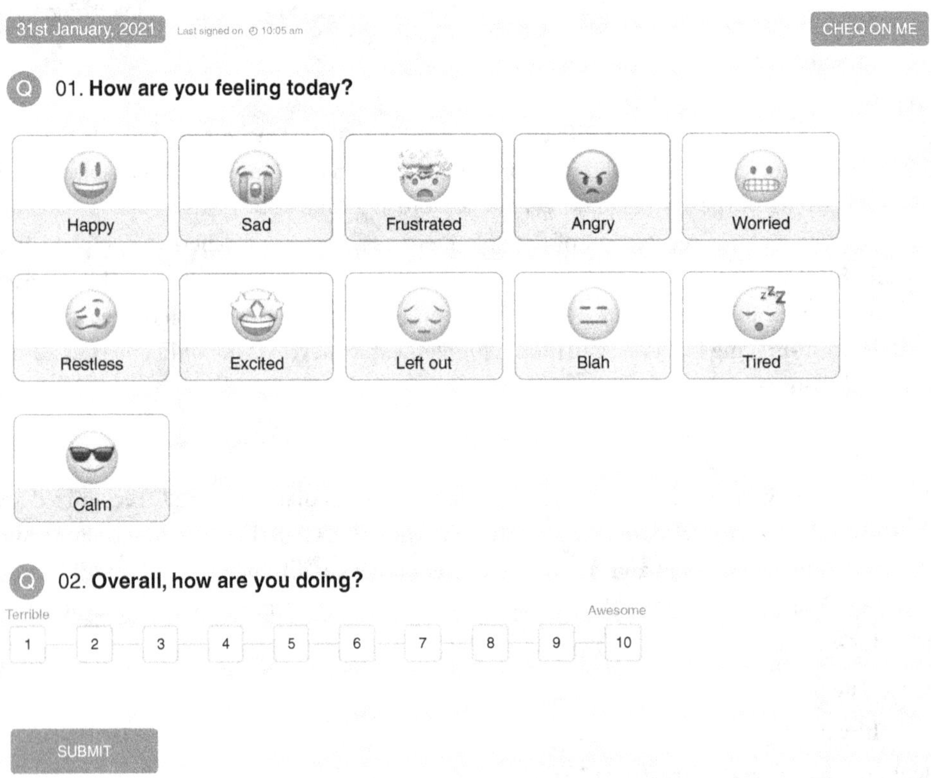

EXHIBIT 4.16 WellCheq online daily check-in tool. Used with permission.

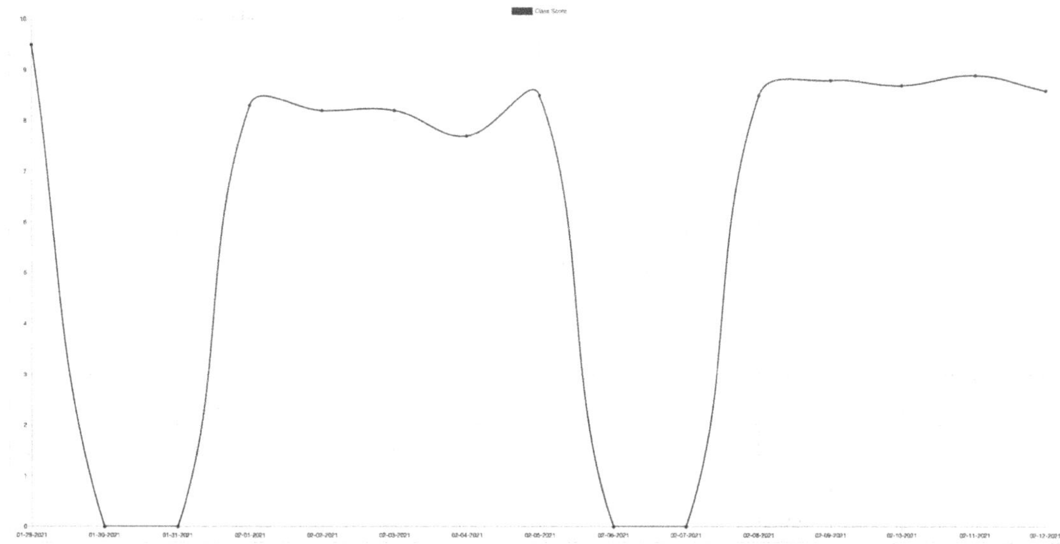

FIGURE 4.1 WellCheq Cumulative Daily Report on "How are you doing?" over a 2-week period. Used with permission.

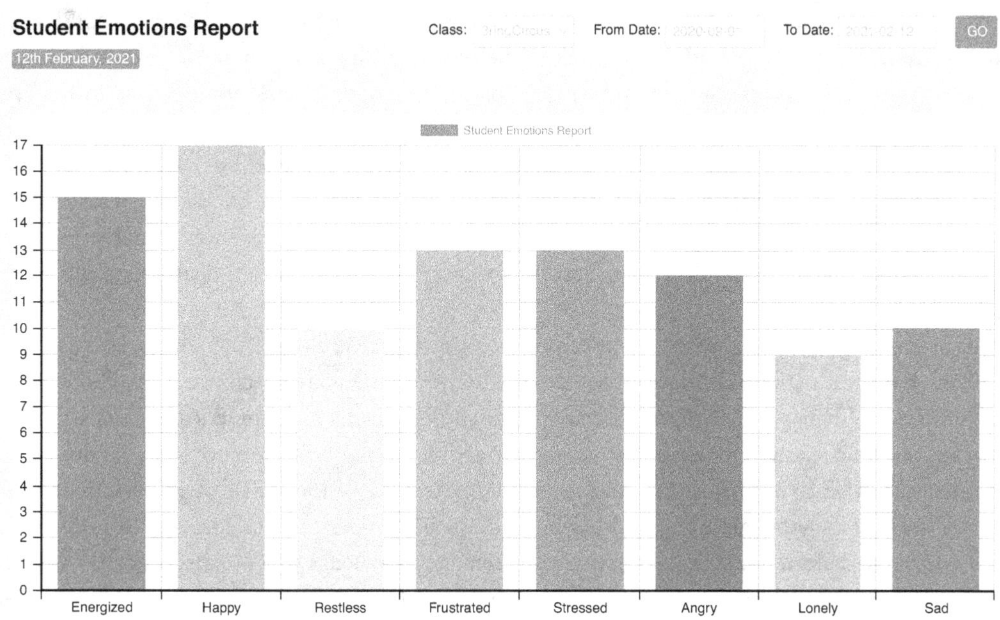

FIGURE 4.2 WellCheq Cumulative Emotions Report on "How are you feeling today?" over multimonth period. Used with permission.

far-right portion of the illustration, it might be interesting to know what was going on in the classroom between February 9 and 12, or what took place in February for a rating of 10 across all students in the classroom.

An important feature of the app its ability to create a query for the Student Emotions Report (Figure 4.2), which can be set to be emailed daily to the classroom teacher and other school personnel for an identified period of time. This type of data analysis allow you to gauge how students are functioning within a particular classroom and can, in fact, inform the need for specific classroom lessons. The ease of use of this tool makes it a wonderful and convenient way to collect data quickly and be able to respond to student needs in real time.

What Can Your Assessment Efforts Look Like?

As you can see, there are a variety of assessments that can be used for screening and intervention purposes. It is possible to utilize more than one assessment and, in some cases, it is advisable to use more than one, if in fact you are providing counseling services that are intended to address more than one issue. When it comes to screening, my two favorites are the SRSS and SAEBRS, due to their comprehensive nature and ease of use for purposes such as identification of possible participants for individual or group counseling. Now, you might feel a bit overwhelmed after reading through all of these potential assessments. But remember, each of these serves as an opportunity to gather data, monitor progress, or inform the types of services that you are providing. Each serves a purpose and that is where you want to start. Let's consider a few scenarios.

Jessica is an elementary counselor with 5 years of experience at this grade level; however, it is her first year at Beachside Elementary. She wants to better understand the classroom dynamics and climate in her upper-grade classrooms. So she decides to administer the My Class Inventory (MCI-SFR; Sink & Spencer, 2005) to her fourth-, fifth-, and sixth-grade teachers as well as to the students in those grades during the month of October. By using this instrument she will be able to better understand the classroom climate in relation to the four areas measured by the MCI-SFR: satisfaction, friction, competition, and cohesiveness. The results of this assessment, for example, might illustrate for Jessica which classrooms are in need of core curricular classroom lessons in the area of conflict resolution. Subsequent to delivering the classroom lessons, Jessica could then administer the MCI again in a posttest manner to evaluate the effectiveness of those lessons. In essence, the MCI is serving as both a needs assessment, as well as a pre–posttest for the actual intervention. Additionally, Jessica could consider the use of the parent version to gain another valuable perspective on classroom climate. This data then becomes a part of the data-driven decision-making that contributes to her CSCP.

In another example, Jamal is a high school counselor serving the junior class (11th grade). While his school has a high graduation rate, the percentage of students who pursue postsecondary options is less than desired. Jamal believes that this is due in part to students lacking awareness and understanding about college life, admissions procedures, and financial aid, among other topics. Thus, he decides to administer the CAKE to all 11th-grade students at the beginning of the school year. By utilizing this assessment early in the year, Jamal can decide what is in the best interest of students. Perhaps the results will show that the majority of students do possess adequate knowledge about college admissions, but that a subset of students are lacking in competence. This would illustrate that Jamal would do best to prioritize small-group counseling for those targeted students. On the other hand, if the results of the CAKE illustrated that few students possessed knowledge about college admissions, then Jamal could decide to provide core curricular classroom lessons to all 11th graders by meeting with them through their English courses.

Finally, let's consider Sarah, a district supervisor who oversees all 127 school counselors in her district. As one of her annual goals for the academic year, she desires to have all schools working toward the development and implementation of a data-driven CSCP. In order to do this, Sarah could first start by administering the School Counseling Program Implementation Survey (SCPIS; Clemens et al., 2010) to all 127 school counselors to see what their current status is, from nonexistent to full implementation.

This data would then allow her to provide appropriate professional development opportunities that address the areas that her school counselors are most in need of support. Similar to the previous examples, the SCPIS could be administered every 6 months over a 3-year period to provide progress monitoring to both the school counselors and Sarah.

Conclusions

You have made it this far through the book, which means you now have a foundational understanding of our profession and the importance of being a data-driven school counselor, as well as an understanding of the process of assessment and data collection and its value in a CSCP. Even further, you have been exposed to a variety of assessments that you can utilize. But it is also important to recognize there is value in utilizing informal assessments, which are typically created by a practitioner for their own use. In the next chapter, we discuss how your data-driven decision-making can be achieved by focusing on the development of informal assessments that yield participation data ASCA Mindsets & Behavior data, and outcome data across grade levels and domains. While we have highlighted a number of free, valid, and reliable instruments, as well as a few informal assessments that can help inform your data-driven decision-making and strengthen the implementation of a CSCP, there are a number of other resources (see Tools and Resources) that provide databases or access to a variety of instruments and other relevant resources.

Additional Reading

Barna, J., Wilkerson, K., & Morgan, S. (2015). An overview of comprehensive school counseling program assessment instruments to inform future research. *ACA Counseling VISTAS*. https://www.counseling.org/docs/default-source/vistas/article_65915a22f16116603abcacff0000bee5e7.pdf?sfvrsn=f4c422c_4.

Hatch, T., Duarte, D. R., & De Gregorio, L. K. (2018). *Hatching results for elementary school counseling: Implementing core curriculum and other tier one activities*. Corwin.

Hatch, T., Kruger, A., Pablo, N., & Triplett, W. (2020). *Hatching tier two and three interventions in your elementary school counseling program*. Corwin.

Hatch, T., Triplett, W., Duarte, D., & Gomez, V. (2019). *Hatching results for secondary school counseling: implementing core curriculum, individual student planning, and other tier one activities*. Corwin.

Whitcomb, S. A. (2018). *Behavioral, social, and emotional assessment of children and adolescents*. Routledge.

Tools and Resources

- Association for Career and Technical Education has a wealth of resources, assessments, and professional development opportunities (https://www.acteonline.org/)
- Career OneStop is used to search for your state or local workforce development office and to access relevant career-focused resources and opportunities (https://www.careeronestop.org/)
- Center on Positive Behavioral Interventions & Supports, *School Climate Survey Suite* (https://www.pbis.org/resource/school-climate-survey-suite)
- Collaborative for Academic and Social–Emotional Learning (CASEL) Compendium (Preschool and Elementary; https://casel.org/wp-content/uploads/2016/06/compendium-of-preschool-through-elementary-school-social-emotional-learning-and-associated-assessment-measures.pdf)
- College, Career, Readiness, & Life Framework from Hobson's, which contains excellent resources to support the utilization of Naviance (https://www.hobsons.com/resources/cclr-framework-booklet/)

- College Sanity, where you can access interactive versions of the CAKE instrument, as well as a survey about college counseling services (www.collegesanity.com)
- Comprehensive, Integrated Three-Tiered Model of Prevention (Ci3T) provides comprehensive information about systematic screening and access to a variety of free assessments (https://www.ci3t.org/screening)
- CRAAFT, where you can access the instrument (http://crafft.org/)
- Measuring SEL with CASEL, where you can locate research about social–emotional learning and review the database of instruments that measure SEL (https://measuringsel.casel.org/)
- Mendocino County Office of Education has two excellent resources, one focused on college and career resources, including the Career Continuum (https://sites.google.com/site/mcoecareerresources/home) and the other on career exploration (https://sites.google.com/site/mcoecareerexploration/creating-a-career-culture)
- National Center on Safe Supportive Learning Environments provides the *School Climate Survey Compendium*, which is an excellent resource serving as a review of school climate surveys that may be best for yours setting (https://safesupportivelearning.ed.gov/topic-research/school-climate-measurement/school-climate-survey-compendium)
- *RAND Education Assessment Finder* (https://www.rand.org/education-and-labor/projects/assessments.html)
- RoadTrip Nation is a comprehensive resource for career exploration and development, including classroom curriculum and a video library with interviews of people discussing their career paths (https://roadtripnation.com/explore)
- When I Grow Up campaign offers a free career-related curriculum (https://www.wrksolutions.com/for-individuals/career-exploration/when-i-grow-up)

Key Points

- School counselors are in a unique position to regularly use formal assessments as a part of their day-to-day responsibility and as a part of their data-driven CSCP.
- If you find an instrument in a book or journal article, school counselors should consider reaching out directly to the author/researcher(s) of the instrument to ask for access. Many people are more than willing to provide free access or a copy of the instrument.
- While not always easily accessible, free, valid, and reliable instruments that school counselors can utilize are available and should be used in conjunction with other information assessments.
- There are a variety of instruments that school counselors can use to measure progress within each of the ASCA domains: academic, career, and social–emotional.

Questions for Reflection

- When selecting an instrument, think to yourself: What do I want to know about students or their classrooms?
- How am I going to decide which students would benefit from small-group counseling? How will I know what to focus our sessions on?
- As a result of this data, what do I know? What are my next steps?
- If you want to use a screener for elementary students, what instrument might you select and why? What about for secondary students?

Online Access to Instruments

CAKE (http://www.collegesanity.com/college-knowledge/)
CAYCI-SES (http://cayci.osu.edu/surveys/surveys-and-technical-reports/)
CRAFFT (https://crafft.org/)

C-SSRS (http://www.cssrs.columbia.edu)
EDSCLS (https://safesupportivelearning.ed.gov/edscls)
KADS-6 (https://teenmentalhealth.org/wp-content/uploads/2014/09/6-KADS.pdf)
Kuder (https://www.kuder.com/solutions/kuder-career-planning-system/assessments/)
MCI Measures (https://sites.google.com/site/chrissinkwebsite/social-emotional-learng-and-development/assessments)
My Career Story (http://www.vocopher.com/CSI/CCI_workbook.pdf)
Naviance (https://www.hobsons.com/solution/naviance/)
O*Net Interest Profile (https://www.onetcenter.org/IP.html)
SAEBRS (https://ebi.missouri.edu/wp-content/uploads/2014/03/EBA-Brief-SAEBRS.pdf)
SCARS (https://www.cscoreumass.org/sc-resources)
SCAS (https://www.scaswebsite.com/)
SCCI (http://www.vocopher.com/ms/scci/SCCI_Master.pdf)
SCPIS (https://www.cscoreumass.org/sc-resources)
SDQ (https://sdqinfo.org/)
SRSS-IE (https://www.ci3t.org/screening)
WellCheq (https://wellcheq.com/)
Xello (https://xello.world/en/)
YRBS (https://www.cdc.gov/healthyyouth/data/yrbs/questionnaires.htm)

References

American School Counselor Association. (2016). *ASCA ethical standards for school counselors.* https://www.schoolcounselor.org/getmedia/f041cbd0-7004-47a5-ba01-3a5d657c6743/Ethical-Standards.pdf

American School Counselor Association. (2019). *ASCA national model: A framework for school counseling programs* (4th ed.). American School Counselor Association.

Anderson-Butcher, D., Amorose, A. J., Iachini, A., & Ball, A. (2013). *Community and Youth Collaborative Institute school experience surveys.* College of Social Work, The Ohio State University.

Bardhoshi, G., Cobb, N., & Erford, B. T. (2019). Determining evidence-based outcomes in school-aged youth: Free-access instruments for school counselor use. *Professional School Counseling, 22*(1b). https://doi.org/10.1177/2156759X19834431

Clemens, E., Carey, J., & Harrington, K. (2010). The School Counseling Program Implementation Survey: Initial Instrument Development and Exploratory Factor Analysis. *Professional School Counseling,* 14(2), 125–134. Retrieved June 27, 2021, from http://www.jstor.org/stable/42732941

Corrigan, M. J., Loneck, B., & Videka, L. (2007). The development and preliminary validation of the adolescent domain screening inventory: A substance use prevention tool. *Research on Social Work Practice, 17*(3), 348–357. https://doi.org/10.1177/1049731506295158

Durand, V. M., & Crimmins, D. B. (1992). *The Motivation Assessment Scale (MAS) administration guide.* Monaco & Associates.

Goodman, R. (1997). The strengths and difficulties questionnaire: A research note. *Journal of Child Psychology and Psychiatry, 38,* 581–586. https://doi.org/10.1111/j.1469-7610.1997.tb01545.x

Knight, J. R. (2018). *CRAAFT self-administered and clinical interview versions.* Boston Children's Hospital. https://crafft.org/

Kutcher, S. (2008). *Kutcher Adolescent Depression Scale.* https://teenmentalhealth.org/wp-content/uploads/2014/09/6-KADS.pdf

Lane, K. L., & Menzies, H. M. (2009). *Student Risk Screening Scale for Internalizing and Externalizing (SRSS-IE).* http://www.ci3t.org/screening

Lane, K. L., Oakes, W. P., Cantwell, E. D., Schatschneider, C., Menzies, H., Crittenden, M., & Messenger, M. (2016). Student Risk Screening Scale for Internalizing and Externalizing Behaviors: Preliminary cut scores to support data-informed decision making in middle and high schools. *Behavioral Disorders, 42*(1), 271–284. https://doi.org/10.17988/bd-16-115.1

Lane, K. L., Oakes, W. P., Swogger, E. D., Schatschneider, C., Menzies, H. M., & Sanchez, J. (2015). Student Risk Screening Scale for Internalizing and Externalizing Behaviors: Preliminary cut scores to support data-informed decision making. *Behavioral Disorders, 40*(3), 159–170. https://doi.org/10.17988/0198-7429-40.3.159

Neukrug, E., Peterson, C. H., Bonner, M., & Lomas, G. I. (2013). A national survey of assessment instruments taught by counselor educators. *Counselor Education and Supervision*, *52*, 207–221. https://doi.org/10.1002/j.1556-6978.2013.00038.x

Posner, K. (n.d.). *Columbia-Suicide Severity Rating Scale (C-SSRS) columbia university medical Center; Center for suicide risk assessment*. http://www.cssrs.columbia.edu/

Poynton, T. A., Ruiz, B., & Lapan, R. T. (2019). Development and validation of the college admissions knowledge evaluation. *Professional School Counseling*, *22*(1a), 98–103. https://doi.org/10.1177/2156759X19834441

Savickas, M. L., & Hartung, P. J. (2012). *My career story: An autobiographical workbook for life-career success*. www.vocopher.com

Savickas, M. L., Porfeli, E. J., Hilton, T. L., & Savickas, S. (2018). The Student Career Construction Inventory. *Journal of Vocational Behavior*, *106*, 138–152. https://doi.org/10.1016/j.jvb.2018.01.009

Sink, C. A., & Spencer, L. R. (2005). My Class Inventory-Short Form as an accountability tool for elementary school counselors to measure classroom climate. *Professional School Counseling*, *9*, 37–48. https://doi.org/10.5330/prsc.9.1.y720844684111402

Spence, S. H. (1998). A measure of anxiety symptoms among children. *Behaviour Research and Therapy*, *36*(5), 545–566. https://doi.org/10.1016/s0005-7967(98)00034-5

5

DATA-DRIVEN SCHOOL COUNSELING THROUGH INFORMAL ASSESSMENT

Data-Driven School Counseling Through Informal Assessment

The very notion that school counselors use data to inform their practices and programming should not be novel. In fact, just as with other educator roles, from teachers to administrators, we must use data to know where our efforts are most needed and illustrate where they are most effective. Dimmitt et al. (2007) emphasize that data-based decision-making can only take place when there is a school context that facilitates such as process. In this chapter, we discuss the use of needs assessments and program evaluation, as well as the three types of data that are a part of a data-driven school counselor's daily functioning, working at any school level. Through informal assessment, each of the following types of data serves a purpose and provides valuable information: participation, Mindsets & Behaviors, and outcome data. Given that we are now operating under the guidelines of the fourth edition of the *American School Counselor Association (ASCA) National Model,* which has undergone some revisions, we also address those language changes. Importantly, we provide developmentally appropriate examples of each type of data at each school level.

There is no doubt that the role of the school counselor has evolved over the years. Perhaps one of the most striking changes in recent years, aside from the nomenclature change from *guidance counselor* to *school counselor* is promotion of the competence inherent within the new name (Lambie & Williamson, 2004; Zyromski et al., 2019) is that the use of data to drive one's comprehensive school counseling program (CSCP) has become an imperative. School counselors, like other educators, are faced with the expectations of conducting their responsibilities with data in mind. In fact, ASCA has a position statement, *The School Counselor & School Counseling Programs* (2017), that specifically outlines what constitutes a CSCP. When you consider what a data-driven CSCP looks like, we recommend turning to this position statement, which highlights the following elements:

- Design of a school counseling program;
- Data-informed annual goals along with the measured impact of direct services delivery;
- Data-informed classroom, small-group and closing-the-gap activities and interventions;
- Calendars reflecting appropriate use of time aligned with ASCA National Model recommendation that 80% of time is spent in direct and indirect services to students;
- Collection and analysis of results data from classroom, small-group and closing-the-gap activities and interventions (American School Counselor Association [ASCA], 2017).

Stone and Dahir (2007) eloquently explain the importance of using data stating, "Closely examining critical data elements that identify the needs of your students and the schoolwide issues that cloud success is the first step to inform and guide the development of an accountable school counseling program" (p. 17). Thus, using data informs both the "what" and the "why" by meeting our student needs in intentional ways. Furthermore, when considering the rationale of why one must be a data-driven school counselor, there has been considerable research conducted by scholars in recent years that illustrates the positive outcomes (i.e., increased feelings of school safety, higher achievement scores, higher attendance rates, decrease in suspension rates) of implementing a data-driven CSCP (see Burkhard et al., 2012; Carey et al., 2012; Carey & Martin, 2015; Dimmitt & Wilkerson, 2012; Lapan et al., 2001; Sink et al., 2008; Sink & Stroh, 2003; Wilkerson et al., 2013).

Keep in mind that data does not only come from formal assessments, such as the Student Risk Screening Scale—Internalizing & Externalizing Behaviors (SSRS-IE; Lane & Menzies, 2009) or the Community and Youth Collaborative Institute-School Experience Surveys (CAYCI-SES; Anderson-Butcher et al., 2013), but also informal assessments. School counselors create such informal assessments every time they design a pre–postassessment for students. Counselors are typically trained, as a part of their counselor preparation program, but often overlook or undervalue it, equating the role of assessment solely with special education eligibility. However, in recent years, it has also become more challenging to carry out the role that school counselors have been trained for. In fact, Lambie et al. (2019) describe that due to shifts in educational priorities, many school counselors have lost sight of their professional identity, that of a trained counselor. Yet, being able to illustrate the important and critical work that you do, through data, is an opportunity to advocate for your students, your role, your CSCP, and your profession. Consider the following scenario:

Yet, being able to illustrate the important and critical work that you do, through data, is an opportunity to advocate for your students, your role, your CSCP, and your profession.

> Kevin is a school counselor at a K-8 center who holds responsibility for all sixth-grade through eighth-grade students. He likes to conduct groups as he believes it is the best way to reach a greater number of students with similar concerns or challenges, especially in light of his high caseload of 740:1 (nearly three times the ASCA recommended ratio). When the principal approaches Kevin about the need for him to proctor the upcoming standardized testing season, he is at a crossroad. How can Kevin illustrate the importance and value of his group counseling and need to stick with appropriate responsibilities, while also maintaining a good working relationship with his administration?

In the event that Kevin was simply conducting group counseling because he enjoys it and sees the potential value of meeting the needs of multiple students at one time, but is not collecting any data from it, he may have difficulties garnering the necessary support of his administrator and nothing would prevent him from being responsible for a noncounseling responsibility, such as test proctoring. On the other hand, if Kevin was a data-driven school counselor who has used data to inform others of who will be in his groups, say those who earned two or more Ds or Fs during the first quarter, and then also is collecting data throughout the group counseling process (i.e., pre and post), he would be able to illustrate not only his intentions for group participation, but also the effectiveness of his groups. This seems like a much more sound rationale as to why Kevin cannot be responsible for test proctoring, and one that his administration would be more likely to recognize and will seek a more suitable staff member.

ASCA National Model Fourth-Edition Revisions

With the introduction of a revision to the National Model comes changes to the nomenclature and organization of its contents. Notably, changes were made with respect to the naming of the types of data that school counselors produce and analyze. The term used to describe who the participants are within an activity has changed from *process data* to *participation data* to more accurately illustrate the targeted audience. For instance, 127 fourth graders participated in 4 weekly sessions of 30 minutes of core curricular classroom lessons on effective communication, problem-solving skills, and handling conflict. This statement simply illustrates the "who" aspect of data *perception data* has changed to *Mindsets & Behaviors data* to coincide with ASCA's *Mindsets & Behaviors for Student Success* (2014). This change allows further understanding of what can be targeted in terms of learning or understanding by the students. For example, a school counselor could design a pre–posttest of Likert-scale items that allow for illustration of changes in students' mindsets and behaviors. Using the mindset, *Self-confidence in ability to succeed* (M.2), an item on the assessment could be "I believe that I can succeed in school" using a 5-point Likert scale, with one being "no belief in my success" and five being "complete belief in my success." A pretest to posttest change would be a way of showing change or improvement in a students' mindset. Lastly, the fourth edition of the National Model remains consistent with previous versions in the use of "outcome data" referring to types of data that can illustrate intended changes in achievement, attendance, or discipline/behavior. The critical question that should be answered with outcome data is "*How are students different as a result of their participation in a specific intervention or activity?*" In sum, while the names have changed from *process data* to *participation data*, and from *perception data* to *Mindsets & Behaviors data*, their intent of illustrating the school counselor's role and impact on students remains the same.

Needs Assessments and Program Evaluation

As a data-driven school counselor, one of your first opportunities to engage with data is through a needs-assessment process. When you arrive as a new school counselor to a school site, you may find yourself wondering "what are the students, staff, and parents/caregivers like?" With this thought, you are desiring to know about these individuals through the lens of data. Dimmitt et al. (2007) describe *needs assessment* as "a formal process of gathering information from a range of sources about their perceptions of the needs of the student population and the importance of particular curricular focus or specific interventions" (p. 38).

Your intent is to learn more about the needs from your stakeholders and to inform the work that you will carry out in the future. One of the challenges is that school counselors find themselves desiring a quick, ready-to-use needs assessment, but yet very few exist since our schools are each unique and ever changing. Instead of feeling deflated by this circumstance, consider that you should be designing a needs assessment that captures exactly the elements that you want to know more about. So, the one-size-fits-all approach does not really work well here. Rather, meet with your school counselor colleagues or student intervention team at the beginning of the year to discuss and collaborate on what information it is that you desire to learn more about. Then, consider which audiences you want to learn from: students, parents/caregivers, teachers, administration, or community members. For example, the school counselor may want to find out from teachers what topics they believe are most needed for core curricular classroom lessons. If given the opportunity, parents/caregivers might identify that small-group counseling opportunities that focus on divorce and loss/grief are desired.

One online platform that many school counselors utilize for need-assessment purposes, specific to the social-emotional domain, and highly recommend is Panorama (www.panoramaed.com). The two main surveys are designated into three categories: student surveys, upper elementary for grades 3 to 5 and secondary school for grades 6 to 12; teacher survey; and family engagement survey. In addition to serving as a comprehensive platform for surveying school climate, there is an extensive resource library that contains

TABLE 5.1 MEASURES WITHIN THE PANORAMA PLATFORM

MEASURE NAME	SEL GROUP	RECOMMENDED OR SUPPLEMENTAL MEASURES
Grit	Student Competencies	Recommended
Growth Mindset	Student Competencies	Recommended
Self-Management	Student Competencies	Recommended
Social Awareness	Student Competencies	Recommended
Self-Efficacy	Student Competencies	Recommended
School Climate—Student	Student Supports and Environment	Recommended
Teacher–Student Relationships	Student Supports and Environment	Recommended
Sense of Belonging	Student Supports and Environment	Recommended
School Safety	Student Supports and Environment	Recommended
Teacher Self-Reflection	Teacher Skills and Perspectives	Recommended
Professional Learning About SEL	Teacher Skills and Perspectives	Recommended
School Climate—Teacher	Teacher Skills and Perspectives	Recommended
Resources for Student Support	Teacher Skills and Perspectives	Recommended
Background Questions	Other	Recommended
Learning Strategies	Student Competencies	Supplemental
Classroom Effort	Student Competencies	Supplemental
Social Perspective-Taking	Student Competencies	Supplemental
Self-efficacy about Specific Subjects	Student Competencies	Supplemental
Emotion Regulation	Student Competencies	Supplemental
Engagement	Student Supports and Environment	Supplemental
Rigorous Expectations	Student Supports and Environment	Supplemental
Valuing of Specific Subjects	Student Supports and Environment	Supplemental
Valuing of School	Student Supports and Environment	Supplemental
Educating All Students	Teacher Skills and Perspectives	Supplemental

the formal assessments that can be used within their platform, but they also have some downloadable databases such as *Student Check-ins Question Bank, Family-School Relationships Survey,* and many more guiding documents, templates, and best practices from districts across the country. With the comprehensive nature of the tool, it is also possible for schools/districts to build their own survey that best meets their needs. See Table 5.1 for the subscales (measures) and their alignment with a particular social–emotional learning (SEL) domain (Student Competencies, Student Supports and Environment, Teacher Skills and Perspectives), and whether they are available in the recommended or supplement measures materials.

In addition to assessment, it is also important to consider what your program evaluation efforts look like. Imagine is coming up on the end of the school year and you find yourself wondering about the impacts of your efforts and your entire CSCP. Of course, you will have outcome data (discussed in more detail later in the chapter) that can illustrate "how students are different as a result of your intervention." But, what about evaluating your comprehensive program through feedback from your stakeholders. Again, wouldn't it be great if such an evaluation was already created for you? But every school counselor and every CSCP is different. Thus, you need to consider what it is that you have implemented this year and use that as your basis for evaluation. You can absolutely use the same concepts used when you design your needs assessment for your program evaluation by focusing on what it is that you want to learn. Since I know many of you may still be thinking about where to even begin, we recommend starting with basic instruments provided from the Center for School Counseling Outcome Research and Evaluation (CSCORE). Here you will find instruments that are organized by role (administrator, counselor, teacher, parent/caregiver), school level (elementary, middle, or high), and Spanish-language versions are available for the parent/caregiver survey. Lastly, we encourage you to gain inspiration from what other school counselors have created for their needs assessments and program evaluation surveys by searching relevant blogs from *School Counselor Stephanie*, *Confident Counselors*, and *Exploring School Counseling.*

Participation Data

As we know, numbers speak to school administrators, giving them an understanding of their school's capacity and functioning, both in terms of teachers and students. From the school counselor's perspective, numbers speak in that they illustrate progress or change in student achievement, behavior, or other outcomes. This particular type of data is focused on just reporting concrete facts, including how many students, which students, what did the students participate in, by what means, and when? The following statement would represent participation data: Seven students in the ninth grade, who are designated as Level-1 English-language learners and earned a non passing grade in their English class, participated in a small group for six, 30-minute sessions during the second semester. As you can see, the statement simply provides a way to document all of these elements. Typically, we consider this a basic level of data that it is not showing change or outcome. Review Table 5.2, which provides examples of participation data across the ASCA domains and is organized by grade level.

Now, let's consider the following scenario:

> *It is late January and Shawnee, an elementary school counselor, is meeting with an assistant principal, José, who just began working at her school. During the meeting, José inquires about what Shawnee has spent her time doing during the fall semester, as he is new to working at the elementary level and unclear about what a school counselors' role entails in this setting.*

Wow, this is an excellent opportunity to illustrate Shawnee's efforts in the previous semester. In her implementation of a CSCP, she has consistently been collecting participation data, which makes it very easy for her to provide documentation to Jose about her efforts. She explains:

> Well, given the transitions that take place at the beginning of the year, I really prioritize getting into all kindergarten and first-grade classrooms as soon as I can in September. I make myself visible by presenting introductory get-to-know-your-school counselor lessons. In fact, I reached all five kindergarten classrooms and all but one first-grade classroom, meaning that 109 students have participated in the 20-minute "Meet the Counselor" classroom lesson. Moreover, I am pleased to share with you

TABLE 5.2 EXAMPLES OF PARTICIPATION DATA ACROSS DOMAINS AND GRADE LEVEL

SCHOOL LEVEL	ASCA DOMAIN	EXAMPLE
Elementary	Academic	97% of all third graders (N = 54) participated in the 4-week "Do Your Best for Success" test-taking strategies core curricular classroom unit.
	Career	67 students in the fifth grade attended the transition-to-middle school presentation delivered by the school counseling team at the feeder school.
	Social–emotional	18 students participated in a 6-week group counseling session focused on anger management and coping skills.
Middle school	Academic	15 sixth graders attended a small-group counseling experience focused on motivation.
	Career	128 seventh graders attended a career-day event at the local community college.
	Social–emotional	92% of eighth graders (N = 86) attending a school-wide assembly focused on understanding and identifying signs of suicidal ideation.
High school	Academic	19 out of 27 students, who were failing Algebra 1, completed a 4-week organizational skills boot camp.
	Career	47% of 11th graders who earned one or more F in the first semester attended a 6-week afterschool tutoring club.
	Social–emotional	100% of ninth graders participated in a curricular unit on healthy relationships and decision-making.

> that based on my needs assessments conducted early in the school year, completed by teachers, parents/caregivers, and students, I was able to provide four different small groups and conduct a series of parent education workshops aimed at meeting their needs.

Of course, the needs of each school level are different. At the middle school level, there tends to be more of an emphasis on time management and organization skills, as well as academic success. Let's see how participation data could be helpful at this level:

> During October's faculty meeting, a majority of the seventh-grade teachers describe concerns about many students struggling with classroom behaviors that are negatively impacting the learning environment. Accordingly, the seventh-grade school counselor, Jessica, decides that she will provide two classroom lessons: one focused on respecting one another, and another focused on conflict resolution. At December's faculty meeting, Jessica is able to report to her colleagues that she has conducted classroom lessons for more than 200 students in the seventh grade, directly answering a need that was identified by teachers.

In this scenario, rather than a proactive measure like what was described in the elementary example, a responsive measure was taken to address a need that was identified by the grade-level teachers. It is imperative for school counselors to remember that they need to be both proactive to meet the perceived needs of students, as well as responsible to the identified needs of students. Such an effort is also a great public relations move for the school counselor, so that other teachers can see explicitly how the school counselor can support successful classroom operations, dynamics, and ultimately, student success.

At the high school level, the emphasis on academic achievement only intensifies. Whether it be enrollment in advanced placement (AP) courses or ensuring that students have opportunities for career technical education (CTE), administrators and school counselors are interested in these numbers:

> Hillside High School has historically provided only a limited number of AP course offerings each academic year. However, the school counselor, Jeannie, has analyzed the previous years' AP enrollment patterns and learned only Caucasian students have applied for AP courses. As a result, Jeannie decided to make a targeted effort to meet individually with all 10th-grade students whose grades meet the eligibility for AP courses. At the end of this effort, Jeannie mets with 218 students who are eligible for AP courses.

While it cannot be assumed that all students who are eligible for AP courses will enroll, perhaps, the school counselors' efforts in educating them on the possibility and expectations can result in increasing the number of students who enroll and successfully complete these courses.

Importantly, participation data illustrate the opportunities and experiences that school counselors have afforded students toward increasing achievement and other successes. We know you might still be wondering about whether this category of data is important or not, so consider this: Your school administrator says to you, "I haven't really seen you much lately. What have you been up to?" This right here is *exactly* why participation data is important; it illustrates or rather tracks your efforts and who is benefitting. Additionally, this category of data is valuable for you to be able to see where you are investing your efforts. For example, at the high school level, by reviewing the participation data, it was noticed that the school counseling team devoted a disproportionate amount of time and effort toward the 12th-grade class, while neglecting many of the ninth graders (except those who were failing three or more courses). This would not be known if they were not documenting participation data.

Mindsets & Behavior Data

As indicated, following the shift from the third to the fourth edition of the ASCA National Model, the term *perception data* was changed to *Mindsets & Behaviors data* to more accurately reflect what constitutes this form of data (ASCA, 2019a, 2019b). Remember that this type of data should focus on describing individuals' attitudes, skills, and knowledge, known as "ASK" When considering how you will assess student change or growth, you want to make sure that you are measuring all elements of the ASK and link them together in questions or statements in the following way:

- *Attitudes*: Statements that describe what you want students to believe.
- *Skills*: Statements that describe what you want students to do.
- *Knowledge*: Statements that describe what students know.

If you are finding it challenging to know how to develop such statements, begin with looking at the ASCA (2014) *Mindsets & Behaviors for Student Success* for some ideas. For example, *M 2. Self-confidence in ability to succeed,* may be one of the mindsets that you wish to focus on. To measure this, one of the questions that you may include on your pretest could be, "I believe that I can be successful in school this year" using a Likert scale to measure to what degree students agree with this statement. Then, you will implement some form of counseling intervention or other supports followed by your posttest. Ultimately, the hope would be that your data could illustrate that your intervention has positively impacted the students' mindset focused around ability to succeed. Just think of how compelling and powerful this data can be to stakeholders and to your CSCP. Similarly, you can review the Mindsets & Behaviors, Category 2: Behavior Standards to identify potential areas for addressing knowledge and skill statements for your pre–posttest.

We highly encourage you to utilize Chapter 6 of *Making Data Work* (fourth edition) in your quest toward becoming a data-driven school counselor, which provides readers with excellent illustrations of

TABLE 5.3 EXAMPLES OF MINDSETS & BEHAVIOR DATA ACROSS GRADE LEVEL AND ASCA ACROSS DOMAINS

SCHOOL LEVEL	ASCA DOMAIN	EXAMPLE (MOST LIKELY COULD ASK THE QUESTION ON A PRE–POSTASSESSMENT)
Elementary	Academic	68% of fourth graders believe that earning high grades in school is important. (*Attitude*)
	Career	91% of fifth graders are able to identify two career clusters. (*Knowledge*)
	Social–emotional	Seven out of eight students are able to develop a plan for making new friends. (*Skill*)
Middle school	Academic	91% of eighth graders know the high school graduation requirements. (*Knowledge*)
	Career	45% of sixth graders report they do not need to go to college. (*Attitude*)
	Social–emotional	80% of students could identify two strategies for managing their stress. (*Skill*)
High school	Academic	47% of ninth graders believe coming to school every day contributes to their grades. (*Attitude*)
	Career	Most of the senior class (79%) knows how to prioritize their time and responsibilities. (*Knowledge*)
	Social-emotional	89% of the group participants can de-escalate their emotion (anger) within 60 seconds. (*Skill*)

ASCA, American School Counselor Association.

what informal assessments can be quickly created to provide you with Mindsets & Behavior data. Above all, keep in mind that effective data-driven decision-making comes from keen intentionality and focus on your established student-outcome goals.

To emphasize the "why is this category of data is important," let's again consider your school administrator's question of "What have you been up to lately?" Beyond just letting stakeholders (like your principal) know what you have been doing, in terms of providing direct services, find a way of collecting relevant and insightful data that can be informative for your next step of providing counseling interventions or other supports. Go beyond just saying, "Well, I've been in four third-grade classrooms today." Instead, say "I've visited four third-grade classrooms and have learned that 31% of those students believe that homework is important." Now, we have some compelling data that drives the work you do next. Clearly, the school counselor(s) can deliver core curricular lessons, maybe a unit on "Doing Your Best Work" to increase the attitudes or beliefs of those third graders. From this section, walk away remembering that the Mindsets & Behaviors data are your compelling data that inform what you do next. Additionally, Table 5.3 has some examples of Mindsets & Behaviors data organized by school level, domain, and category within ASK classification.

Outcome Data

As you can see, different types of data have different purposes. Many stakeholders would say that the most important data is outcome data; however, data-driven school counselors know that all three types are important. In order to illustrate outcome data, we need to consider "how did the counseling intervention or activity impact students' success in their area(s) of achievement, attendance, discipline?" Within the educational realm, teachers and counselors alike are expected to positively impact student

TABLE 5.4 EXAMPLES OF OUTCOME DATA ACROSS GRADE LEVEL AND INTENDED OUTCOME

SCHOOL LEVEL	DESIRED OUTCOME	EXAMPLE
Elementary	Attendance	Total number of absences for the identified group of students (first–third graders with five or more absences) in the first semester was 57, which (N = 46) will be compared to the second trimester and we hope will illustrate a decrease in absences by 15%.
	Achievement	The number of third graders who scored below proficient on the state standardized test will decrease by 20%, from 60 to 48 students.
	Discipline/behavioral	The number of disciplinary referrals being reported from students who ride the North route bus will decrease by 35% from 71 referrals to 47.
Middle school	Attendance	The school-wide attendance rate will increase by 2% from 89% to 91% by the end of the second trimester.
	Achievement	By the end of the school year, the passing rate on the Algebra I end-of-course exam will increase by 4% from 77% to 81%.
	Discipline/behavioral	The number of dress code violations among the seventh-grade class will decrease from 50 to 15 violations in the second semester.
High school	Attendance	By the end of the second quarter, ninth-grade AVID students who earned at least 1 D or F will decrease from 27 to 12 students.
	Achievement	The truancy rate among the 12th-grade class will decrease from 18% to 11%.
	Discipline/behavioral	The number of 12th-grade students who complete the FAFSA will increase from 47% to 70% by January 31st.

AVID, advancement via individual determination; FAFSA, Free Application for Federal Student Aid.

success and learning outcomes. This form of data allows school counselors to do just that. Table 5.4 describes some examples of proposed outcomes according to grade level and desired outcome area.

Now, we must also consider additional sources of information and data that illustrate your impact. A CSCP that most effectively benefits students is achievable when school counselors intentionally focus on assessment and data-collection efforts that support their role in providing direct and indirect service to students. Qualitative methods include having follow-up conversations with teachers who have made student referrals, interviews with students who have previously participated in small groups, and focus groups with parents/caregivers whose children have participated in a specific counseling intervention, such as individual counseling. Quantitative methods may come from asking those students who have previously participated in small groups to rate their experience of the group or perhaps ask for feedback about the content and clarity of core curricular classroom lessons that you conducted for 10th graders on academic motivation.

A CSCP that most effectively benefits students is achievable when school counselors intentionally focus on assessment and data-collection efforts that support their role in providing direct and indirect service to students.

Let's apply these concepts of participation data, Mindsets & Behaviors data, and outcome data to the following scenario:

> Coastal Middle School has developed an annual student outcome goal: "By the end of the academic year, eighth-grade students who earned less than a 2.1 grade point average (GPA) during the first semester will increase their GPA by 0.5."

A data-driven school counselor will consider how to use readily available school data (i.e., course grades, standardized achievement tests, attendance) in conjunction with school counselor-led data to inform their practice and illustrate effectiveness.

Now, we need to keep in mind what data we can collect to determine the effectiveness of the intervention related to this goal. The first step would be to consider who will be participating in the targeted intervention. In this case, through running a query in the school's student information system, a report yielded that there are 26 students who meet this criteria. This would be your participation data. Next, you would want to consider the Mindsets & Behaviors data that you could collect. Perhaps you know that these 26 students are all enrolled in a fourth-or fifth-period study hall. You could utilize this opportunity to have each of them complete a pretest that addresses questions about their attitudes, skills, and knowledge relevant to their targeted goal. For instance, "I believe that I can be successful in school this year" would be an excellent question to have as a Likert scale-type question. The intent would be that this rating would improve from pretest to posttest, as a result of your counseling intervention and/or other school supports. Remember not to make your pre–posttest too long with frivolous questions, rather stick to those that fall into one of the three categories of ASK. Next, you would consider what is the most appropriate and feasible intervention. This will look different at each school. Nonetheless, we encourage you to consider what evidence-based programs or curricula exist. For example, at one school, it may be possible to implement the *Student Success Skills* classroom curriculum during the study hall periods. Whereas, in another school, it may be more feasible and realistic to implement the *Student Success Skills* small-group curriculum or *MindUp* curriculum during the study hall period or a different designated time, such as the lunch period. Finally, you should consider what outcome data can be collected. Of course, in this scenario, we would want to focus on course grades to illustrate whether the goal was met or not. But we also could and should be considering what other outcomes there may be. For example, your posttest may be administered to students 2 weeks following the end of the intervention. A data-driven school counselor will consider how to use readily available school data (i.e., course grades, standardized achievement tests, attendance) in conjunction with school counselor-led data to inform their practice and illustrate effectiveness. You may also be able to convey with the data how students' ASK have been impacted by the counseling intervention.

Pre–Posttests

By now, it is evident that school counselors *need* to collect data. One of the most common methods is through the use of pre–posttesting, which can come from the use of formal assessments such as the Spence Children's Anxiety Scale (SCAS), but also through informal assessments like pre–posttests that school counselors often create. One of the most critical elements is to consider what it is that you want to measure, and by that, you must think about *how you want students to be different as a result of our counseling intervention or support.* Within this, you must additionally consider what intervention efforts are feasible for your school's circumstances. Hatch et al. (2019) emphasize that creating pre- and postassessments requires school counselors to have skill and careful attention to what it is that you want to learn by asking yourself the following questions:

- What do you want students to *believe?*
- What do you want students to *know*?
- What *skill* do you want students to demonstrate?

Earlier in the chapter, we mentioned the acronym of ASK, but would be remiss to not provide a bit more detail into the development of these critical questions.

Developing Pre–Posttest Items

When constructing items to include in your survey, there are some development aspects to keep in mind. First, do not overcomplicate things and ask too many questions; rather, stick to including only items that have a direct relation to your goal and intervention. A good rule of thumb is to have no more than 10 items on a pre–posttest, perhaps even fewer considering what is developmentally appropriate. Also, you want to consider what is appropriate in terms of how you communicate. While using emojis, other characters, or a thumbs up/down, may be the best way to communicate with elementary-level students, it may not be best for high school-level students. Thus, as you are creating your questions you want to do so in a way that is developmentally appropriate in terms of language and format. Asking a 10th-grade student to rate their level of satisfaction with a particular experience may work, while the concept of satisfaction for a second grader will most likely get lost in translation. Word selection is important, too; you want to refrain from asking questions that lead to a particular response or have a negative connotation to them. For instance, would you consider this to be an appropriate item: At school, you must follow the rules even if you do not agree with them (using a 5-point Likert scale of agreement from "strongly disagree" to "strongly agree"). While there may be an appropriate intent for this item, it definitely could be revised to be more appropriate. How you phrase and format items on your pre–posttests can dramatically impact the responses that you will receive from students.

How you phrase and format items on your pre–posttests can dramatically impact the responses that you will receive from students.

Types of Scales

In order to have an effective item on your pre–posttests, you must consider the type of output that you want (i.e., the type of answer). Although the concept may seem simple enough, it does take practice at crafting items that are well written and in alignment with your intended intervention efforts. Some types of questions lend themselves better to certain types of answer scales. For instance, giving consideration to the developmental level of high school students, it would be more appropriate to provide a multiple-choice answer format to a knowledge question than a true/false (as students could simply guess and have a 50–50 chance of being correct and thus skew your data about what students actually learned). Similarly, attitude questions lend themselves best to Likert-scale items, as we typically do not function in dichotomous thinking: either you do or do not believe something. Instead, attitude questions are focused on illustrating 'to what extent. As a general rule of thumb:

Open-ended/free response: A good option for when description or context is needed,

Multiple choice: A good option for when there is an exact or specific answer desired,

Likert scale: A good option for items that measure intensity, agreement, and importance

True/false: A good option when measuring a concrete skill that requires knowledge obtained from intervention (I can calculate my current GPA.).

Most important, start with the basic pragmatic principle from Hatch et al. (2018): "Teach what you assess; assess what you teach." We recommend that you collaborate with other colleagues and develop a pool of items that you can share with one another, rather than reinventing the wheel. Tables 5.5 through 5.7 provide examples of what a few of your pre–posttest questions directly related to a counseling intervention may look like, at each school level, across the three ASCA domains.

TABLE 5.5 EXAMPLES OF ELEMENTARY SCHOOL PRE–POSTTEST QUESTIONS IN THE SOCIAL–EMOTIONAL DEVELOPMENT DOMAIN

School Level: Elementary		
Intervention: Core curricular classroom lesson unit, four lessons delivered to all third-grade students (*N* = 97 students) during the month of February		
ASCA Mindset & Behavior Standard(s) being addressed: B-SS.2: Create positive and supportive relationships with other students.		
TYPE OF DATA BEING ELICITED	**STATEMENT**	**TYPE OF ANSWER BEING ELICITED**
Attitude	Making friends is important.	Likert scale Not important, little bit important, important, very important
Skill	I can make new friends at school.	True/False
Knowledge	List three ways to make new friends.	Open-ended/free response

TABLE 5.6 EXAMPLES OF MIDDLE SCHOOL PRE–POSTTEST QUESTIONS IN THE ACADEMIC DEVELOPMENT DOMAIN

School Level: Middle School		
Intervention: Six-week small-group counseling intervention, organizational bootcamp for sixth graders who earned two or more Ds/Fs during first 6 weeks of trimester 1.		
ASCA Mindset & Behavior Standard(s) being addressed: B-LS.3: Use time management, organization, and study skills.		
TYPE OF DATA BEING ELICITED	**STATEMENT**	**TYPE OF ANSWER BEING ELICITED**
Attitude	If I study, I can pass any test.	*Likert scale* Strongly disagree, disagree, neither agree nor disagree, agree, strongly agree
Attitude	To what extent are you willing to use your planner to write your homework assignments each day?	*Likert scale* Definitely will not, probably will not, not sure, probably will, definitely will
Skill	I can create an afterschool schedule to get my homework completed.	*Likert scale* Probably not, maybe, quite likely, definitely
Knowledge	Which of the following is a good study strategy?	*Multiple choice* Wait until the night before to begin studying; ask a friend what they are studying; *review notes that you took in class*; take a nap

TABLE 5.7 EXAMPLES OF HIGH SCHOOL PRE–POSTTEST QUESTIONS IN THE CAREER DEVELOPMENT DOMAIN

School Level: High School
Intervention: Core curricular classroom lessons (two sessions) in all ninth grade English courses during the month of October
ASCA Mindset & Behavior Standard(s) being addressed: B-LS.7: Identify short-term and long-term academic, career, and social–emotional goals.B-LS.8: Actively engage in challenging coursework.

(*continued*)

TABLE 5.7 EXAMPLE OF HIGH SCHOOL PRE–POSTTEST QUESTIONS IN THE CAREER DEVELOPMENT DOMAIN (*continued*)

<table>
<tr><th>TYPE OF DATA BEING ELICITED</th><th colspan="2">STATEMENT</th><th>TYPE OF ANSWER BEING ELICITED</th></tr>
<tr><td>Attitude</td><td colspan="2">Meeting my short-term goals can help me attain my long-term goals.</td><td>Likert scale
Strongly disagree, disagree, neither agree nor disagree, agree, strongly agree</td></tr>
<tr><td>Attitude</td><td colspan="2">I believe that I can successfully graduate high school.</td><td>Likert scale
Probably not, maybe, quite likely, definitely</td></tr>
<tr><td>Skill</td><td colspan="2">Describe what an effective afterschool schedule looks like.</td><td>Open-ended/free response</td></tr>
<tr><td rowspan="7">Skill</td><td colspan="2">Christian earned the following grades. What is his GPA?</td><td rowspan="7">Multiple choice
1.0; 1.5; 2.0; 2.5; 3.0</td></tr>
<tr><td>Algebra I</td><td>B</td></tr>
<tr><td>Biology</td><td>B</td></tr>
<tr><td>Art History</td><td>A</td></tr>
<tr><td>World History</td><td>C</td></tr>
<tr><td>PE</td><td>A</td></tr>
<tr><td>Sign Language 1</td><td>C</td></tr>
<tr><td>Knowledge</td><td colspan="2">Which of the following is a long-term goal?</td><td>Multiple choice
Finish my homework before I go to bed; enroll in honors/AP courses next year; earn a B+ or higher on my persuasive essay due next week</td></tr>
<tr><td>Knowledge</td><td colspan="2">What is the minimum GPA that you may earn to graduate from Beachside High School?</td><td>Multiple choice
1.75; 2.0; 2.5; 2.75; 3.0</td></tr>
</table>

AP, advanced placement; GPA, grade point average; PE, physical education.

Conclusions

Your CSCP is truly driven by the data that you create and collect, which ultimately supports the "how" and "why" of what you do for and with students on a daily basis. Young and Kaffenberger (2019) have conceptualized a cyclical process (Figure 5.1) that precisely illustrates the how and why school counselors use data.

Importantly, their comprehensive process addresses aspects such as systemic change, creating annual student outcome goals, utilizing evidence-based interventions, and using assessment to monitor students' progress. Although you now have an understanding of the types of data that a school counselor should utilize as a part of their CSCP, you may be wondering about the logistical aspects of how you collect data. In the next chapter, we share practical tips and considerations for collecting and analyzing data, and even highlight some technological tools that can make the assessment process much easier and less scary than many may think.

Additional Reading

Hatch, T. (2014). *The use of data in school counseling: Hatching results for students, programs, and the profession.* Corwin.

Holcomb-McCoy, C. (2007). *School counseling to close the achievement gap: A social justice framework for success.* Corwin Press.

Holcomb-McCoy, C., Gonzalez, I., & Johnston, G. (2009). School counselor dispositions as predictors of data usage. *Professional School Counseling, 12*, 343–351. https://doi.org/10.1177%2F2156759X0901200504

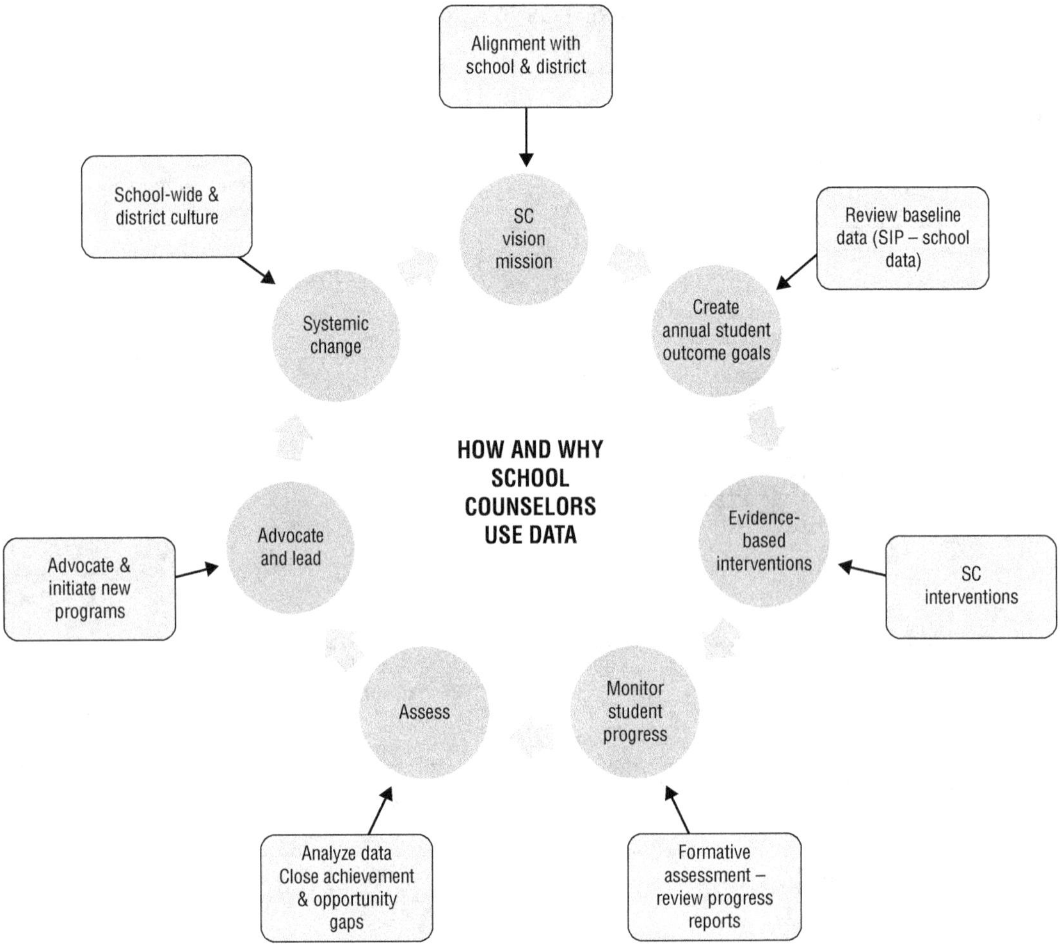

FIGURE 5.1 How and why school counselors use data. Used with permission.

SC, school counselor; SIP, school improvement plan.

Perera-Diltz, D. M., & Mason, K. L. (2010). An exploration of accountability practices of school counselors: A national study. *Journal of Professional Counseling: Practice, Theory, and Research, 38*, 52–70.

Young, A., & Kaffenberger, C. (2011). The beliefs and practices of school counselors who use data to implement comprehensive school counseling programs. *Professional School Counseling, 15*, 67–76. https://doi.org/10.1177/2156759X1101500204

Tools and Resources

- *Confident Counselors* discusses how to create a counseling needs assessment using Google Forms (https://confidentcounselors.com/2017/05/09/creating-a-school-counseling-needs-assessment-using-google-forms/).
- *Exploring School Counseling* offers an entire section of the blog, specifically devoted to data collection and includes the 21 Day Data Challenge (http://exploringschoolcounseling.blogspot.com/search/label/data%20collection).
- *Panorama Education* provides a comprehensive online platform for data collection and analysis of social–emotional learning, multi-tiered systems of support (MTSS)/response to intervention (RTI) efforts, school climate, and college and career-readiness tracking (https://www.panoramaed.com/resources).

- *Simply Imperfect Counselor* has an excellent blog posting for those school counselors just starting their data-driven journey (https://simplyimperfectcounselor.com/beginners-guide-to-school-counseling-data/).
- *School Counselor Stephanie* has an excellent blog posting about needs assessments (http://school counselorstephanie.com/2018/09/29/needs-assessments-in-school-counseling/).
- Student Success Skills Curriculums offers a variety of developmentally appropriate, evidence-based curricula that support social–emotional learning and development, academic success skills, and college/career success skills (https://studentsuccessskills.com/).

Key Points

- School counselors need to identify sources of data from readily available sources and through their own efforts.
- It takes skills and practice to develop effective pre–posttest items that reflect attitudes, skills, and knowledge.
- Whether participation data, Mindsets & Behaviors data, or outcome data, all data types serve a purpose and have value in your CSCP and in illustrating its impact on student success and well-being.

Questions for Reflection

- Describe how each of the three categories of data (participation, Mindsets & Behaviors, outcome) are important and contribute to the implementation of a CSCP.
- Reflect upon and identify which types of data you are currently collecting in your school. If you are not collecting any data, consider what the existing barriers are.
- How can outcome data help you more fully implement a CSCP?

References

American School Counselor Association. (2014). *Mindsets and behaviors for student success: K-12 college-and career-readiness standards for every student.* Author https://www.schoolcounselor.org/getmedia/7428a787-a452-4abb-afec-d78ec77870cd/Mindsets-Behaviors.pdf

American School Counselor Association. (2017). *The school counselor and school counseling programs.* https://www.schoolcounselor.org/Standards-Positions/Position-Statements/ASCA-Position-Statements/The-School-Counselor-and-School-Counseling-Program

American School Counselor Association. (2019a). *ASCA National Model: A framework for school counseling programs* (4th ed.). American School Counselor Association.

American School Counselor Association. (2019b). *ASCA National Model implementation guide* (2nd ed.). American School Counselor Association.

Anderson-Butcher, D., Amorose, A.J., Iachini, A., & Ball, A. (2013). *Community and Youth Collaborative Institute School Experience Surveys.* Columbus, OH: College of Social Work, The Ohio State University.

Burkhard, A. W., Gillen, M., Martinez, M. J., & Skytte, S. (2012). Implementation challenges and training needs for comprehensive school counseling programs in Wisconsin high schools. *Professional School Counseling, 16,* 136–145. https://doi.org/10.5330/psc.n.2012-16.136

Carey, J. C., Harrington, K., Martin, I., & Stevens, D. (2012). A statewide evaluation of the outcomes of the implementation of ASCA National Model school counseling programs in high schools in Utah. *Professional School Counseling, 16,* 89–99. https://doi.org/10.5330/psc.n.2012-16.89

Carey, J. C., & Martin, I. (2015). *A review of the major school counseling policy studies in the United States: 2000–2014.* Center for School Counseling Outcome Research and Evaluation.

Dimmitt, C., Carey, J. C., & Hatch, T. (2007). *Evidence-based school counseling: Making a difference with data-driven practices.* Corwin Press.

Dimmitt, C., & Wilkerson, B. (2012). Comprehensive school counseling in Rhode Island: Access to services and student outcomes. *Professional School Counseling, 16,* 125–135. https://doi.org/10.5330/psc.n.2012-16.125

Hatch, T., Duarte, D., De Gregorio, L. K. (2018). *Hatching results for elementary school counseling: Implementing core curriculum and other tier one activities.* Corwin.

Hatch, T., Triplett, W., Duarte, D., & Gomez, V. (2019). *Hatching results for secondary school counseling: Implementing core curriculum, student planning and other tier one activities.* Corwin.

Lambie, G. W., Stickl Haugen, J., Borland, J. R., & Campbell, L. O. (2019). Who took "counseling" out of the role of professional school counselors in the United States? *Journal of School-Based Counseling Policy and Evaluation, 1*(3), 51–61. https://doi.org/10.25774/7kjb-bt85

Lambie, G. W., & Williamson, L. L. (2004). The challenge to change from guidance counseling to professional school counseling: A historical proposition. *Professional School Counseling, 8*, 124–131.

Lane, K. L., & Menzies, H. M. (2009). *Student Risk Screening Scale for Early Internalizing and Externalizing Behavior (SRSS-IE).* Retrieved from http://www.ci3t.org/screening#srssie

Lapan, R. T., Gysbers, N. C., & Petroski, G. F. (2001). Helping seventh graders be safe and successful: A statewide study of the impact of comprehensive guidance and counseling programs. *Professional School Counseling, 6*, 186–198

Sink, C. A., Akos, P., Turnbull, R. J., & Mvududu, N. (2008). An investigation of comprehensive school counseling programs and academic achievement in Washington State middle schools. *Professional School Counseling, 12*, 43–53. https://doi.org/10.5330/psc.n.2010-12.43

Sink, C. A., & Stroh, H. R. (2003). Raising achievement test scores of early elementary school students through comprehensive school counseling programs. *Professional School Counseling, 6*(5), 350–365

Stone, C. B., & Dahir, C. A. (2007). *School counselor accountability: A measure of student success.* Pearson/Merrill Prentice Hall.

Wilkerson, K., Pérusse, R., & Hughes, A. (2013). Comprehensive school counseling programs and student achievement outcomes: A comparative analysis of RAMP versus nonRAMP schools. *Professional School Counseling, 16*, 172–184. https://doi.org/10.1177/2156759x1701600302

Young, A., & Kaffenberger, C. (2019). *Making DATA work* (4th ed.). American School Counselor Association.

Zyromski, B., Hudson, T. D., Baker, E., & Granello, D. (2019). Guidance counselors or school counselors: How the name of the profession influences perceptions of competence. *Professional School Counseling, 22*, 1–10. https://doi.org/10.1177/2156759X19855654

6

USING TECHNOLOGY AND ACCOUNTABILITY REPORTS TO PROMOTE YOUR COMPREHENSIVE SCHOOL COUNSELING PROGRAM

Accountability Comes in Many Forms

Perhaps best articulated by Dimmitt et al. (2007), school counselors' work is fast paced and never-ending; thus, you must constantly make decisions about the most effective ways to use your time to best impact student outcomes. Long gone are the days when school counselors simply sat in their offices and waited for the work to come to them, operating in a reactive fashion. Sadly, one of the consequences of this action (or lack thereof) is that other stakeholders did not learn about the critical work that we could and should do. In this chapter, we highlight technology tools to simplify your assessment and data-collection and analysis efforts, ways to document your accountability and effectiveness to stakeholders, and best practices for showcasing your comprehensive school counseling program (CSCP) and its impact on student outcomes.

By this point in the book, you have become familiar with the reasons for having a data-driven, comprehensive school counseling program and the importance of assessment and data collection. In fact, the key documents from our professional school counseling organization emphasize that we have a professional imperative to have attitudes, skills, and knowledge around assessment and data collection. Did you realize that the word *data* occurs 29 times and *assessment* occurs 12 times in the *ASCA School Counselor Professional Standards & Competencies* (American School Counselor Association [ASCA], 2019)? Yet, research has shown that technology is underutilized by school counselors, particularly when it comes to presenting results to key stakeholders (Mason et al., 2019)

Did you realize that the word *data* occurs 29 times and *assessment* occurs 12 times in the *ASCA School Counselor Professional Standards & Competencies*?

Now it is time to consider what your accountability can look like when utilizing various technological tools and accountability approaches. An important caveat to remember is that you should never go at this alone. Rather than flying solo, consider how you can best collaborate with stakeholders throughout your efforts, not just during the implementation of your intervention efforts. For example, think about how you might collaborate with your school counselor colleagues when it comes to the promotion of your CSCP. Perhaps you have a computer teacher who has advanced Excel skills and may be able to assist in communicating progress or changes in student growth or performance. Maybe you have a yearbook teacher or activity coordinator who is excellent at publicizing events and activities.

Collaboration is key for successful school counselors. But beyond that human resource capital, school counselors also have an extensive collection of technological tools that can support one's assessment and data collection efforts. We are all very aware of the concept "work smarter, not harder." With the high caseloads and often unrealistic responsibilities placed upon counselors, it is imperative to learn how to best navigate your circumstances and take advantage of tools and opportunities that present themselves. Let's discuss a few technological tools that can be utilized in a number of ways in the development and implementation of your CSCP.

Tools to Aid in Data Collection

When school counselors are asked, "How do you know that your effort/intervention was effective," how can they respond? Sadly, there is not much of a response to give if they are not collecting data. Yes, it is great to be able to say the behavior of my student Angel has improved. But how do you know? This is the power of data, being able to show that what you are doing is effective (or not effective, which is also important). When I (Sandra) first started as a school counselor my years ago, data collection was rather difficult and required concerted preparation and coordination. In fact, I still remember the first time I was creating a needs assessment, sitting at my computer simply typing out questions that I wanted answers to as a new school counselor. I had no rhyme or reason or tools to really aid me in the process. I photocopied pretests on white paper, posttests on blue paper to help keep myself organized. I coordinated with teachers to conduct pre–posttests prior to and after my core curricular classroom lessons, taking away previous instructional minutes. Then I spent a substantial amount of time entering data into Excel and then analyzing and disaggregating the data to make sense of my work. And yes, I am a number person so I enjoyed the data side of things, but I also knew that my time could be utilized more effectively. While we will specifically discuss a few key technologies, we also encourage you to check out *50+ Tech Tools for School Counselors* (Cleveland & Sharp, 2019) for some excellent ideas on how to utilize technology in your school counseling practice, especially Chapter 2 on data-collection tools and Chapter 4 on tools to promote your CSCP.

Google Suite

One of the benefits of Google Workspace is that you can have everything under one platform with tools that integrate well with one another and support your daily activities as a school counselor. For instance, you could build a Google Site that serves as your school counseling website separate from your school's website. This would allow you to have full oversight and management of the content and functions. Also, you would be able to directly integrate documents that you create with other Google tools into your website. For instance, with Google Forms you can collect needs-assessment data from stakeholders such as parents/caregivers and community members could be integrated into a webpage. Also, your Closing-the-Gap Action Plan/Results Report could be created as a Google Doc that you directly connect into the appropriate area of your website. For such integration, we recommend exploring Google Sites, Google Docs, Google Sheets, and Google Slides. Another helpful tool that is part of the suite that you may consider utilizing for student engagement during core curricular classroom lessons is Jamboard, which serves as an interactive whiteboard with direct-link access for students or others to participate in discussion or other activities.

Interactive Presentation and Polling Tools

In addition to using Google Forms as a means of data collection, there are a number of polling tools that could be used during the delivery of core curricular classroom lessons or with your small-group counseling interventions. Let's imagine that you are preparing a lesson for seventh graders on decision-making skills. Your presentation can be delivered through Nearpod, which is a digital presentation tool that offers a variety of functions for both the presenter and the audience. In real time, you can add open-ended questions, polling functions, or even student contributions to the actual slides. Audience participation can take place via computer or phone app. Another technological tool for your consideration is Mentimeter, which affords users an interactive presentation mode and data-collection tool, with many functions for audience engagement, simply be entering a six-digit code. While there are free and paid versions, the free version has a two-question limit on presentations. A third tool that combines polling and interactive presentations is Poll Everywhere. One of the great features about this tool is that you can download the app for integration with PowerPoint, Keynote, or Google Slides and simply add polls to your existing presentations. For those who are looking to streamline their direct data-collection efforts and audience engagement, you may consider using a quick response (QR) code as a way to direct participants to a poll or survey, rather than having to give them a website link or an access code. The use of a QR code can help facilitate the completion of your data-collection efforts, especially if you have a long or confusing URL. We recommend QR Code Generator, which is an app available for free and allows you to create a QR code, add a logo or text, and download as an image for inclusion in a presentation or even on a website. See Figure 6.1 for an example of how an interactive presentation can use these tools.

School Counselor's Use of Time Analysis

What happens when you put a software developer with a school counselor? You get School Counselor Use-of-Time Analysis (SCUTA), an online platform that allows schools and districts to develop a data-driven, evidence-based CSCP that follows the ASCA National Model. This is one of our favorite tools for school counselors to be able to effectively manage all aspects and data elements of their CSCP. Its tag line says it all: *The School Counselor's Advocate*. This integrated system allows you to create a data summary of your school, create and implement lesson plans, identify annual student outcome goals, build Mindset & Behavior action plans, document your annual administrative conference, and track activities of your advisory council. Additional features, including being able to conduct a use-of-time

Figure 6.1 Illustration of integrating Mentimeter and a QR code into an interactive presentation. Used with permission.

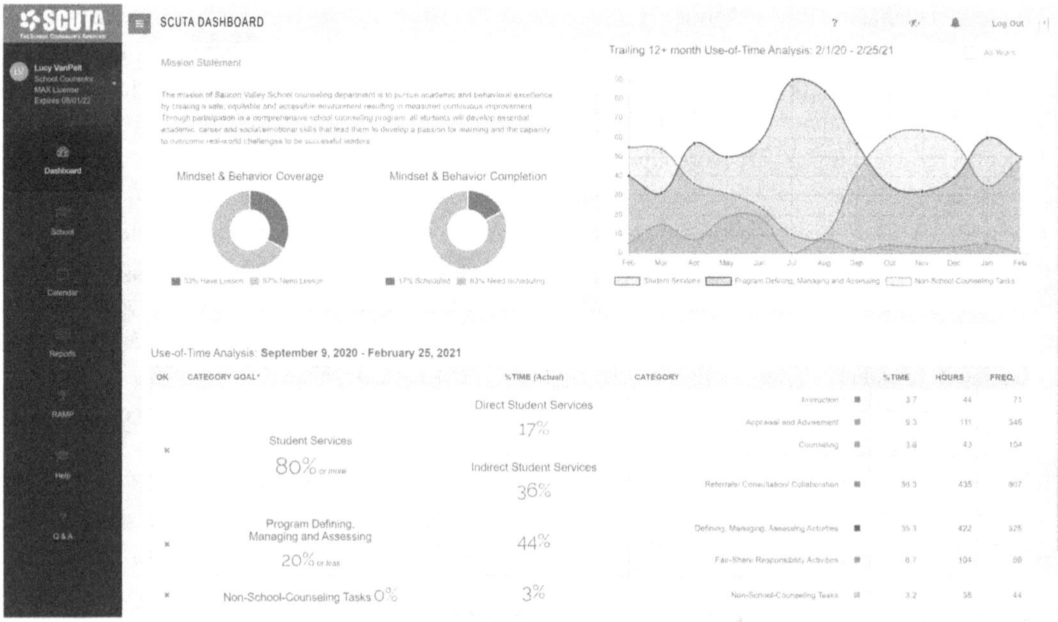

Figure 6.2 School Counselor Use-of-Time Analysis: User dashboard depicting the various functions of the platform. Used with permission.

analysis for a specific period of time, search a database of lessons aligned with the ASCA Mindsets and Behaviors, and ability to integrate with your Google or Microsoft calendar. All activities can be communicated to stakeholders via the real-time portal, printed copies, or portable document format (PDF) documents to best meet your stakeholders' needs.

Let's highlight some of the key features that may be of interest to you. First, the SCUTA dashboard offers users an easy-to-use and navigate homepage that follows the organizational structure of the ASCA National Model, as illustrated in Figure 6.2. As you begin to consider your data-driven efforts, one of your first steps is to get an understanding of your school's data and current operations, which can be captured in your School Data Summary (Exhibit 6.1), and to identify which areas of school data you would like to prioritize in the implementation of your CSCP.

Once you have an idea of your starting points, you can then focus on deciding on interventions that address the ASCA Mindsets & Behaviors for your action plan (Figure 6.3). Upon completion, SCUTA creates a summary of the completed activities addressed in your action plan (Exhibit 6.2) and your desired outcomes.

It is important to note that you are also able to document your Annual Student Outcome Goal Plan (Figure 6.4), which can easily be shared or distributed to stakeholders. SCUTA also offers the opportunity to track your data in a variety of ways, such as through a 1-month snapshot of your entire activities (Figure 6.5), with the Use-of-Time Pareto Analysis. This type of summary of your work can become especially important in your conversations with administration about your use of time and may be of benefit during your annual administrative conference as a way of comparing the intended use of time versus actual use of time (Exhibit 6.3).

According to the developer, Steve Zaharakis, there are numerous versions of the platform to best serve your needs: SCUTA Lite, Pro, MAX, R, and SD. Those just starting their data journey may want to consider Lite, which you can try for free (see the Tools and Resources section for the link). The Pro version allows you to answer the question most frequently posed by administration:

SCHOOL DATA SUMMARY

1. **Identify who in the building can help you.** Who is your data expert; who can help you interpret the data?
   - **Administration, Principle, DOE:**
     Principal, Assistant Principals and CAR; VDOE reports and PowerSchool reports
   - **School Counseling department:**
     Part-time clerical assistant is available as needed (up to 425 hours per school year). This person helps with filing and sorting documents, copying records for new students and students who are withdrawing, and processing specialty center/Governor's Scho
   - **Data manager/registrar:**
     Registrar coordinates/oversees the registration of new students, files information in cumulative files, manages incoming phone calls for the school counseling department, manages visitors to the office, processes residency issues, and many other tasks as
   - **Attendance assistant clerk , Career and college center assistant , Teachers:**
     n/a
   - **Other staff:**
     n/a
   - **Volunteers and other:**
     n/a

2. **Identify the school improvement plan goals.**
   - **My school has a School Improvement Plan**
     Math and Reading Improvement, as well as Chronic Attendance/Engagement improvement
   - **In which areas can the school counseling program support the work?**
     Achievement and Attendance/Engagement

3. **Review available school data reports for previous years to identify trends.**
   - **What is working well according to your school data reports?**
     - Achievement
     - Attendance
     - Discipline
   - **Highlight possible areas of need according to your school data reports**
     - Achievement
     - Attendance
     - Discipline
   - **Identified underperforming groups:**
     ATTENDANCE/ENGAGEMENT: A total of 34 students missed 10% or more of enrolled days during the 2019-2020 school year (this was a 39.3% decrease from the 2018-2019 school year, but only captured September 2019-March 2020). 34.4% of chronically absent studen

4. **Compare your school's data with district and state data or other comparable data points.**
   - **Opportunities for improvement based on school disctric/state comparsion**
     We need to provide targeted assistance and interventions to the various subgroups within our student population who are seeing negative outcomes in our outcome data, for both attendance/engagement and achievement. EL, Hispanic Male and Female, and Africa

5. **Identify what else you need to know.**
   - **Any additional items you need know.**
     Since schools closed in March 2020, we feel that our outcome data is skewed. As a result, we want to gather baseline data for this year's goals at the end of the first semester for both achievement and attendance/engagement.

Exhibit 6.1 School Counselor Use-of-Time Analysis: School Data Summary. Used with permission.

SCHOOL DATA SUMMARY

6. Identify and prioritize data points you will address through your school counseling program.

Priority	Need	Data Point	How it will be addressed through the School Counseling Program
1	Achievement	During the 2019-2020 school year, 48 students who failed one or more core classes. This is a 42.9% decrease in failures compared to the previous school year, but (15 EL - 31.25%; 13 SWD - 27.08%; 16 students parents don't speak English - 33.33%) of group	School Counselors will provide supports/interventions to students struggling academically - classroom lessons, individual and small group counseling, contacts with teachers and parents. We need to improve communication with non-English speaking parents.
1	Attendance	During the 2019-2020 school year, 34 students were chronically absent. This number represents 2.98% of our student body. This year, we will focus on attendance as it relates to student engagement (students who miss 10+ days first semester).	School Counselors will provide supports and interventions to chronically absent students - classroom lessons, individual and small group counseling, and contacts with parents. We also need to improve communication with non-English speaking families.

Exhibit 6.1 (*continued*)

"What do you do?" with features that can document your vision and mission statement, annual student outcome goals, and track your participation, Mindsets & Behaviors data, and outcome data. The MAX version offers more extensive features beyond Pro, including closing-the-gap reporting, action plans/results, documentation of your core curricular classroom lessons, and even a library of ready-to-go lessons.

In addition to being an invaluable tool for practicing school counselors, there is also a University Version for those teaching in school counselor preparation programs. School counselor educators can utilize the platform to teach about the various aspects of a data-driven CSCP during a school counseling orientation courses, CSCPs, or fieldwork courses, depending upon the setup of your preparation program. Also, there is a newly developed feature of practicum and internship timesheet tracking for completion of field-experience hours.

Excel Add-Ins

In addition to utilizing a comprehensive platform like SCUTA, school counselors can take advantage of a number of tools that integrate with other common technologies, such as Microsoft Excel. This is an excellent choice for those who do not have the resources to purchase systems, as well as for those who have some competency or comfort in using Microsoft Office. However, note that it may be necessary for you to work with your information technology (IT) department for permission to download these add-ins to your district-managed computer.

Time Elapsed Analysis and Reporting System

The Microsoft Excel add-in, Time Elapsed Analysis and Reporting System (TEARS) designed by Dr. Russ Sabella, is a tool that allows school counselors to automate the calculation of time spent on their various tasks and then provides two visual representations (table and graph) of the categories of time spent. In our opinion, this is an excellent tool for those who already utilize Microsoft Outlook to manage their schedules. What is great is that you can personalize the categories for which you want

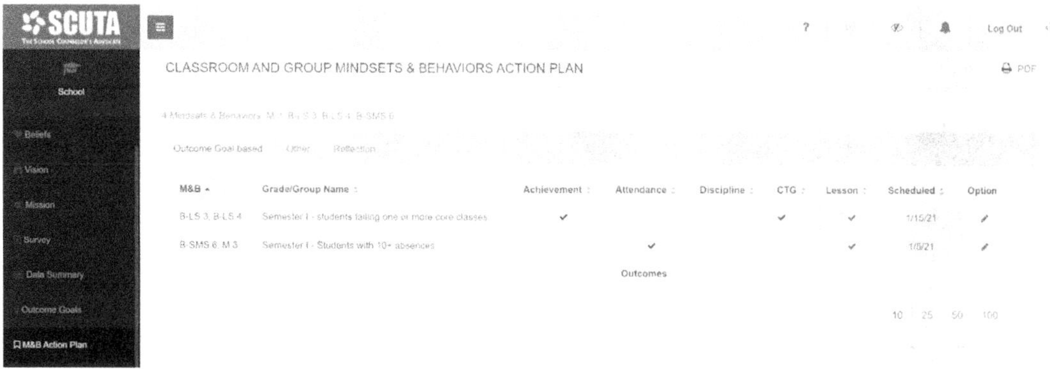

Figure 6.3 School Counselor Use-of-Time Analysis: Mindsets & Behaviors Action Plan. Used with permission.

CLASSROOM AND GROUP MINDSETS & BEHAVIORS ACTION PLAN

3.U1 CLASSROOM AND GROUP MINDSETS & BEHAVIORS ACTION PLAN

The ASCA Mindsets & Behaviors guide the planning and delivery of all student activities and interventions. The purpose of the classroom and group Mindsets & Behaviors action plan is to provide an overview of the delivery of direct services in large group (LG), classroom (Class) and small group (SG) settings. This plan presents the topics addressed, and the annual calendar presents schedule of all classroom and groups activities.

Use the classroom and group Mindsets & Behaviors action plan to identify all ASCA Mindsets & Behaviors addressed through classroom and group activities. While some activities address multiple ASCA Mindsets & Behaviors, list the activity with the primary mindset or behavior addressed by the activity. It is not necessary to repeat activities with all ASCA Mindsets & Behaviors addressed through that activity.

School Name: ABC Middle School

Mindsets	Activity	Participants	Class/LG	SG
M 1: Belief in development of whole self, including a healthy balance of mental, social/emotional and physical well-being	◦ Mindfulness Monday Lessons	◦ 8th Graders grade: 393 students: 205M, 188F 32x 30 lesson (average) 9/21/20, 10/5/20, 10/12/20, 10/19/20, 11/2/20, 11/9/20, 11/16/20, 11/24/20, 11/30/20, 12/7/20, 12/14/20, 1/4/21, 1/11/21, 1/25/21, 2/1/21, 2/8/21, 2/22/21, 3/1/21, 3/8/21, 3/15/21, 3/22/21, 3/29/21, 4/12/21, 4/19/21, 4/26/21, 5/3/21, 5/10/21, 5/17/21, 5/24/21, 6/7/21, 6/14/21, 10/26/20	X	
M 2: Self-confidence in ability to succeed				
M 3: Sense of belonging in the school environment	◦ Counselor Intro Lesson - 8th grade	◦ 8th Graders grade: 393 students: 205M, 188F 30 minute lesson 9/17/20	X	
M 4: Understanding that postsecondary education and life-long learning are necessary for long-term career success				
M 5: Belief in using abilities to their fullest to achieve high-quality results and outcomes				
M 6: Positive attitude toward work and learning	◦ How do You Measure Success?	◦ 8th Graders grade: 393 students: 205M, 188F 45 minute lesson 1/14/21	X	

Exhibit 6.2 School Counselor Use-of-Time Analysis: Mindsets & Behaviors Action Plan, summary of completed activities. Used with permission.

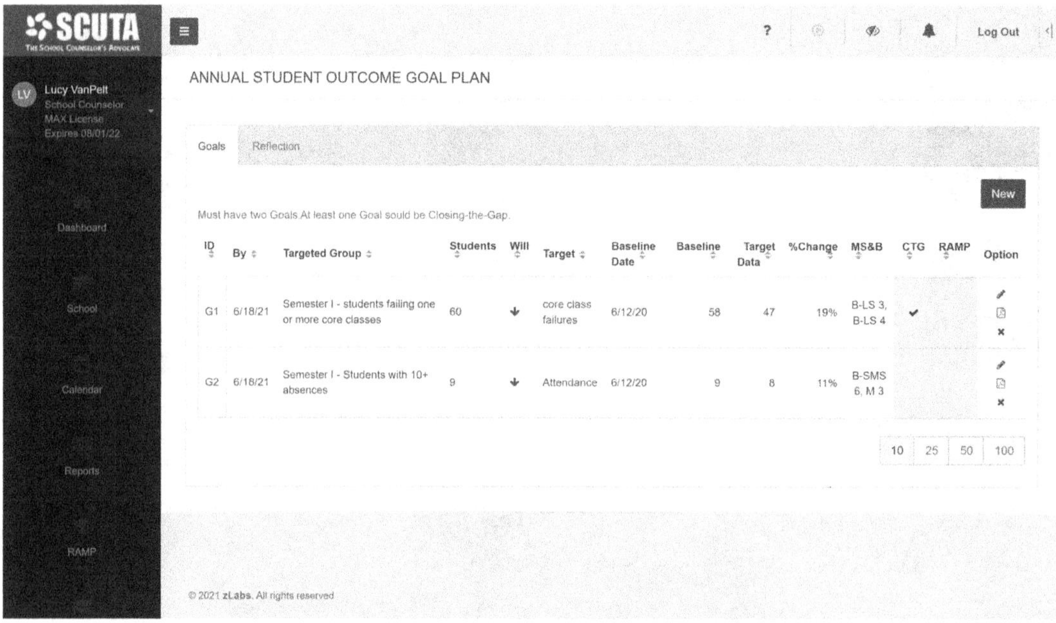

Figure 6.4 School Counselor Use-of-Time Analysis: Annual Student Outcome Goal Plan. Used with permission.

Figure 6.5 School Counselor Use-of-Time Analysis: Use-of-Time Pareto Analysis (1-month summary). Used with permission.

to analyze your time. For instance, your student intervention team meeting process might be called a *Student Study Team, Student Intervention Team*, or *Response-to-Intervention Team*; no matter their name, they can be documented appropriately. Similarly, if you want to separately document virtual core curricular classroom lesson and those lessons held face-to-face, you could have two categories. One of the benefits of having your raw data in Excel is that you are able to disaggregate or filter your entries to focus on specific activities or outcomes (Figure 6.6). Additionally, using the raw data, you are able to create visuals that illustrate how your time is being spent as a bar graph showing comparisons of time

ANNUAL ADMINISTRATIVE CONFERENCE

School Counselor: Lucy VanPelt *ABC Middle School 2020-21*

After a review of the school data, the following priorities were identified:

During the 2019-2020 school year, 48 students who failed one or more core classes. This is a 42.9% decrease in failures compared to the previous school year, but (15 EL - 31.25%; 13 SWD - 27.08%; 16 students parents don't speak English - 33.33%) of group
During the 2019-2020 school year, 34 students were chronically absent. This number represents 2.98% of our student body. This year, we will focus on attendance as it relates to student engagement (students who miss 10+ days first semester).

Based on these priorities, the following goals were identified:

	Annual Student Outcome Goals
1	By the 12th of June 2020, Semester I - Students with 10+ absences students will decrease their Attendance by 11% from 9 *(6/12/20)* to 8.
2	By the 12th of June 2020, Semester I - students failing one or more core classes will decrease their core class failures by 19% from 58 *(6/12/20)* to 47.

School Counselor Use of Time			
A minimum of 80% of time is recommended for direct and indirect student services and 20% or less in program planning and school support.			
Use of Time from Previous School Year			
Direct Student Services	Indirect Student Services	Program Planning and School Support	Non-School- Counseling Duties
25%	26.2%	40.1%	8.6%
Use of Time Plan for Current School Year			
Direct Student Services	Indirect Student Services	Program Planning and School Support	Non-School- Counseling Duties
50%	30%	20%	0%

Ratio and Caseload

The recommended ratio is one school counselor per 250 students.

Ratio One School Counselor Per 393 Students

Exhibit 6.3 School Counselor Use-of-Time Analysis: Annual administrative conference document completed following the meeting between school counselor and administrator. Used with permission.

across categories (Figure 6.7) or as a pie chart, which can illustrate the portion of your total hours invested in each category (Figure 6.8).

Auto Closing-the-Gap

Also developed by Dr. Sabella, the Auto Closing-the-Gap (AutoCTG) is a free Excel add-in that is easy to download. The intent of this tool is to assist you in creating Closing-the-Gap reports by utilizing an Excel spreadsheet in conjunction with a PowerPoint (PPT) presentation file. All you need to do is download the ZIP file provided by Dr. Sabella and then revise the data that you are using in your Excel spreadsheet. Note that there are written instructions and a video tutorial to help guide you in this process.

ANNUAL ADMINISTRATIVE CONFERENCE

Ratio and Caseload

Caseload definded by:	☐ Alpha Assigned: Last names beginning with: ☑ Grade Level: Students in grades: Lowest Grade : 8th ☐ All students in building ☐ Other:

Program Implementation Plan to Address Priorities

Attach the following documents for review and discussion during the conference:

- Classroom and Group Mindsets & Behaviors Action Plan
- Closing-the-Gap Action Plan
- Annual Calendar

Advisory Council
The school counseling advisory council will meet to provide feedback and input on the school counseling program.

Fall Meeting Date	12/10/19
Spring Meeting Date:	05/18/20, 05/17/21
Proposed Members:	Melanie P., Victoria C., Janis J., Erica M., Sarah F., Lindsay H., Beverley D., Lesley H., Liz P., Marcea S., Elane E., Angela M.

Professional Development

I plan to participate in the following professional development based on annual student outcome goals and my School Counselor Professional Standards & Competencies self-assessment.

Date(s)	Topic	Cost
03/05/21	Virtual VSCA Conference	$0
03/04/21	Virtual VSCA Conference	$0
02/24/21	homebound coordinator training	$0
12/11/20	safe schools training	$0
12/03/20	Attendance/Engagement Virtual Workshop	$0
11/04/20	specialty center application training (virtual)	$0
10/09/20	SCUTA help	$0
09/14/20	ASCA Summer Camp Webinar - ASCA Model Templates	$0
09/05/20	Restraint and Seclusion training	$0
09/05/20	safe schools training and restraint/seclusion training	$0
08/31/20	Fall 2020 Resilience Module for Adults and K–12 Students	$0

Exhibit 6.3 (*continued*)

ANNUAL ADMINISTRATIVE CONFERENCE

Date(s)	Topic	Cost
08/31/20	ASCA Model templates (summer camp)	$0
08/27/20	Microsoft Teams for School Counselors	$0
08/24/20	Schoology Course - Part 2	$0
08/24/20	ASCA - writng competencies (summer camp)	$0
08/23/20	Nearpod training	$0
08/20/20	Loom training	$0
08/17/20	Second Step Webinar	$0
08/17/20	ASCA - Evidence-Based Activities and Interventions - Part 2 (summer camp)	$0
08/17/20	ASCA - Evidence-Based Activities and Interventions - Part I (summer camp)	$0
08/12/20	Microsoft Teams videos	$0
08/12/20	Nearpod training	$0
08/12/20	Second Step seminar	$0
08/11/20	Tier 1 Virtual School Counseling for Midle School	$0
08/10/20	ASCA - Lesson Planning (summer camp)	$0
08/10/20	Distance Learning Playbook with Doug F.	$0
08/05/20	ASCA - Calendars, Lesson Plans, Classroom Instruction Results Reports, Small Group Results Reports, and Closing the Gap Action Plan and Results (summer camp)	$0
08/04/20	Schoology course and virtual instruction training	$0
08/03/20	ASCA - Action Plans & Results (summer camp)	$0
08/03/20	ASCA - Goals and Mindsets (summer camp)	$0
08/02/20	Confident Counselor's Virtual Conference - August 1-2, 2020	$0

School and District Committees and Professional Work		
Group	**Time Commitment**	**School Counselor's Role**
MTSS Team BIP meeting, MTSS Team Child Find Meeting, MTSS Team 6th Grade IT Meeting, MTSS Team conference to discuss behavioral concerns, MTSS Team Intervention Team - 6th grade, MTSS Team child find meeting, MTSS Team Intervention Team, MTSS Team IT Meeting, MTSS Team Intervention Team Meeting, MTSS Team eligibility meeting, MTSS Team child find, MTSS Team intervention team, MTSS Team, MTSS Team intervention team meeting, updating IT resource map, MTSS Team Eligibility Meeting, prep for department meeting, prep for meeting, prep for career investigations training, prep for second step training, prep for faculty presentation, MTSS Team IT Team meeting, MTSS Team eligibililty meeting, department meeting, MTSS Team 8th Grade RTI	64.25 hours 65 times/	

Exhibit 6.3 (*continued*)

ANNUAL ADMINISTRATIVE CONFERENCE

School and District Committees and Professional Work		
Group/School Counselor	**Time Commitment**	**School Counselor's Role**
MTSS Team child find meeting	2.25 hours 3 times/	organizer
School Counselor	0.75 hour	prep for meetings
MTSS Team General RTI Meeting, MTSS Team 8th Grade RTI, MTSS Team Eligibility Meeting, MTSS Team finalize eligibility paperwork, MTSS Team eligibility meeting	16.25 hours 17 times/	participant
School Counselor	1 hour	prep work for faculty meeting
School Counselor	2.5 hours 3 times/	prep for department meeting

Budget Materials and Supplies
Annual budget: $250
Material and Supplies needed: colored paper, copy paper, pencils, pens, staples, paper clips, folders, envelopes, tissues,stress balls, fidget cubes, binders, binder dividers, candy, and snacks for incentives

School Counselor Availability/Office Organization
The school counseling office will be open for students/parents/teachers from 9/9/20 to 6/19/21
My hours will be from 08:00 AM to 03:30 PM (if flexible scheduling is used).
The career center will be open from 08:00 AM to 03:30 PM

Role and Responsibilities of Other Staff and Volunteers

School Counseling Department Assistant

Assists registrar with records.

Attendance Assistant/Clerk
Part-time clerical assistant is available as needed (up to 425 hours per school year). This person helps with filing and sorting documents, copying records for new students and students who are withdrawing, and processing specialty center/Governor's School applications, course information forms, ACP's, etc.

Data Manager/Registrar
Registrar coordinates/oversees the registration of new students, files information in cumulative files, manages incoming phone calls for the school counseling department, manages visitors to the office, processes residency issues, and many other tasks as assigned.

College and Career Center Assistant

Other Staf

Volunteers

Lucy VanPelt
School Counselor Signature — *Date Signed*

Melanie P.
Administrative Signature — *Date Signed*

Exhibit 6.3 (*continued*)

Once you have the desired data in spreadsheet format, it will automatically create visual representations of your data for you. Figure 6.9 illustrates how your data can be transformed into visuals that document the change in desired outcomes such as decrease in absences or referrals. In addition, a 10-slide PPT template is provided for you to present and showcase your findings to stakeholders (Figure 6.10).

EZAnalyze and EZAnalyze TimeTracker

Another school counselor educator and researcher, Dr. Timothy Poynton, has created the free Excel add-ins EZAnalyze and EZTimeTracker. This pair of tools has easy-to-follow manuals and tutorials that guide you through how to complete a variety of tasks. For instance, *EZAnalyze* allows you to complete all of the basic descriptive statistics, disaggregate your data so that you can better understand it, and transform your data into visual representations such as pie charts and bar graphs, as illustrated in Exhibit 6.4.

This tool can be particularly helpful for compiling data contained in your accountability reports. Additionally, the *EZAnalyze TimeTracker* serves as a way for you to track your activities in a variety of formats, such as reporting all activity with an individual student or within a small group (Figure 6.11). For those of you whose administration requests some form of documentation of your activities, this may serve as a worthwhile tool, especially the Summary Report function.

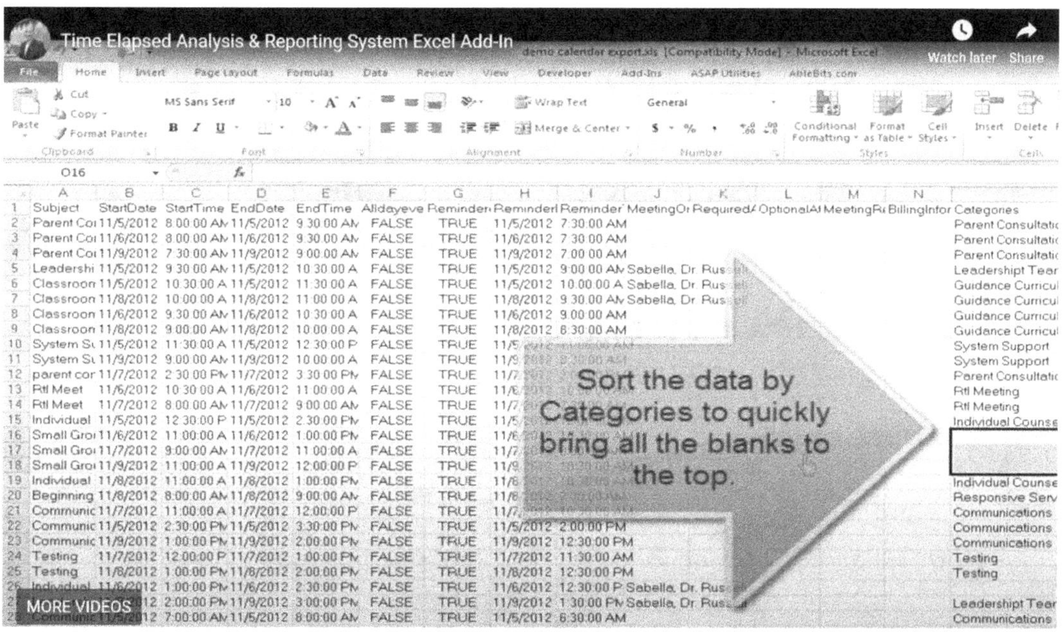

Figure 6.6 Raw data produced from Time Elapsed Analysis and Reporting System. Used with permission.

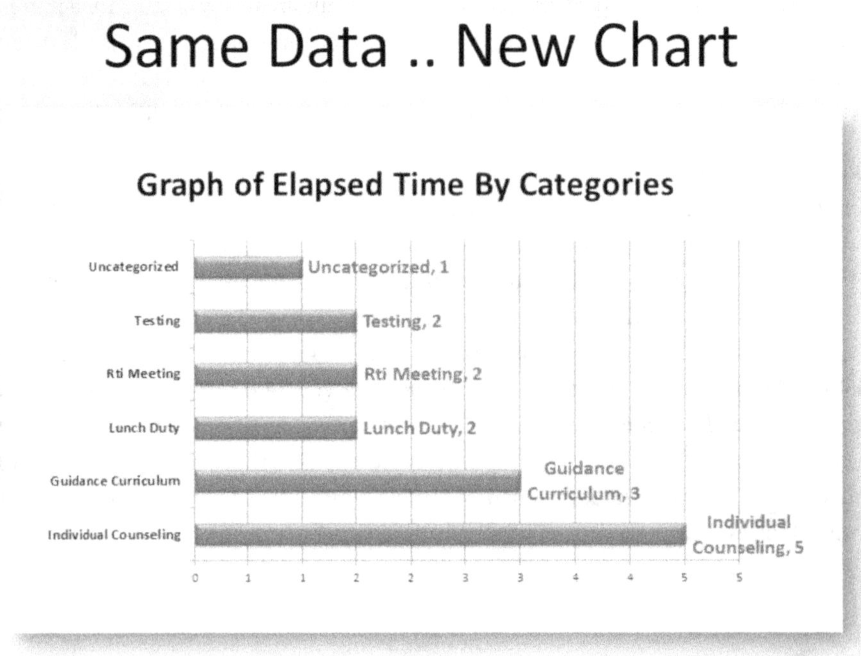

Figure 6.7 Visual representation produced in the Time Elapsed Analysis and Reporting System (bar graph). Used with permission.

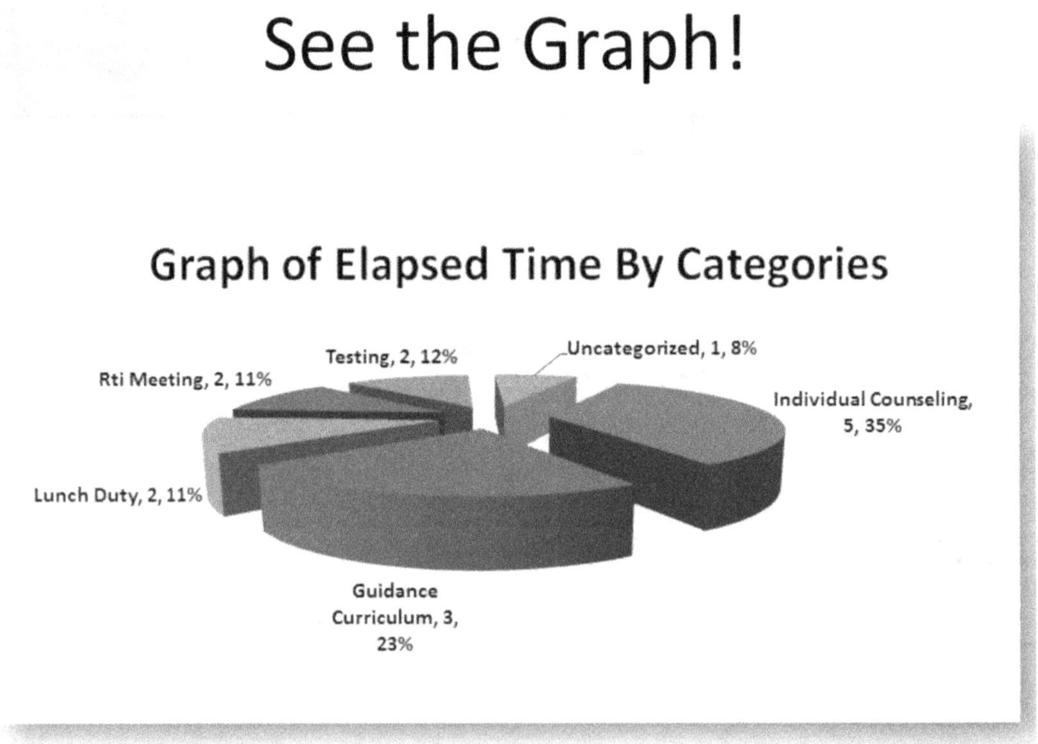

Figure 6.8 Visual representation produced in the Time Elapsed Analysis and Reporting System (pie chart). Used with permission.

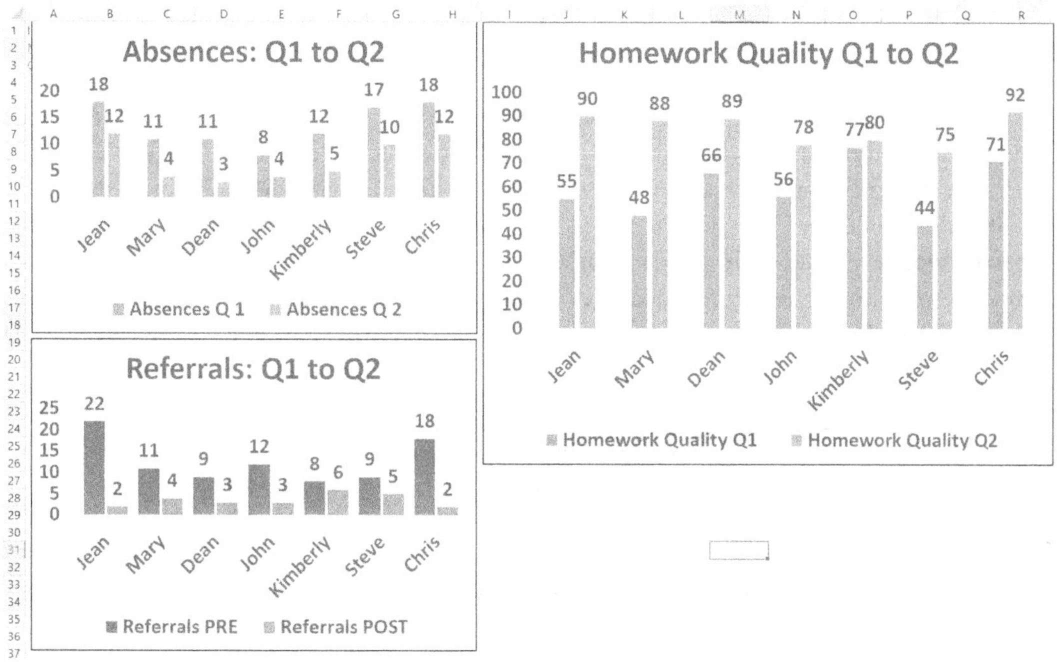

Figure 6.9 Charts produced using the Auto Closing-the-Gap Tool. Used with permission.

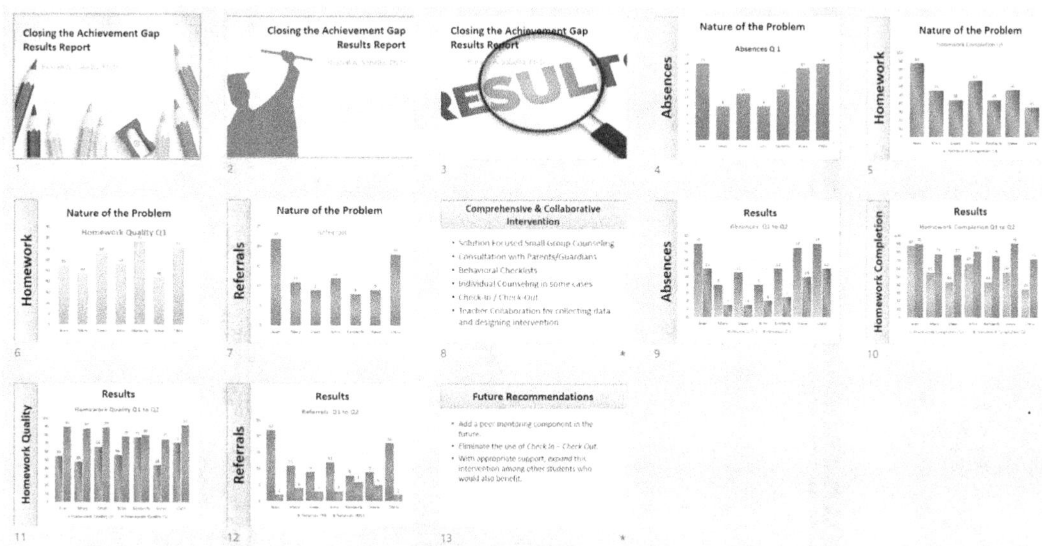

Figure 6.10 Template for presenting results using the Auto Closing-the-Gap Tool. Used with permission.

WellCheq

Although the WellCheq assessment is covered in Chapter 4, here we want to highlight one of its strengths: The online portal includes a variety of data-analysis tools perfect for your accountability reports. With its two simple questions (Exhibit 6.5), you will not get overwhelmed by the data. Instead, you can quickly have a snapshot of how students are doing in real time, according to the developmentally appropriate categories, including happy, angry, sad, blah, worried, that are part of question one.

For question two, students are asked to rate "Overall, how are you doing?" using a solution-focused counseling approach as a scaling question of 1 (terrible) to 10 (awesome). What is excellent about this tool is that teachers and counselors can have a quick and easy way to monitor students and intentionally

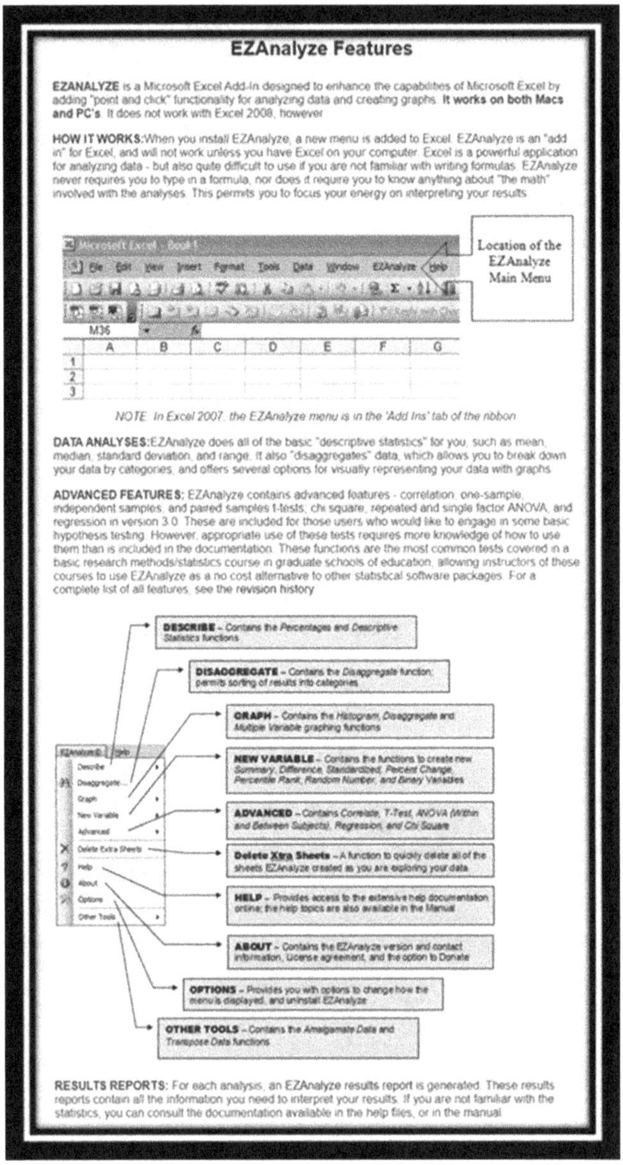

EZAnalyze Features

EZANALYZE is a Microsoft Excel Add-In designed to enhance the capabilities of Microsoft Excel by adding "point and click" functionality for analyzing data and creating graphs. **It works on both Macs and PC's**. It does not work with Excel 2008, however.

HOW IT WORKS: When you install EZAnalyze, a new menu is added to Excel. EZAnalyze is an "add in" for Excel, and will not work unless you have Excel on your computer. Excel is a powerful application for analyzing data - but also quite difficult to use if you are not familiar with writing formulas. EZAnalyze never requires you to type in a formula, nor does it require you to know anything about "the math" involved with the analyses. This permits you to focus your energy on interpreting your results.

NOTE: In Excel 2007, the EZAnalyze menu is in the 'Add Ins' tab of the ribbon

DATA ANALYSES: EZAnalyze does all of the basic "descriptive statistics" for you, such as mean, median, standard deviation, and range. It also "disaggregates" data, which allows you to break down your data by categories, and offers several options for visually representing your data with graphs.

ADVANCED FEATURES: EZAnalyze contains advanced features - correlation, one-sample, independent samples, and paired samples t-tests; chi square, repeated and single factor ANOVA, and regression in version 3.0. These are included for those users who would like to engage in some basic hypothesis testing. However, appropriate use of these tests requires more knowledge of how to use them than is included in the documentation. These functions are the most common tests covered in a basic research methods/statistics course in graduate schools of education, allowing instructors of these courses to use EZAnalyze as a no cost alternative to other statistical software packages. For a complete list of all features, see the revision history.

DESCRIBE – Contains the *Percentages* and *Descriptive Statistics* functions

DISAGGREGATE – Contains the *Disaggregate* function; permits sorting of results into categories

GRAPH – Contains the *Histogram*, *Disaggregate* and *Multiple Variable* graphing functions

NEW VARIABLE – Contains the functions to create new *Summary, Difference, Standardized, Percent Change, Percentile Rank, Random Number, and Binary* Variables

ADVANCED – Contains *Correlate, T-Test, ANOVA (Within and Between Subjects), Regression, and Chi Square*

Delete Xtra Sheets – A function to quickly delete all of the sheets EZAnalyze created as you are exploring your data

HELP – Provides access to the extensive help documentation online; the help topics are also available in the Manual

ABOUT – Contains the EZAnalyze version and contact information, License agreement, and the option to Donate

OPTIONS – Provides you with options to change how the menu is displayed, and uninstall EZAnalyze

OTHER TOOLS – Contains the *Amalgamate Data* and *Transpose Data* functions

RESULTS REPORTS: For each analysis, an EZAnalyze results report is generated. These results reports contain all the information you need to interpret your results. If you are not familiar with the statistics, you can consult the documentation available in the help files, or in the manual.

Exhibit 6.4 Features of EZAnalyze Excel add-in. Used with permission.

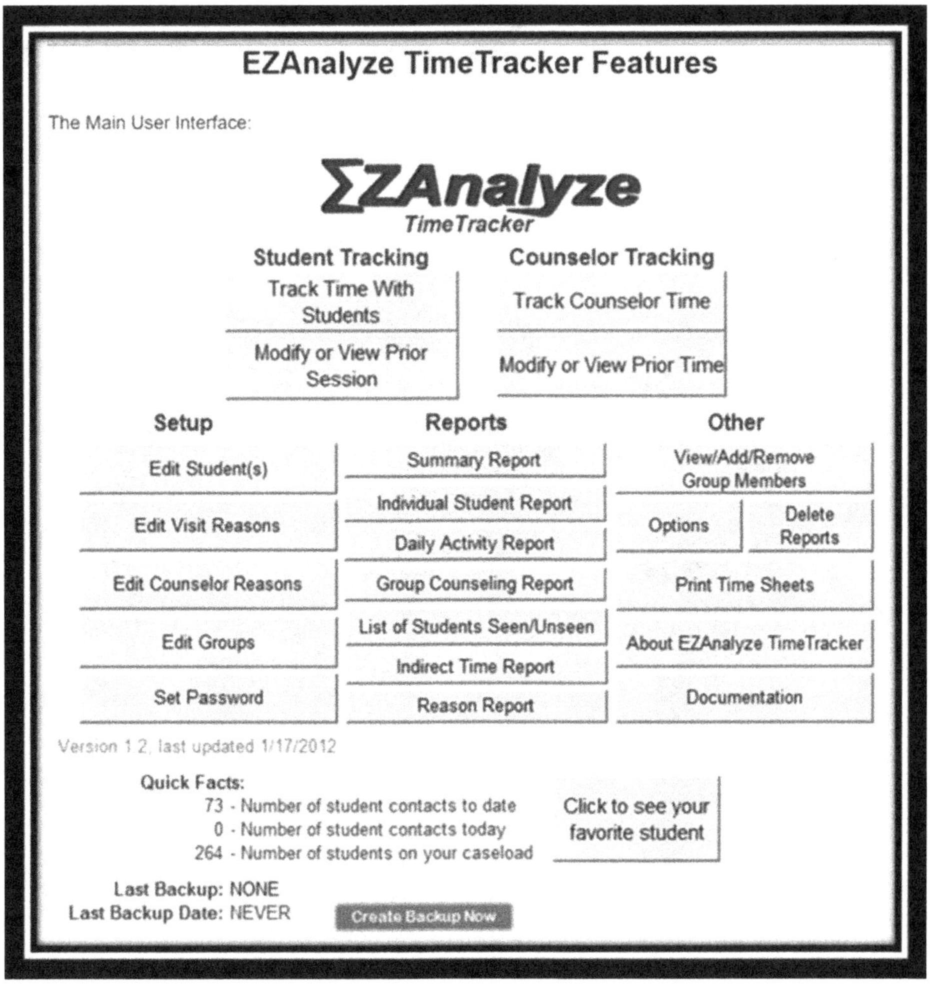

Figure 6.11 Features of EZAnalyze Time Tracker Excel add-in. Used with permission.

check-in with those who self-report a low score as illustrated in Figure 6.12. Also, helpful for teachers and school counselors is the *Student Emotions Report*, which can be queried for one day or an extended period of time (see Figure 6.13). Based upon the trends, this can help guide the topics needed for core curricular lessons with a specific teacher/classroom.

Approaches to Documenting Your Accountability

While it is widely known that K-12 public schools across the United States are highly data-driven and focused on accountability for all educators, the focus on school counseling programs seems to be much less specific. Yet, Section A.3 of the *ASCA Ethical Standards* (2016) is specifically focused on data-informed school counseling programs. Moreover, school districts and administrators want to know how school counselors are utilizing their time, and importantly, making a difference in the lives of students, families, and teachers. Just as each school is unique in its composition and there is no "one size fits all," there are a variety of accountability reporting frameworks to choose from. Our

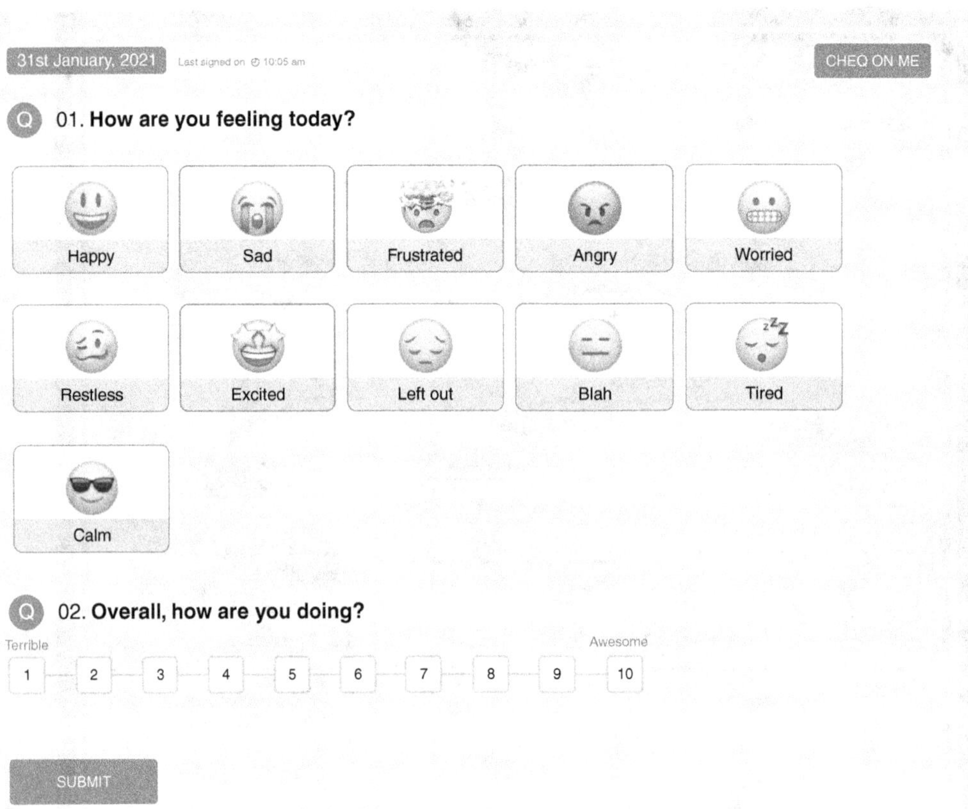

Exhibit 6.5 WellCheq Check-in Tool (two items). Used with permission.

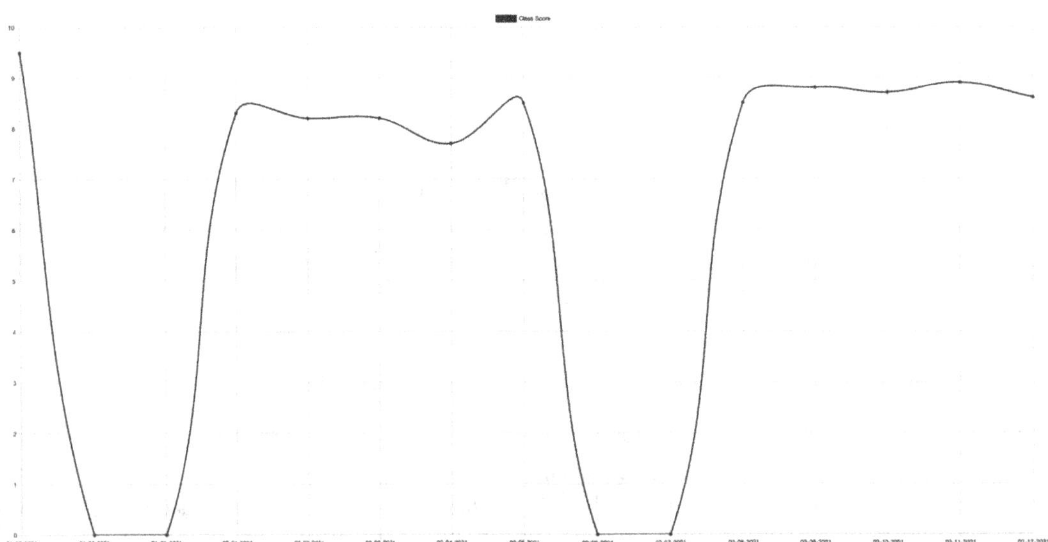

Figure 6.12 WellCheq query of student responses to "Overall, how are you doing?" over a 2-week period. Used with permission.

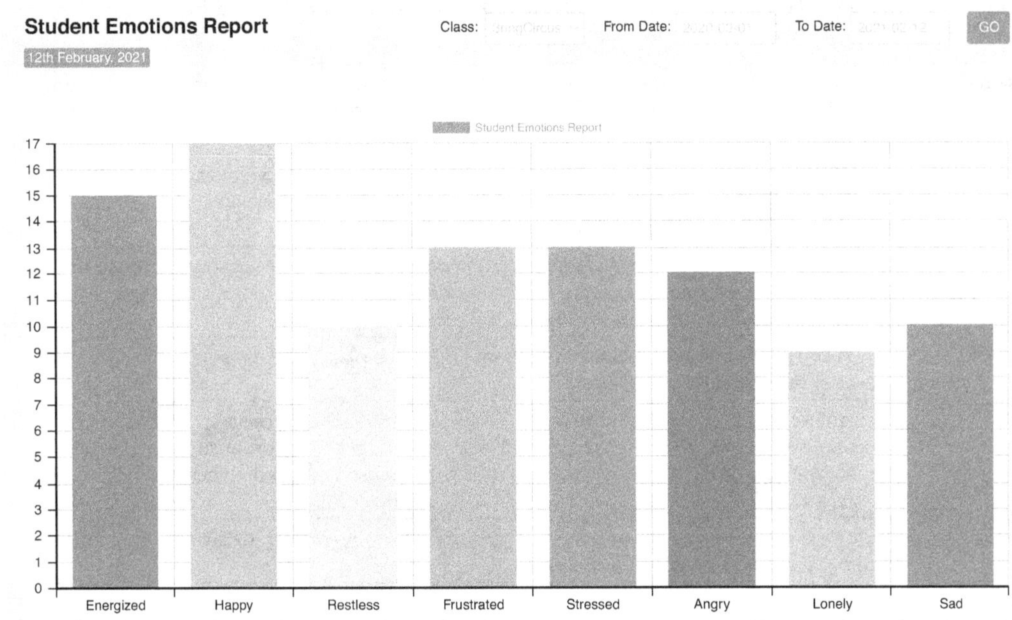

Figure 6.13 WellCheq Student Emotions Report cumulative responses for the academic year within one classroom. Used with permission.

recommendation is to review each of them and see which framework best meets the needs of your school's CSCP.

Mission, Elements, Analyze, Stakeholders, Unite, Reanalyze, and Educate

Dahir and Stone (2003) developed the seven-step accountability process of Mission, Elements, Analyze, Stakeholders, Unite, Reanalyze, and Educate (MEASURE) as a means for supporting school counselor accountability and showcasing the critical impact school counselors have on students (Table 6.1). This process helps school counselors move beyond just documenting the counting of tasks to accurately depict the impact of their work by considering seven important elements: mission, elements, analyze, stakeholders, unite, reanalyze, and educate. For further information on accountability efforts following this framework of a results report, we encourage you to review School Counselor Accountability: A MEASURE of Student Success by Dr. Carolyn Stone (Dahir & Stone, 2003).

Goals, Results, Impact Statement, and Program Implications

Brott (2006) conceptualized a simple accountability framework for school counselors to succinctly share with stakeholders their success over time within a CSCP. Through an action research lens, school counselors can view their work through a continuous improvement approach: GRIP. The acronym GRIP stands for goals, results, impact statement, and program implications (Table 6.2). Overall, the intention is for school counselors to actively and regularly generate ideas for improving and strengthening their CSCP, and communicate these in a brief, easy-to-understand way.

TABLE 6.1 EXPLANATION OF THE SEVEN STEP ACCOUNTABILITY REPORTING PROCESS DEVELOPED BY DAHIR AND STONE (2003)

Mission	Just as the school has a mission statement, the comprehensive school counseling program should have a mission that aligns with the goals of the school's annual improvement plan and the appropriate roles and responsibilities for school counselors.
Elements	Identify critical data elements that are important from the perspective of various stakeholders. For example, attendance rates, course enrollment patterns, and behavioral referrals are just a few examples of data elements that you may consider.
Analyze	Once you have identified data elements, break down the data (AKA disaggregate), so that you have a clearer understanding of the unique needs at your school and how these elements are impacting student achievement and personal success.
Stakeholders	When considering the intervention efforts that may take place, also consider which stakeholders you need to collaborate with.
Unite	Remember that this should not be a solo endeavor by the school counselor; rather, focus on what collaborations will be necessary for the greatest level of support or success to positively impact the data. Your intervention efforts should be focused on creating action plans that can deliver success.
Reanalyze	Following targeted and developmentally appropriate interventions, review the outcome data, and see the positive impact on students.
Educate	Demonstrate how your targeted efforts impacted students by showing all stakeholders the results (i.e., consider through your website, newsletters, memos, PTA/PTO meetings, etc.)

PTA, Parent–Teacher Association; PTO, Parent–Teacher Organization.

TABLE 6.2 EXPLANATION OF THE FOUR ELEMENTS OF THE ACCOUNTABILITY REPORTING PROCESS DEVELOPED BY BROTT (2006)

Goal	Establish specific goals that the intervention will address in terms of measurable behaviors or outcomes. Briefly identify in a paragraph the basics in terms of the when, where, who, and how. Make sure to include how you will be measuring impact (i.e., formal assessments, needs assessments, pre–posttests, etc.) and aligning to the most recent version of the ASCA National Model and ASCA Mindsets & Behaviors.
Results	Think of this section as the "so what?" being documented. For example, as a result of conducting a 6-week group counseling session for seventh graders failing two or more courses, all participants were able to increase their attendance by 25% and their overall course grades by about 0.75 grade points. Group participants also increased their beliefs about being able to succeed in school. It would be appropriate to use charts and others means of illustrating the results.
Impact statement	Think of this section as identifying statements that illustrate both quantitative and qualitative aspects of data. Your statements have the opportunity to be very compelling and to support the critical impact on student behavior and academic performance.
Program implications	Now that your intervention has been completed and you know its impact, what do you make of it? Reflect on the following questions for continuous improvement: What aspects were successful? What aspects were not successful? What should I continue to do, and what should I revise? What do I need? What will happen next?

ASCA, American School Counselor Association.

Making DATA Work

Young and Kaffenberger (2019) developed a process known as *DATA* to help school counselors implement a data-driven CSCP through a structured process that yields a one-page report capturing key areas. This four-step process is as follows: Design, Ask, Track, Announce (DATA). As was emphasized in Chapter 5, it is imperative that school counselors work with intentionality. By utilizing the DATA process, you are able to answer pragmatic questions. Within the Design action step you answer, "What is your goal?" Within the Ask action step, you answer, "How will you achieve your goal?" In the Track action step, you answer, "How will you analyze the data?" Last, in the Announce action step, you address, "How will you share your results?" The first two questions can be adequately answered by what is discussed in previous chapters. But in terms of analyzing data and sharing your results, we encourage you to consider what technological tools and other resources can best serve your efforts in these two components. For more information, we suggested reading *Making DATA Work* (fourth edition; Young & Kaffenberger, 2019).

Support Personnel Accountability Report Card

Various forms of school and district report cards exist throughout the country. Often, these reports are widely focused on metrics of the entire student or educator population. Similar to a school's improvement plan, the work that school counselors do both directly and indirectly impacts the metrics that you see. Yet, these documents do not typically illustrate the counselors' efforts to address student success in any or all of the three domains: academic, career, and social–emotional. However, the Support Personnel Accountability Report Card (SPARC) is an exception. According to its website (n.d.), the SPARC was initially developed by an advisory group of Los Angeles County counselors, counselor supervisors, counselor educators, and the California Department of Education staff, modeled after the School Accountability Report Card that is utilized in California. Initially, the document highlighted all three domains: academic, career, and personal/social development in alignment with the third edition of the ASCA National Model, as illustrated by Lakeland High School's SPARC (Exhibit 6.6). However, the document has evolved in recent years to specifically illustrate school's efforts toward students' career and college readiness. You will notice in Exhibit 6.7 that Hillview Middle School's SPARC shows how educators addressed college and career readiness across the school through core curricular classroom lessons and other school activities. Blair Middle and High School's SPARC (Exhibit 6.8) illustrates career readiness efforts through an annual college day, the completion of 4-year academic plans, and documentation of course enrollment patterns in dual enrollment coursework.

Although a voluntary, continuous improvement process, participation in the SPARC gives schools an opportunity to publish a document that identifies key student outcomes achieved through collaboration and to publicize their plans for continued success in direct alignment with ASCA's National Model and the core functions of a school counselor or school counseling team.

School Counseling Program Profile

For school counselor educators and district-level school counseling supervisors, the School Counseling Program Profile (SC PRO) may serve as a great starting point for getting individuals new to being data driven started on their journey. According to its website, the California Association of School Counselors (CASC, n.d.) has designed an initiative in collaboration with various school counselor preparation programs throughout the state to have school counselor trainees create and publish documents that "reflect collaboration, teamwork, and commitment to continuous improvement" with their school counseling site supervisors. These peer-reviewed documents follow a rubric and are aligned with key elements of the ASCA National Model, as well as state-level accreditation and funding mechanisms. The rubric categories are Principal's Message; Our School Counseling Program Team; Our School Counseling Program; Academic, College/Career, and Social Emotional Development; Partners and Programs; Contact Information. In our opinion, reviewing these documents is an excellent first step toward becoming a data-driven school counselor and is developmentally appropriate for school counselor trainees, as well as those who are new to these data-driven approaches. The SC PRO for Marshall

DEPARTMENT OF GUIDANCE & COUNSELING

ACCOUNTABILITY REPORT CARD 2014 - 2015

DIRECTOR OF SCHOOL COUNSELING COMMENTS

In 2014, Lakeland Regional High School was ranked 112th in New Jersey, and was ranked in the Top 20 "Most Improved" schools in New Jersey in 2013.

Lakeland Regional High School's Counseling Department received national recognition as a "Recognized ASCA Model Program" by the American School Counselor Association.

The RAMP designation, awarded to schools whose counseling programs align with the criteria set in the *ASCA National Model*, recognizes schools that are committed to delivering a comprehensive, data-driven school counseling program and creating an exemplary educational environment.

Lakeland Regional High School is one of approximately 450 schools across the country who have received the RAMP designation since the program's inception. Most notably, Lakeland Regional High School is the <u>first</u> and <u>only</u> school in New Jersey to attain this honor!

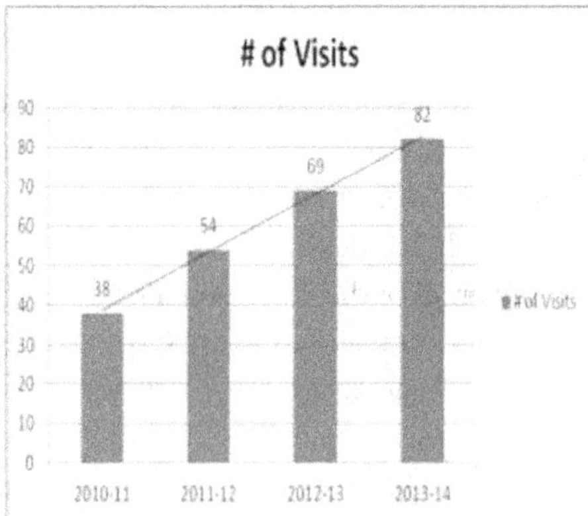

46% increase in 4 years!

INCREASE IN COLLEGES & CAREER/TECHNICAL SCHOOLS VISITING LAKELAND

The number of colleges and career/technical schools visiting Lakeland continues to grow. We firmly believe in providing ample opportunities to our students, so they are knowledgeable about their options beyond high school.

Growth per year has been 15% - 30%, with an overall increase of 46% over the last four years.

GUIDANCE & COUNSELING TEAM

The Guidance & Counseling Department is here to provide expertise in the areas of academic, career and personal / social development. The counselors include:

- Ms. Donna Kerr, School Counselor
- Ms. Lisa Manicone, School Counselor
- Mrs. Dianalyn Matlosz, School Counselor
- Mr. Brian Mulhern, School Counselor
- Mrs. Tara Ross-Salman, School Counselor
- Dr. Ray Danziger, Student Assistance Coordinator
- Mr. Tim Conway, Director of Guidance

Secretaries include: Dawn Phillips, Janet Ross & Nancy Suter

The team of counselors now serves approximately 205 students each, and is dedicated to reaching every student within the Lakeland community. The counselors provide programs and services in the form of classroom guidance lessons, individual (i.e. 4-year plans) and group counseling, consultation with parents, teachers and other educators, referrals to other school support services (i.e. I&RS, Special Services) or community resources, peer assistance, intervention and advocacy at the systemic level, career development, coordination of SWAP, SWAN and LEAP peer leadership programs, review of student testing and assessments, and coordinate state testing. For a list of all services by grade level visit the <u>Guidance website</u>.

INSTANT COLLEGE ADMISSIONS DAY AT LAKELAND!

On December 6, 2013 and January 17, 2014, Lakeland Regional High School held instant decision days with <u>19</u> colleges and technical schools.

Students had the opportunity to sign up in Naviance for one or more colleges and/or technical schools they were interested in, and in one day, find out their admissions decision!

116 total seniors (43.1% of the class) participated in the event with a total number of <u>210 college acceptances</u>.

LAKELAND REGIONAL HIGH SCHOOL | 205 Conklintown Road, Wanaque, NJ 07465 | phone 973.835.1900 | fax 973.835.7932

Exhibit 6.6 Lakeland Regional High School Support Personnel Accountability Report Card in alignment with the third edition of the *ASCA National Model*. Used with permission. ASCA, American School Counselor Association.

ACCOUNTABILITY REPORT CARD 2014 - 2015
"GUIDANCE & COUNSELING"

SCHOOL CLIMATE & SAFETY

The YES, SWAP, and LEAP groups are involved in prevention programming to the students at Lakeland Regional High School as peer leadership groups, and they provide prevention programs to the surround K-8 and middle school districts.

Speak With a Peer (SWAP), Leaders Encouraging Adolescent Progress (LEAP) & Youth Empowering Success (YES) groups are involved in the summer during our 9th grade orientation, throughout the year in the Pathways classes, as well as during our 8th grade open house.

These groups, albeit with slightly different core missions, are an integral part of the school community in helping our students feel safe, serve as mentors, advocating for healthly life habits, anti-bullying messages and assistance with transitioning to the high school.

COLLEGE / CAREER:

On October 16, 2013, Lakeland Regional High School offered its "College Roundtable" program. Representatives included Lafayette College, George Washington University, The College of New Jersey, Quinnipiac University, and SUNY - Oneonta.

The event was well received by students and parents providing insight into the college admissions process, what colleges are expecting and answering attendee's questions.

During the first half of the 2013 – 2014 school year, the Guidance & Counseling Department hosted two college tours. Kutztown / Moravian on October 30, 2013 and the second was to Ramapo College on November 22, 2013.

On January 7, 2014 there was a program "Junior College Planning", which was developed to assist students and parents begin the college planning process. Over 150 students and parents came out for the event, and the program overall received an 97% satisfaction rating.

The Financial Aid Night on January 16th, 2014 provided 100 attendees with an understanding of the Financial Aid process, as well as the various forms of aid available. Attendees received a timely warning to steer clear of a scam from FAFSA.com.

Recent data from ACT shows Lakeland Regional above the state average in English, Reading and overall Composite scores. The number of students taking the ACT at Lakeland is at an all time high. The chart below shows a 25.64% increase over the past 5-years.

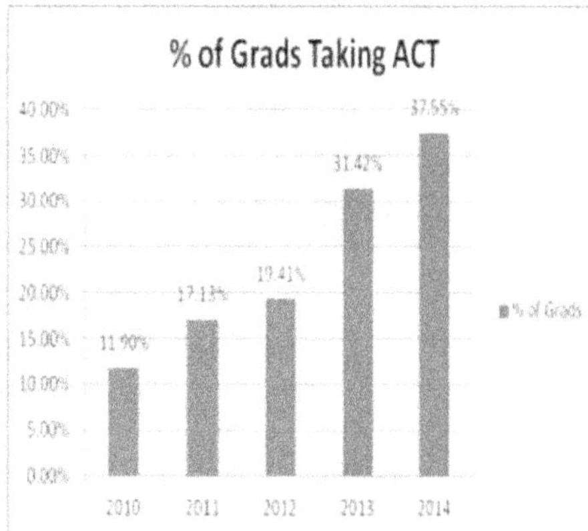

25.64% Increase over 5 Years!

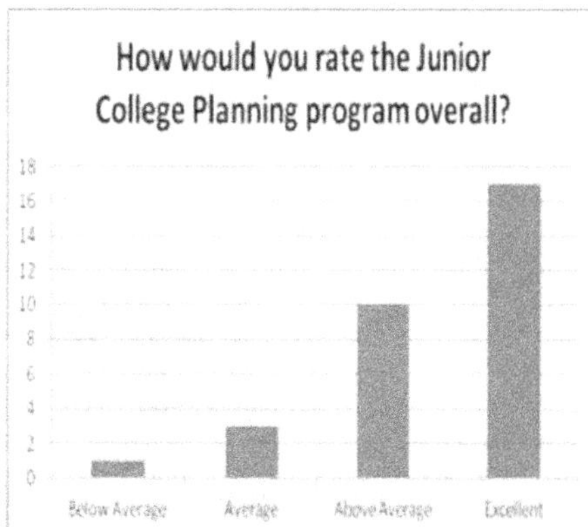

97% satisfaction rating!

LAKELAND REGIONAL HIGH SCHOOL | 205 Conklintown Road, Wanaque, NJ 07465 | phone 973.835.1900 | fax 973.835.7932

Exhibit 6.6 (*continued*)

ACCOUNTABILITY REPORT CARD 2014 - 2015
"GUIDANCE & COUNSELING"

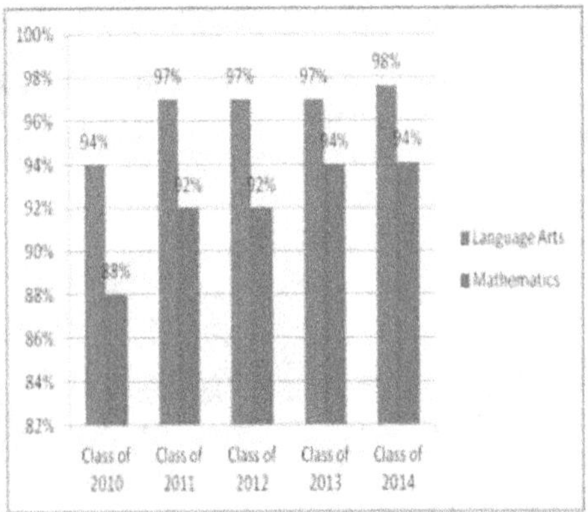

HSPA 5-YEAR TREND

MEASUREMENTS

ACADEMIC:

With the graduating Class of 2014, LRHS saw a higher pass rate of 98% in Language Arts and a steady pass rate of 94% in Mathematics . Overall, 100% of LRHS students passed either the HSPA or the AHSA (Alternative High School Assessment).

Lakeland Regional High School offers 14 Advanced Placement (AP) level courses and 3 dual enrollment college courses for a total of 17 college level courses offered during the school day.

Class of 2014:
AP Scholars = 15
AP Scholars with Honors = 4
AP Scholars with Distinction = 12
156 students took 275 exams

Advanced Placement Courses: English Literature, US History, Music Theory, Art History, U.S. Government & Politics, Comparative Government Spanish, Calculus AB, Statistics, Computer Science, Biology, Chemistry, Environmental Science, and European History.

*See LRHS school profile for additional data!

PERSONAL / SOCIAL:

Lakeland Regional High School offers counseling groups for students who are "at-risk" and for students who are experiencing challenges in their lives (i.e. anxiety).

In spring 2014, we ran an academic support group, which was based off student interest, teacher referral and failing grades in two or more classes. Overall, the group improvement showed a 7-point increase in grades (Q3 to Q4). The failure rate was reduced from 13 courses to 6 courses, which was a 54% decrease in failures.

One student stated, "I'm grateful for Teacher A and Counselor K for not giving up on me and for pushing me forward when I wanted to give up". Another stated, "... made me change my attitude towards everything.. and to never stop trying".

FOCUS FOR IMPROVEMENT

The Guidance & Counseling Department sets rigorous goals and standards that are in alignment with the districts vision and mission. During the 2013 – 2014 school year our major goals include:

- Goal was a reduction of course failures for identified 9th & 10th grade students by 5%. The goal exceeded expectations with a 45.83% reduction in the failure rate.
- The goal was a 20% increase in knowledge and skills for juniors of the post secondary planning process by the end of the school year. Juniors demonstrated a 149% increase in knowledge and skills by the end of the school year.

VOLUNTEER INVOLVEMENT

Parent's are strongly encouraged and welcome to participate in the activities in the Department through the following ways:

- Members of the School Advisory Committee
- Mentors for students involved in "shadow days"
- Guest speakers for "Career Days" or workshops
- Periodic surveys mailed home and online which help guide programs and services

To become involved in one or more of these opportunities, please contact Tim Conway, Director of Guidance at (973) 835-1900 or email at tconway@lakeland.k12.nj.us.

LAKELAND REGIONAL HIGH SCHOOL | 205 Conklintown Road, Wanaque, NJ 07465 | phone 973.835.1900 | fax 973.835.7932

Exhibit 6.6 (*continued*)

ACCOUNTABILITY REPORT CARD 2014 - 2015
"GUIDANCE & COUNSELING"

DEVELOPMENTS IN 2014 - 2015

Next school year, Lakeland Regional High School seeks to enhance the number of courses being offered through Passaic County Community College (PCCC) and the Dual Enrollment program. Currently, there are 3 courses offered at Lakeland through Seton Hall and Syracuse University for credit. Next year the following courses plan to be offered to eligible juniors and seniors.

- Introduction to Criminal Justice – 3 credits
- Introduction to Sociology – 3 credits
- Child Development I / II – 3 credits (each)
- Emergency Medical Technician (EMT) – 8 credits

Lakeland Regional High School offered "Introduction to Psychology" during summer of 2014 as another Dual Enrollment course through PCCC with 18 total students enrolled. Cost of a 3-credit course is approximately $180.

COMMUNITY PARTNERSHIPS

Connecting with our community is essential to our programs and services for both improved student success and our professional growth.

At this time the department is currently connected with the following community resources:

- Passaic County Community College
- AWARE ASAP
- Chilton Hospital
- Ringwood Recreation Department

ACCOUNTABILITY REPORT CARD
"GUIDANCE & COUNSELING"

www.lakeland.k12.nj.us

HOW WILL AN ADVANCED DEGREE HELP YOU?

Earnings and unemployment rate for people 25 years and over

Unemployment rate in 2009	Level of Education Completed	Mean (average) earnings in 2009
14.60%	Less than a high school diploma	$28,496
9.70%	High school graduate, no college	$40,352
8.60%	Some college, no degree	$46,800
7.00%	Occupational program (trade/vocational school)	$46,696
6.80%	Associate degree	$48,308
5.20%	Bachelor's degree	$71,552
3.90%	Master's degree	$82,628
2.50%	Doctoral degree	$113,308
2.30%	Professional degree	$114,712

205 Conklintown Road | Wanaque, NJ 07465
phone 973.835.1900 | fax 973.835.7932

We value your opinions and suggestions! Please continue to respond to surveys that are sent out, as they help us to shape our programs and services to the Lakeland community! Suggestions may also be submitted to Tim Conway, Director of Guidance at tconway@lakeland.k12.nj.us.

Thank you for your continued support!

Exhibit 6.6 (*continued*)

HILLVIEW MIDDLE SCHOOL

HOME OF THE HAWKS

Hillview Middle School
SPARC 2019-20

Support Personnel Accountability Report Card

A continuous improvement document sponsored by the California Department of Education

Address: 40525 Peonza Lane, Palmdale, Ca 93551
Phone: 661-722-9993 **Fax:** 661-722-9483 **Website:** https://www.westside.k12.ca.us/hv
Principal: Co-Principals Rodney Lots and Jennifer Slater-Sanchez **District:** Westside Union
Grade Levels: 6,7,8 **Enrollment:** 984

Principal's Message

Aside from a clean, technology rich, and safe campus, Hillview Middle School (HMS) offers many strengths to create an atmosphere where students want to learn and feel valued. Members of the Student Support Team (SST) strive to empower students to reach their highest potential by offering a strong core curriculum and consistent support to help facilitate their academic success, social-emotional development and college and career readiness. Students have access to a wide variety of clubs and activities that are both engaging and fun. This not only maintains their interest in learning but also exposes them to different situations and tasks to prepare them for success in a diverse community. We are working to achieve our goals contained in our School Site Plan which are 1) ensure all students are well-equipped with the cognitive, linguistic, interpersonal skills necessary to be successful in a global society and 2) develop and implement programs that support students' academic, behavioral, and socio-emotional growth and success. In an effort to achieve our goals and prepare our students for high school and college, honors and advanced courses are offered which is aligned to the Local Control Accountability Plan (LCAP) goal of access for all students to rigorous courses.

Career and College Readiness Student Outcomes

The SST at HMS strongly believes in our district's vision of promoting students who have acquired the knowledge, skills and attitudes necessary to achieve significant career, educational, civic and personal goals, which will enrich our society as positive role models and responsible citizens. The data below shows students becoming aware of post secondary career choices and understanding how to be college ready by excelling in their classes.

Career Readiness

In the 4th quarter of every year, all of our 8th grade students complete an Interest Profiler assessment through California CareerZone online which will allow them to explore career options by detailing education needed, income potential, and job availability in their particular interest. In addition, these students were given a presentation on post-secondary options, which a pre-test showed, students had little knowledge about community college, vocational school and paying for college. At the end of the presentation, a post-test revealed that all students (368 total) could identify 3 post-secondary options,168 of students had an increased awareness of scholarships and paying for college and 300 students could explain what the benefits of attending a vocational or trade school.

Career Options can be Clearly Described

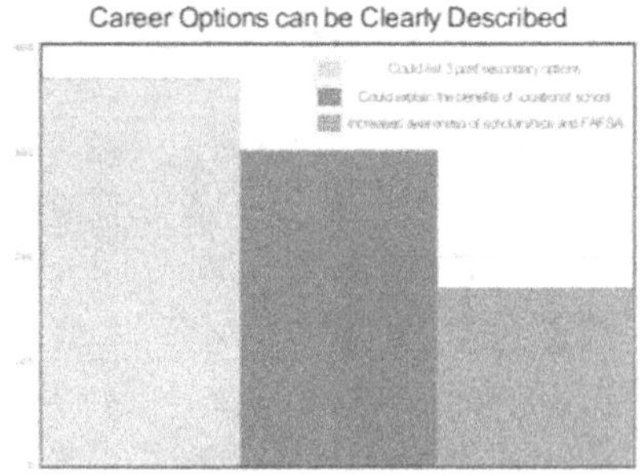

College Readiness

The mission of HMS is to ensure that all students will be prepared to reach high levels of academic achievement as determined by district, state, and national standards. Our SST provides numerous opportunities of support for students to be successful in their classes through lunch time and morning tutoring, learning lab, and math and language arts support classes. All students have access to a rigorous curriculum and honors classes which help to prepare them for the high level of commitment, hard work and dedication they will need for more challenging courses in high school for their college admissions. This chart demonstrates the percentage of students in each grade that have received honor roll and principal's list recognition: 80% of our 6th grade, 38% of our 7th grade, and 45% of our 8th grade classes.

Honor Roll Recognition

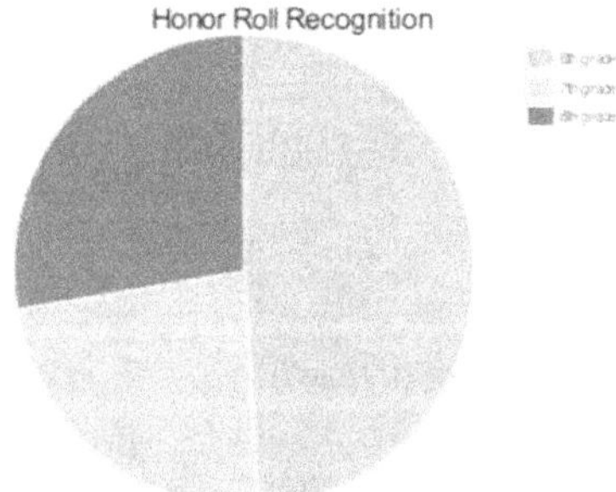

Exhibit 6.7 Support Personnel Accountability Report Card for Hillview Middle School—Updated college and career-readiness format. Used with permission.

21st Century Skills

In order for our students to be successful in their future career endeavors and college goals, members of our SST recognize the importance of all of our students to develop 21st Century Skills. We want our students to be critical thinkers, digitally literate, globally aware, and effective communicators.The SST facilitates a wide range of programs and classes that are available to every student such as Model United Nations, AVID (Advancement Via Individual Determination), ASB (Associated Student Body), and Design and Modeling that foster problem solving, collaboration, and leadership skills. Programs such as these help our students to be ready for high school and college that will set them on their future career path.

Additional Achievements:

- 94% of our 8th grade students took the PSAT.
- 2019 - Became a Unified Champions School for Special Olympics.
- 2017 - Earned early candidacy for WASC (Western Association of Schools and Colleges) accreditation.

Career and College Readiness School Site Programs and Community Partnerships

Our SST is able to provide innovative and engaging opportunities and programs through the support of our many community partnerships such as the West Antelope Valley Educational Foundation (WAVE) that contribute the resources needed to foster growth towards college and career readiness through programs like Vex Robotics, Concert Band, Mathletes, Science Olympiads, and Model United Nations. Counselors participate in professional development through Hatching Results that assists in designing, implementing, evaluating, and improving comprehensive, data-driven school counseling programs that address the diverse needs of all students.

School Site Programs

- Peer Leaders - Are positive role models that assist in creating a safe and inclusive school culture.
- Inclusion League - Special and general education students partnering to build relationships.
- Dancing Feet - Competition dance program that promotes team work and creates self-confidence.
- Science Olympiad and Mathletes - Competitions that provide rigorous, standards-based challenges.
- Associated Student Body (ASB) - Represents the interests and goals of Hillview's total student body.
- Model United Nations - Simulation of UN conferences where students role-play ambassadors to the UN.

Community Partnerships

- Lancaster West Rotary - Offers financial support for several extracurricular programs such as band.
- WAVE Foundation - Provides financial support for innovative student led projects like Lego Robotics.
- Children's Center of the Antelope Valley - This agency provides school based mental health services.
- Boys Town - We use this resource for school wide discipline strategies that teach social skills.
- Hatching Results - Provides training to counselors to create data driven counseling programs.
- Cedar Sinai Blood Mobile - Helps our students learn to be globally aware and locally responsible.

Student Support Team

Hillview's Student Support Team is comprised of highly inclusive professionals that have a complete regard for the progress and personal development of every student. They work to provide an equitable support system for all students to become college and career ready through promoting rich opportunities for learning both within and outside of the classroom. They cultivate a range of partnerships with parents, business owners, and the community to support student learning and progress. In keeping with the Westside Union School District's motto of "Pointing the Path, Providing the Way" our SST works as a collaborative group to provide all students with continued support in academics, social/emotional issues and career and college choices. Our SST members belong to the following professional organizations: Association of School Administrators, American School Counselor Association, California School Counselor Association, California Association of School Psychologist, Computer Using Educators, and Westside Union Teachers Association.

Position	Years	Qualifications
Co-Principal	15	BS, MA, ASC
Co-Principal	5	BA, MA, MA, ASC, Ed.D.
Counselor	12	BA, MS, PPSC
School Psychologist	18	BA, MS, EdD
Teacher/AVID	12	BS

Position	Years	Qualifications
Teacher/ASB Advisor	20	BS
Teacher/CJSF Advisor	16	BA
School Nurse	26	RN, SNC
Campus Climate Assistant	4	AA, District Training
Campus Climate Assistant	13	District Training

SST Contact Name: Jennifer Schmid
Phone: 6617229993
E-mail: j.schmid@westside.k12.ca.us

SPARC Seal
California Department of Education

Exhibit 6.7 (*continued*)

Blair Middle and High School
SPARC 2019-20

Support Personnel Accountability Report Card

A continuous improvement document sponsored by the California Department of Education

Address: 1201 S. Marengo Ave., Pasadena, CA 91106
Phone: 626-396-5820 **Website:** https://www.pusd.us/blair
Principal: David Ibarra **District:** Pasadena Unified School District
Grade Levels: 6-12 **Enrollment:** 988

Principal's Message

The Student Support Team (SST) at Blair High School offers a comprehensive guidance program that abides by the American School Counselor Association's Mindsets and Behaviors for Student Success and the California Standards for the School Counseling Profession. As an International Baccalaureate School, all students are provided with rigorous instruction that supports them in becoming career and college ready. The SST maintains a safe and nurturing school environment that prepares students for career and college readiness via counseling, guidance, support, and resource allocation. Regarding our first goal from last year of improving our graduation rate, some progress has been made. Significant progress was made on the second goal from last year of preparing students for completing a senior portfolio and defense as well as their community service/work based learning hours in order to graduate. One goal for improvement is to reduce suspensions for specific subgroups. A second goal for improvement is to develop and implement a strategic plan for intervening with students at risk for not graduating. The SPARC is aligned to the Local Control Accountability Plan.

Career and College Readiness Student Outcomes

It is important to measure, analyze, and improve student outcomes in order to become more effective in abiding by the American School Counselor Association Mindsets and Behaviors for Student Success and the California Standards for the School Counseling Profession. The student outcomes presented below were achieved through SST members teaching guidance lessons, providing resource allocation, and coordinating multiple college and career preparation opportunities.

Career Readiness

SST members meet with all ninth graders about their future college and career plans. A plan of the classes they will take the throughout high school and into their post-secondary plans is developed. One hundred and thirty ninth graders completed their high school plan in 2019 and one hundred and twenty-four ninth graders did this in 2018. SST members and college access partners do multiple presentations on graduation requirements, college types, and admission requirements. An annual college day where presentations by colleges are done and an annual career day where presentations by career representatives are done further assist students in exploring their options. College and career conferences that are put on by the district, community, and various other organizations are also promoted.

High School Plan Developed

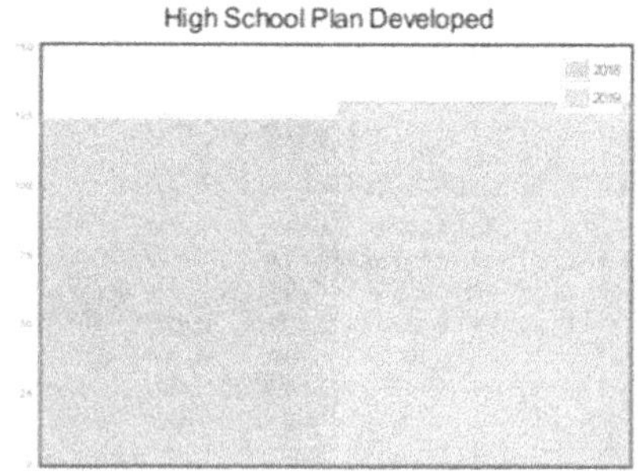

College Readiness

SST members partnered with the local community college to promote and facilitate concurrent and dual enrollment. This was the first year in many years that a dual enrollment course, Political Science 1 (American Government) was offered on our campus and taught by a professor from Pasadena City College. Blair High School students who completed this course received credit for graduation and college. Full International Baccalaureate Diploma candidates had to take Political Science 1 in order to fit all of their other course requirements into the school day. Thirty-one students completed a dual enrollment course in 2019 compared with seven students who completed a concurrent enrollment course in 2018.

Community College Course Completed

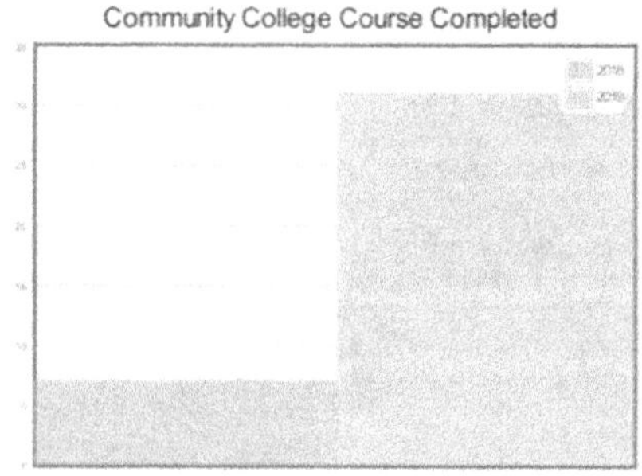

Exhibit 6.8 Support Personnel Accountability Report Card for Blair Middle and High School—Updated college and career-readiness format. Used with permission.

21st Century Skills

As an International Baccalaureate School, 21st Century Skills are embedded into lessons throughout the school. SST members provide resources so that all students are taught the International Baccalaureate Learner Profile of the month, such as Open Minded, Thinkers, Communicators, Knowledgeable, and Principled. Awards are given to students who demonstrate the International Baccalaureate Learner Profile of the Month. Each student is provided a Chromebook to take home and use during class to further develop information, media, and technology literacy. SST members partner with mental health providers and public health providers to assist students in self-management skills so they can achieve their potential.

Additional Achievements:

- Our seniors provided over 2000 work-based learning hours to our local community.
- Ninety percent of our graduates from 2020 were accepted to college.
- Over 30 students completed a college course via concurrent or dual enrollment.

Career and College Readiness School Site Programs and Community Partnerships

The SST collaborates with a variety of school-wide programs and a significant number of community partners in order to further assist students in preparing for career and college readiness success. Providing these programs and developing and maintaining these partnerships are vital to improving students' college and career readiness. There is not enough space to list all of the School Site Programs and Community Partnerships here! Students become more engaged in school and their community through these partnerships

School Site Programs

- College and Career Guidance Exploration: Pasadena City College (PCC), College Access Plan
- Student Workshops: Upward Bound, Talent Search, Cal-SOAP, College Access Plan
- College Admission and Placement Tests: Collegeboard, ACT, International Baccalaureate
- Annual Career Day: Armed Services, Huntington Memorial Hospital, Sassoon Academy
- Annual College Day: University of California, Los Angeles, California State University, PCC
- Personal and Social Support: Pasadena Unified School District Mental Health

Community Partnerships

- Pasadena City College: Application workshops, concurrent and dual enrollment
- Health Careers Academy: Pasadena Public Health, Planned Parenthood, Kaiser Permanente
- Pasadena Education Foundation: Technology, grant writing and assistance, scholarships
- Young and Healthy Families: Access to all types of healthcare for students and families
- University of California, Los Angeles: Personal and social support
- Art Center College of Design: Art classes and guest speakers

Student Support Team

Blair School's SST members abide by the American School Counselor Association Mindsets and Behaviors for Student Success and the California Standards for the School Counseling Profession in order to create an equitable student support system that prepares students for career and college readiness success with 21st Learning Skills. SST members are involved in numerous professional organizations or associations to allow for ongoing professional development and skill attainment. SST members belong to the following organizations: Association of Pasadena School Administrators, California Association of School Counselors, American School Counselor Association, California Association of Marriage and Family Therapists, and National Education Association. Please see the chart below for a partial list of team members, their years of experience, and their highest credential and education level.

Position	Years	Qualifications
Principal	18	MA, Admin Credential
Assistant Principal of High School	15	Ed.D., Admin Credential
Assistant Principal of Middle School	25	MS, Admin Credential
Special Education Coordinator	2	MA
Instructional Coach	20	MA
School Nurse	1	BS

Position	Years	Qualifications
Head Librarian	11	MA
School Counselor	36	MS, PPS Credential
School Counselor	24	MS, PPS Credential
School Psychologist	6	MA, PPS Credential
Senior Clerk Typist	16	High School Diploma
Registrar	22	BS

SST Contact Name: Andrea Cordeiro-Benson
Phone: 626 396-5820 X 80123
E-mail: cordeirobenson.andre@pusd.us

SPARC Seal
California Department of Education

Exhibit 6.8 (*continued*)

Middle School (Exhibit 6.9) provides an excellent model of what you can summarize and promote to stakeholders with this format.

Exemplary Comprehensive School Counseling Programs

In addition to utilizing various forms and approaches to address their accountability, some school counselors have invested considerable time and effort in developing and implementing exemplary CSCPs that are data driven and evidence based. The Recognized ASCA Model Program (RAMP) is a program sponsored by the ASCA and is intended to honor the work of those who have meet the standards for

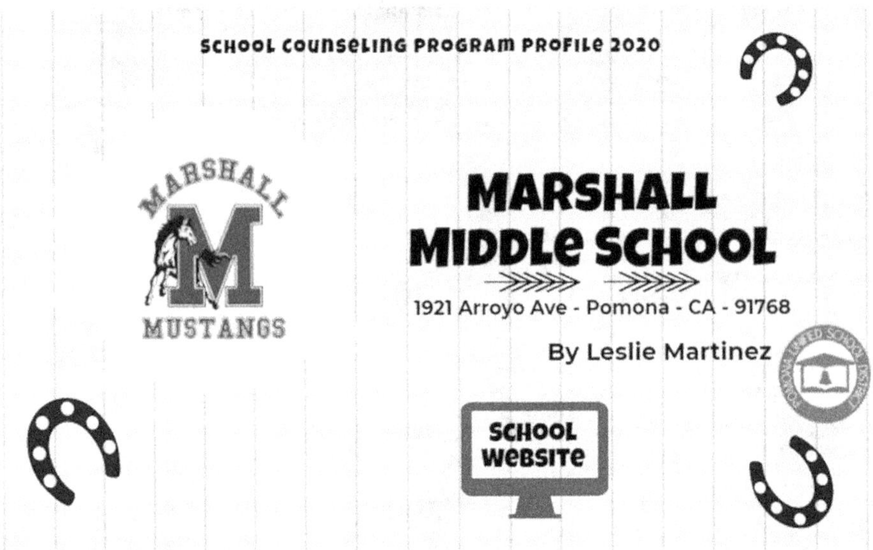

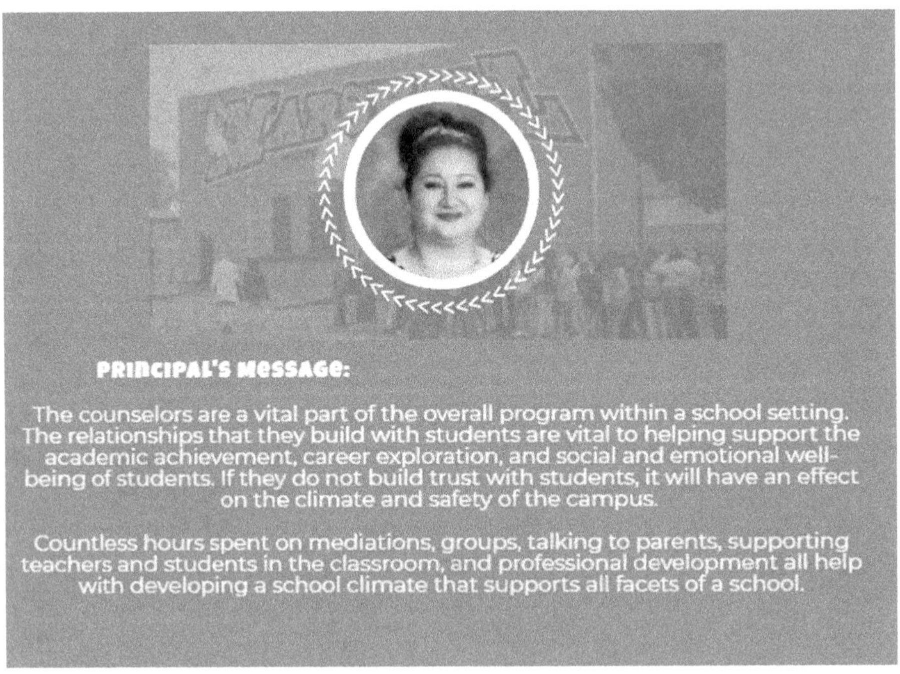

Exhibit 6.9 School Counseling Profile for Marshall Middle School. Used with permission.

Exhibit 6.9 (*continued*)

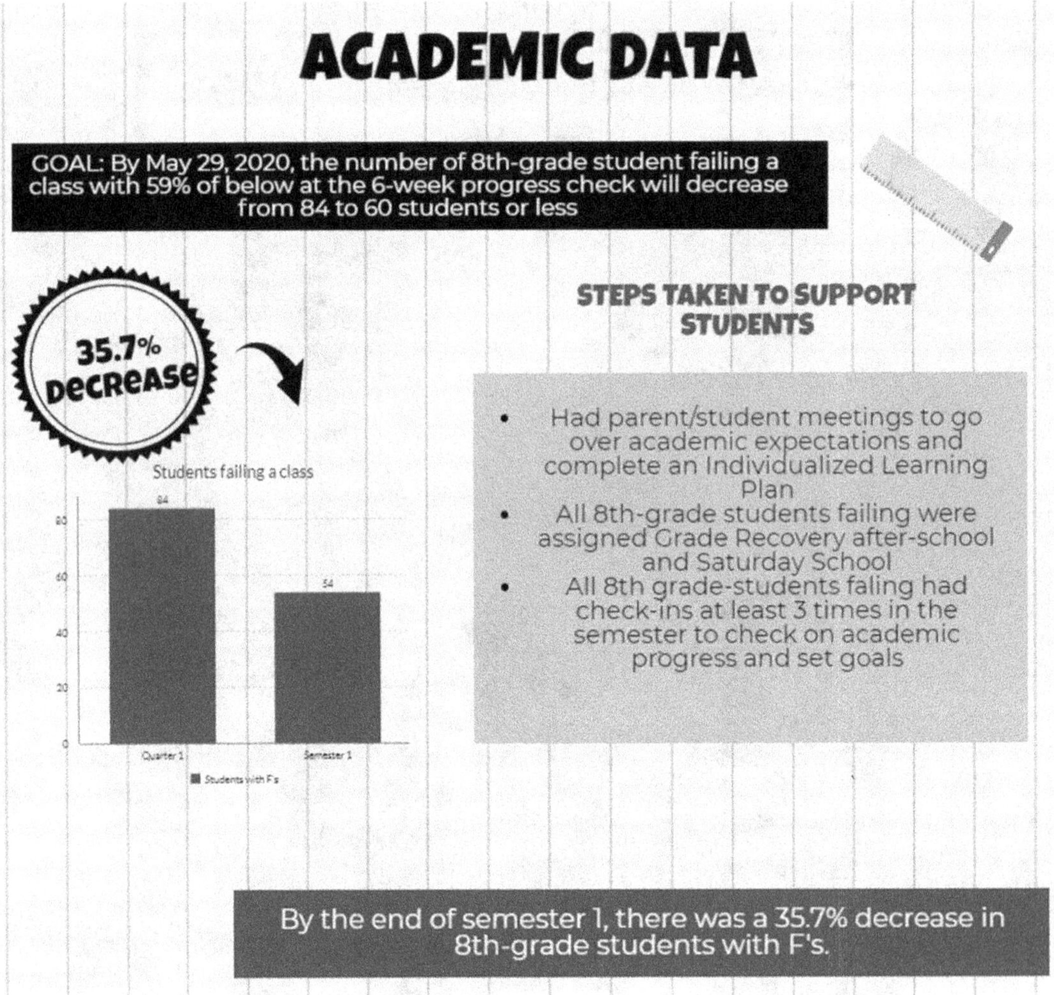

Exhibit 6.9 (*continued*)

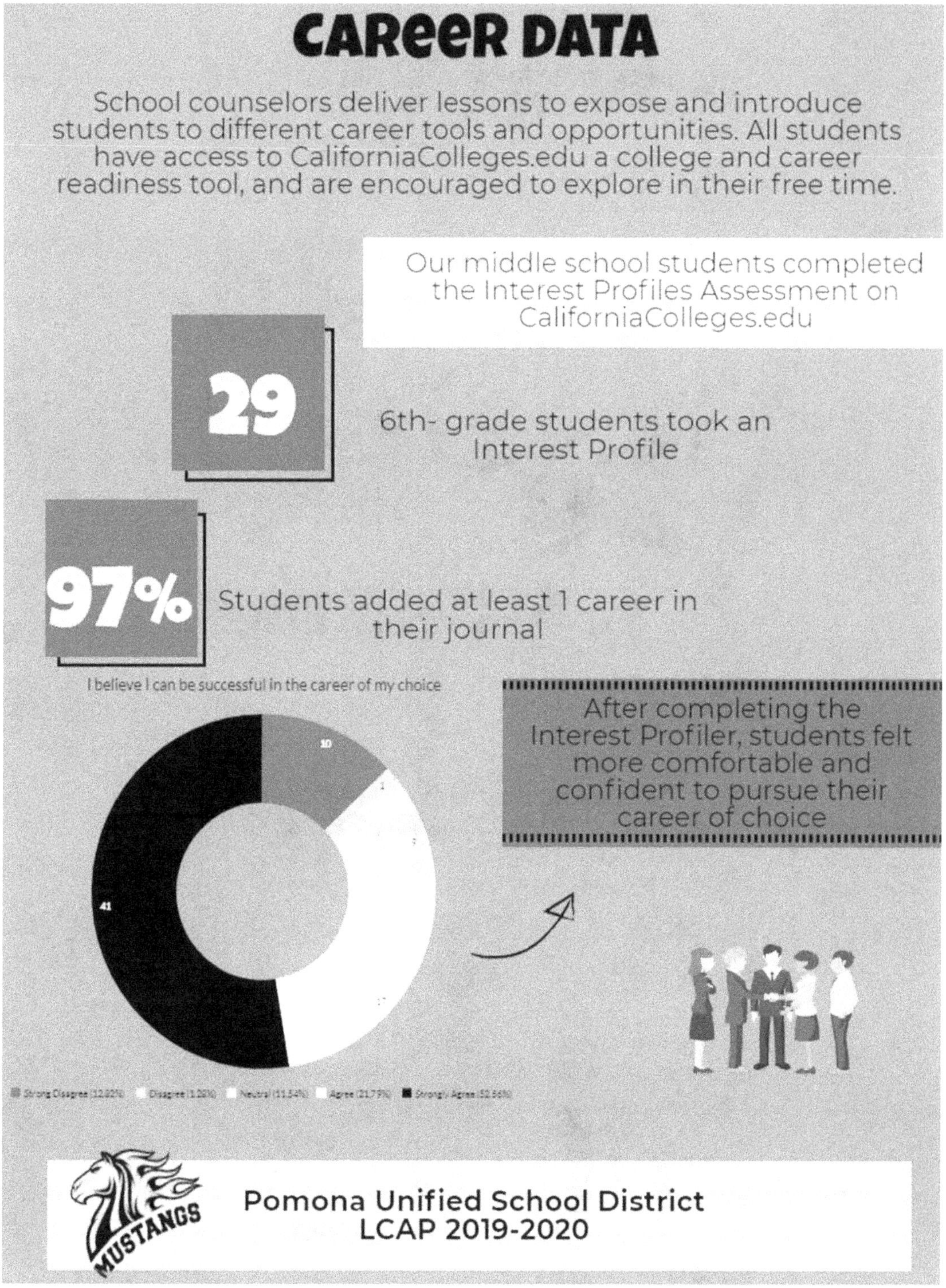

Exhibit 6.9 (*continued*)

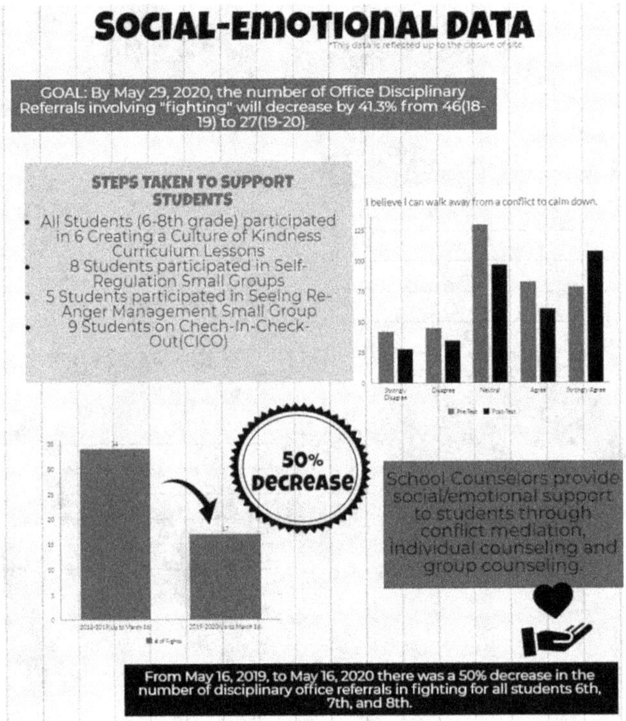

Exhibit 6.9 (*continued*)

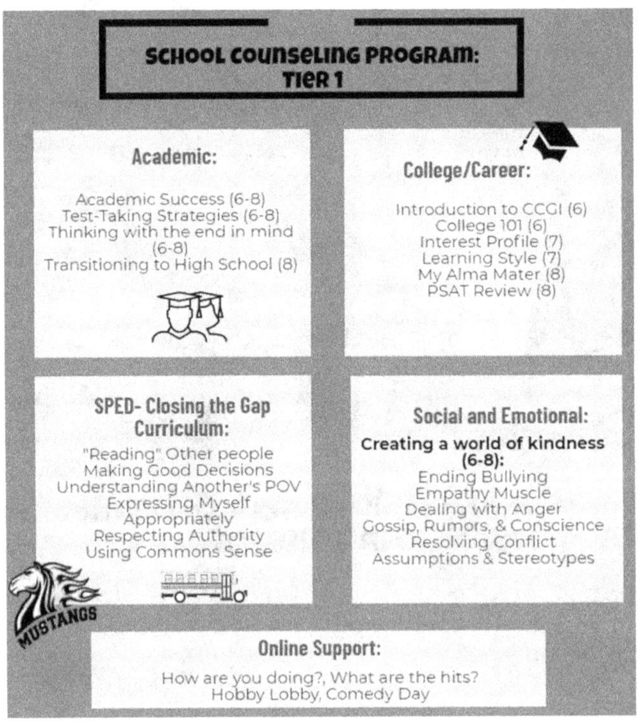

Exhibit 6.9 (*continued*)

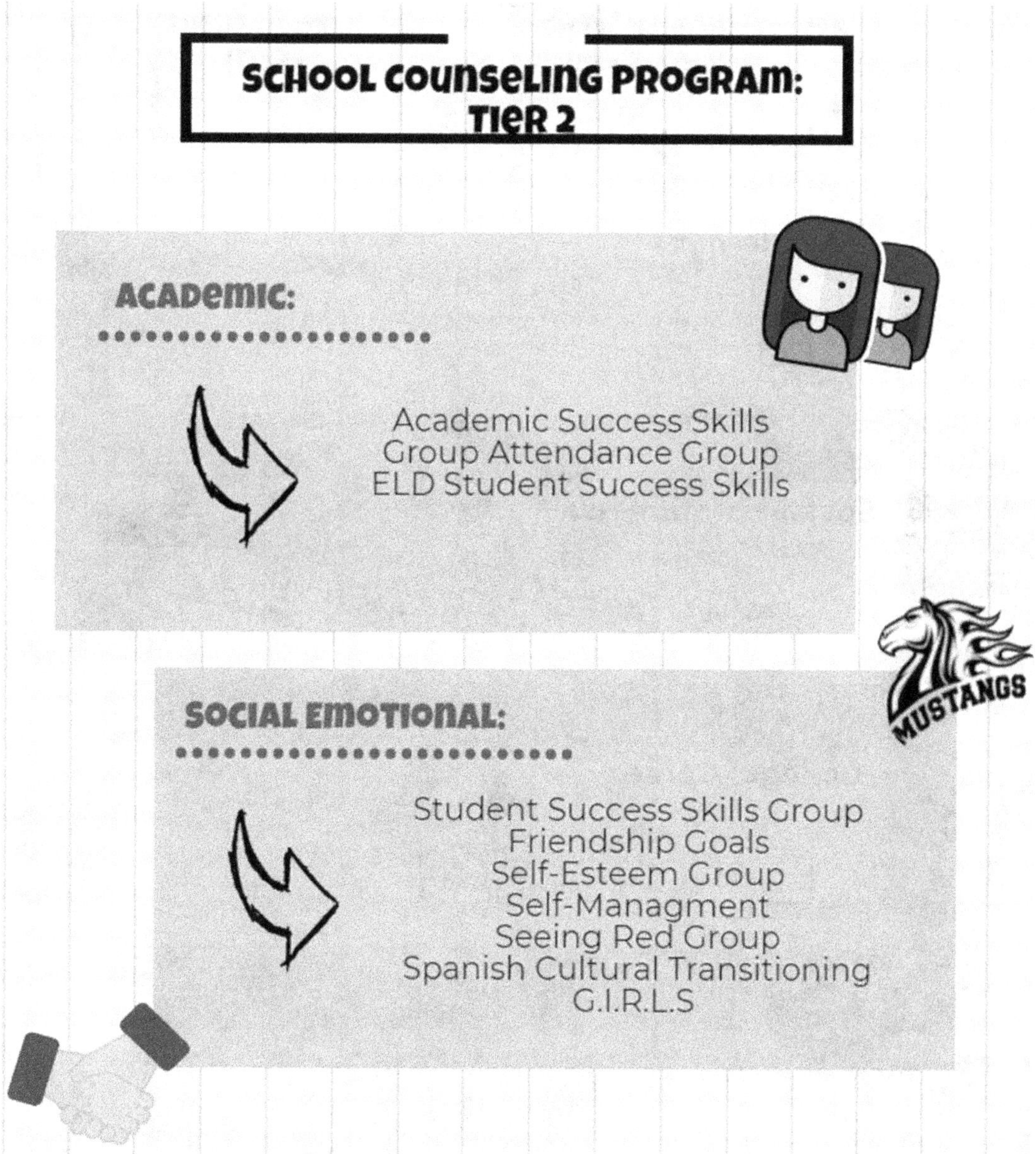

Exhibit 6.9 (*continued*)

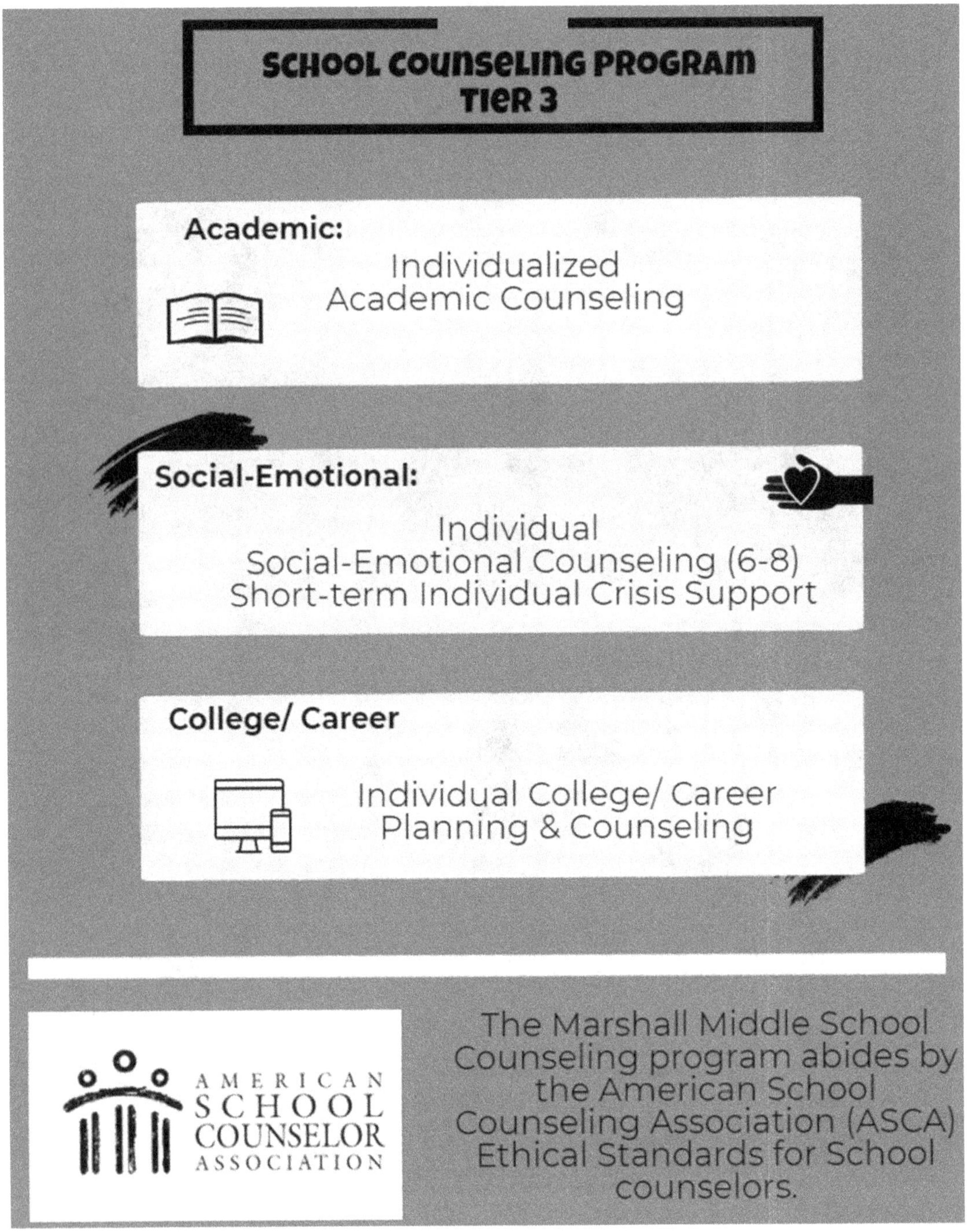

Exhibit 6.9 (*continued*)

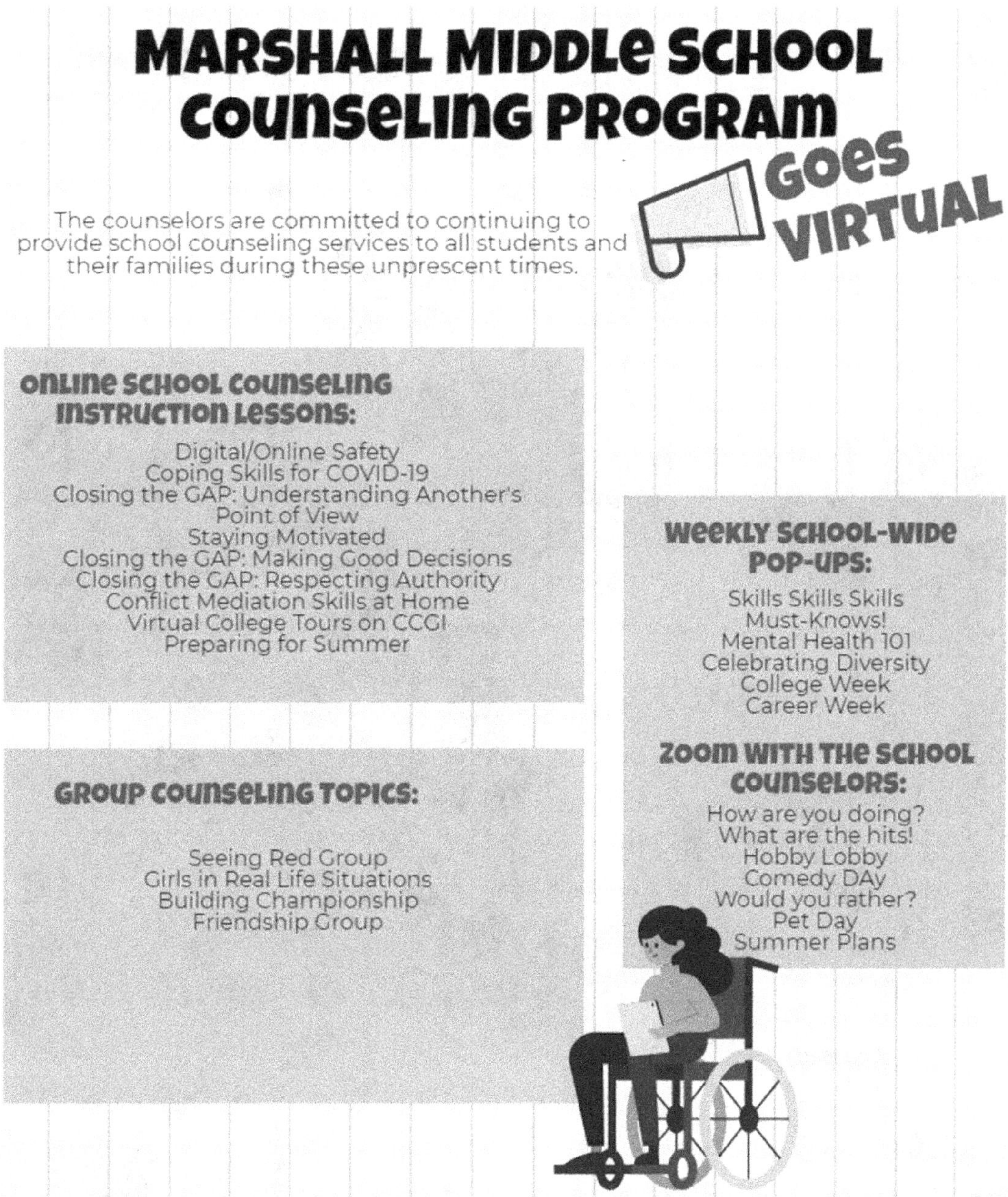

Exhibit 6.9 (*continued*)

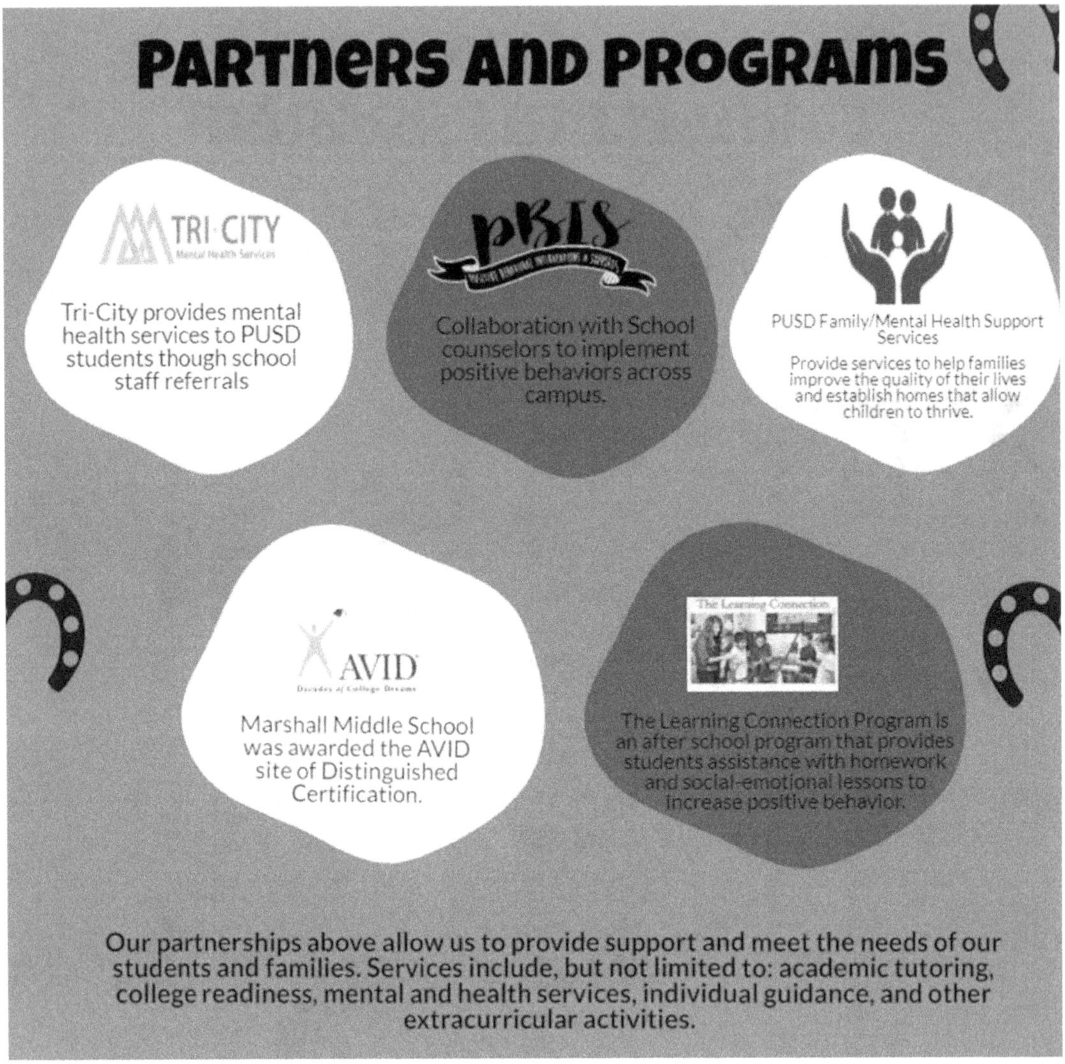

Exhibit 6.9 (*continued*)

excellence. To date, almost 1,000 schools have been acknowledged as RAMP recipients. For those of you who are ready to promote your successful, data-driven CSCP, we encourage you to consider applying for RAMP status. You can access examples of RAMP applications and materials from previous award winners as well as access helpful videos and tutorials from the ASCA library for some inspiration on earning this honorable designation. In terms of the content, the scoring rubric has 10 categories (Table 6.3) and requires the following: in order to qualify for RAMP designation, the application must earn 54 out of 60 points; if a scored application earns 58 points, it is eligible as a RAMP School of Distinction. Your RAMP status is valid for a 5-year period.

According to ASCA (personal communication, February 5, 2021), there are a few states that currently have state-level-approved programs that can also lead to RAMP designation (Missouri, Alabama, and Delaware), as well as others that are working on a similar process. Thus, we encourage you to explore which route is best for you. For example, in Missouri, the Department of Elementary and Secondary Education manages the Gysbers Missouri Comprehensive School Counseling Program Award, named

Exhibit 6.9 (*continued*)

after a nationally renowned school counselor educator, Dr. Norm Gysbers. Meanwhile, in Alabama, The School Counseling Program of Distinction award is a state-level award managed by the Alabama School Counselor Association. In Indiana, there is a comprehensive process known as *Redesigning School Counseling*, which began in 2004 and has awarded nearly 300 recipients the Indiana Gold Star Award, which has also resulted in many RAMP recipients. With assistance from the American Student Achievement Institute (ASAI), those interested in pursuing the process attend a consultation meeting and then monthly webinars to support the various components, which are aligned with ASCA RAMP criteria, before finally submitting their materials to the online portal (ASAI, n.d.).

TABLE 6.3 POINTS ALLOCATION FOR THE RAMP RUBRIC

RUBRIC AREA	POINTS ALLOCATED
Vision and Mission Statements	6
Annual Student Outcome Goals	6
Classroom and Group Mindsets & Behaviors Action Plan	5
Annual Administrative Conference	5
Advisory Council	6
Calendars (Annual and Weekly)	5
Lesson Plans (Classroom and Group)	5
Classroom Instruction Results Report	7
Small-Group Results Report	7
Closing-the Gap Action Plan/Results Report	8
Total (possible)	60

4 points needed to earn RAMP designation.

Best Practices for Showcasing Your Efforts

No one wants their efforts to go to waste, right? This is exactly why it is critical to showcase your efforts, advocate for the important work you do, and convey the impact you make on student behavior and success. Now, I know what you are thinking "this sounds scary" or you don't want to draw attention to yourself. But the truth is, your efforts are important and deserve to be recognized, AND, showcasing your efforts is a part of advocacy on behalf of your students, your role, and your profession as a whole. Hatch et al. (2018) emphasize that sharing your results regardless of their format is important to increase public understanding about the role of a school counselor as well as to build sustainability of your CSCP. We offer you a variety of ways to promote your CSCP.

Flashlight Presentation

Beyond the results reports that we have previously described, you should also consider the format used to convey your key points to stakeholders during public presentations. Knowing your audience is key to having a successful presentation that highlights your data-driven CSCP. For some purposes, having a presentation format may be appropriate, such as when you want to highlight one specific outcome of your CSCP in a brief, 5- to 10-minute presentation, which Hatch named a *Flashlight Presentation* (2018). Unlike the interactive presentations that you may deliver in classrooms, Hatch et al. (2018) recommend you consider how to communicate with stakeholders about the *one*, most important aspect that deserves the attention of your intended audience. But why would you want do this, rather than focus on your entire CSCP? Well, back to the earlier point about knowing your audience. You want to make sure that the concept and results are understood. Some stakeholders may get overwhelmed by a comprehensive presentation. So this alleviates the potential overwhelm. For a template of what your Flashlight Presentation should contain at the elementary level, we encourage you to refer to Chapter 9 of *Hatching Results for Elementary School Counseling: Implementing Core Curriculum and Other Tier One Activities* (Hatch et al., 2018), and for the secondary level,

Knowing your audience is key to having a successful presentation that highlights your data-driven CSCP.

Chapter 10 of *Hatching Results for Secondary School Counseling: Implementing Core Curriculum, Individual Student Planning, and Other Tier One Activities* (Hatch et al., 2019).

One Pagers

We know that time is a hot commodity and that many educators and other stakeholders will not want to read an extensive report or attend a lengthy presentation. So, similar to the Flashlight Presentation approach, it would behoove you to consider how you can highlight your most critical information and results in a one-page document format. The beauty is that we have so many different technological tools that can assist in the promotion. District middle school counselor Jasmine Arellano has trained her colleagues in brief one-page accountability reports to illustrate the impact of their CSCPs, with midyear and end-of-year reports. These reports can include participation data, Mindsets & Behaviors data, and outcome data. For example, Marshall Middle School's midyear report (Exhibit 6.10) highlights the school counselors' work from August to December and includes data that specifically addresses two of their annual student outcome goals, as well as an end-of-year report (Exhibit 6.11) that captures the activity of the school counselor or team for the entire year. Arellano also compiles a cumulative report that reflects the efforts of all of her middle school counselors, which can be distributed to school administration and other relevant stakeholders (Exhibit 6.12).

Promoting at the School-Site Level

At the school-site level, you have the opportunity to connect with a variety of stakeholders. Once you have completed your accountability reports, you can begin publicizing your work by presenting your results to your colleagues during a staff meeting. This provides you with the opportunity to show explicitly how students are different as a result of your school-wide and targeted invention efforts. Remember that many educators forget that school counselors, too, have standards to follow. So try to incorporate important ASCA documents and terms into your presentation. Also can consider publishing specific data from your accountability reports on your school website or in a school newsletter. Here the intent is to educate both stakeholders of parents/caregivers as well as the community at large about what the school counselor's role is and how counselors support student success. It is important to keep in mind that you may have individuals who are unfamiliar with your role, so keep the content developmentally appropriate, while still taking advantage of the opportunity to promote your work.

Promotion at the District Level

Beyond your own school site, you can think about promoting your work within your district, perhaps during school-level meetings, depending upon the size of your district. The accountability work that you are doing is sure to inspire your school counseling colleagues; we must remember to work smarter, not harder, so think about how you can promote your successes, but also discuss the challenges and your process of building and implementing your CSCP, so that others can learn from you and apply this knowledge accordingly to their own school site. Also, at the district level, we encourage you to speak to your local school board members. These are the elected or appointed individuals who are supposed to serve in the best interests of schools and students, just as you do. Again, by promoting the work you do toward student success, you are advocating and educating key stakeholders about the importance of your role. When I [Sandra] speak at a school board meeting. I am always cognizant of the fact that I have a 5-minute window to capture their attention and share what they need to know. As such, I focus my efforts on providing them with a brief one-pager that summarizes the work done

Exhibit 6.10 Marshall Middle School midyear report illustrating progress toward three identified goals.

MARSHALL MIDDLE SCHOOL

Jasmine Arellano, M.S., S.B.B.C., P.P.S
Marlen Purpura, M.A., P.P.S.

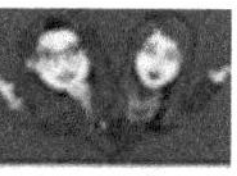

SCHOOL COUNSELING PROGRAM 19/20 END OF THE YEAR REPORT

SCHOOL COUNSELING PROGRAM VISION STATEMENT

The vision of the Marshall Middle School counseling program is that all students will graduate 21st-century ready. Guided by the ASCA Mindset & Behavior Standards for Student Success, students will be equipped with the highest level of social/emotional, academic, and college/career skills to reach their highest potential and sustain personal growth. They will be equipped with the necessary skills to secure a career that aligns with their skills, interests and values. Our resilient and empowered students will advocate for a society that values compassion, diversity, and positive change in an ever-transforming world.

SCHOOL COUNSELING PROGRAM MISSION STATEMENT

The mission of the Marshall Middle School Counseling Program is for all students to have equitable access to a data-driven multi-tier, multi-domain school counseling program designed to support each student in reaching their social/emotional, academic, and college/career potential. We advocate for equity, access, and success for every student through in-class instruction, small groups, individual counseling, and school-wide activities. Through data driven practices we ensure that all students have access to school counseling services that meet students needs. In collaboration with the community, teachers, school staff, parents, and stakeholders, all students will develop the foundational skills to foster a safe learning environment, build resiliency, and empower them to become caring contributing members of our community.

School At-A-Glance
(2019 CA Dashboard Data)

Grade Levels: **6-8**

Enrollment: **524**

Socioeconomically Disadvantaged: **96.9%**

English Language Learners: **25%**

Students with Disabilities: **15.6%**

Foster Youth: **1.9%**

Principal: **Eva Robles**

Assistant Principal: **Maricela Najera**

School Counselors: **Jasmine Arellano & Marlen Purpura**

Marshall Middle School's Counseling program offers a data-driven Comprehension School Counseling Program that focuses on the Academic, Social-Emotional, and College/Career success of our students. Our program is American School Counseling Association (ASCA) Model aligned.

OVERVIEW

Total # of Documented School Counseling Contacts:	Total # of In-Class Instruction Lessons (including online):	Total # of Group Counseling Sessions:	Total # of Conflict Mediations:	Total # of Mental Health Referrals:
11,045	201	110	62	44

Template was created on Piktochart — Page 1

Exhibit 6.11 Marshall Middle School end-of-year report illustrating participation data, Mindsets & Behaviors data, and outcome data.

MARSHALL MIDDLE SCHOOL

Jasmine Arellano, M.S., S.B.B.C., P.P.S
Marlen Purpura, M.A., P.P.S.

School Counseling Program Annual Student Outcome Goal 1:
By May 29, 2020, the number of Office Disciplinary Referrals involving "fighting" will decrease by 41.3% from 46 (18-19) to 27 (19-20).

Mindset & Behavior Standards Addressed:
M1. Belief in development of whole self, including a healthy balance of mental, social/emotional, and physical well-being
B-SMS-2. Demonstrate self-discipline and self-control

IN-CLASS INSTRUCTION LESSONS

- Creating a Culture of Kindness Curriculum
  - Ending Bullying
  - Dealing With Anger
  - Empathy Muscle
  - Detaching from Negativity
  - Gossip, Rumors, & Conscience
  - Resolving Conflicts
  - Redefining Cool
  - Assumptions & Stereotypes

** With the exception of ASRD students, all 6th-8th grade students received these lessons.

PARTICIPATION DATA

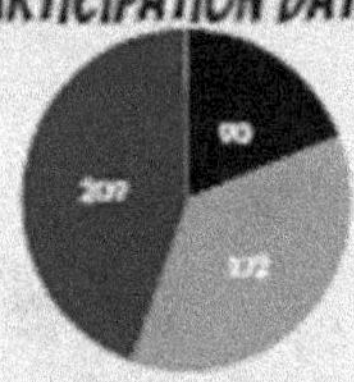

OUTCOME DATA

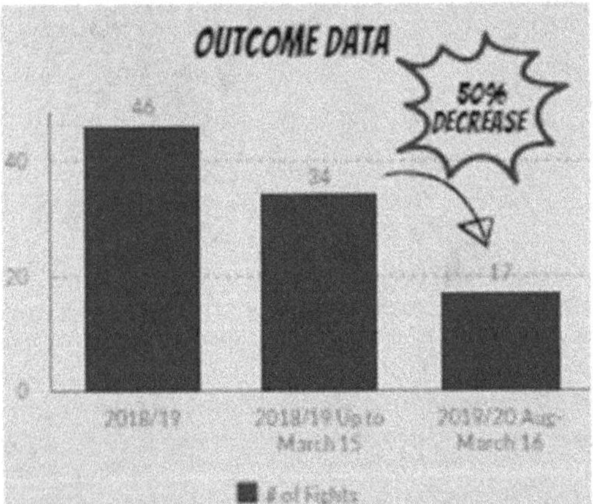

- **Goal met.**
- We had a 50% decrease in fights compared to the 18/19 school year.
- When comparing data points from last school year (March 15th) to this school year (March 16th) we have had 17 less fights.

GROUP COUNSELING TOPICS

- 4 Self-Esteem Groups
- Boys Champions Group
- Managing Conflict Group
- 2 Seeing Red Groups
- Self-Management Group
- Spanish Cultural Transitioning

** All students for all group counseling topics were invited based on PBIS SWIS Data.

INDIVIDUAL COUNSELING/RESPONSIVE COUNSELING/CONFLICT MEDIATIONS/REFERRALS

- Provided students with Individual Counseling based on specific needs
- Conflict Mediations as needed
- Referrals to Mental Health Services

MINDSET & BEHAVIOR DATA

Students able to identify the conflict resolution process.

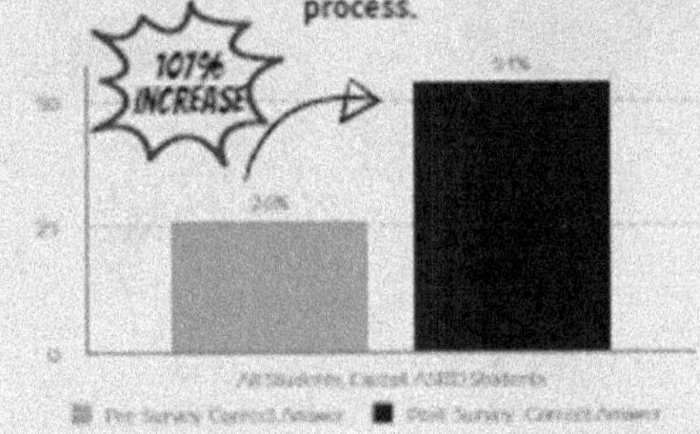

Which part of the brain are we stuck in when we are angry and don't calm down?

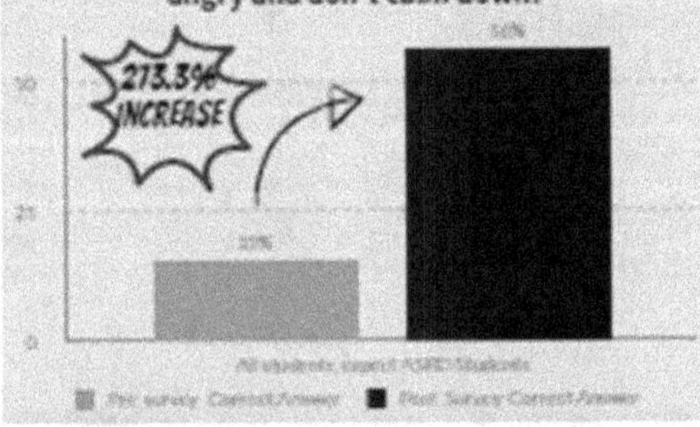

Page 2

Exhibit 6.11 (*continued*)

MARSHALL MIDDLE SCHOOL

Jasmine Arellano, M.S., S.B.B.C., P.P.S
Marlen Purpura, M.A., P.P.S.

School Counseling Program Annual Student Outcome Goal 2:
By May 29, 2020, the number of 8th graders failing a class with a grade average of 59 or below at the end of the first 6 weeks will decrease by 28% from 84 students (end of first six weeks) to 60 students or fewer (end of the school year).

Mindset & Behavior Standards Addressed:
M6. Positive attitude toward work and learning
B-LS-3. Use time-management, organizational skills, and study skills

IN-CLASS INSTRUCTION LESSONS

- Academic Success Skills
  - Organization Skills
  - Time-Management
  - Attendance
- Online Success Skills

** With the exception of ASRD students, all 8th grade students received these lessons.

PARTICIPATION DATA

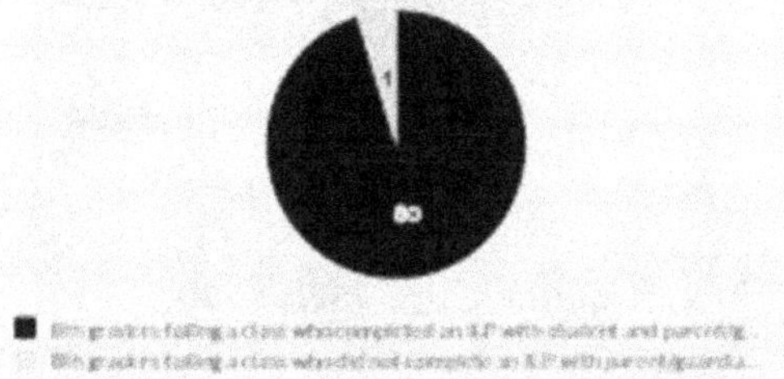

MINDSET & BEHAVIOR DATA

I believe I can pass my classes with a D or higher.

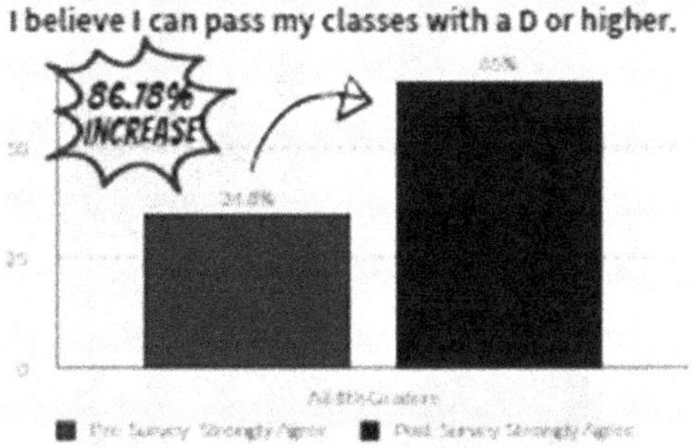

Which of the following is a good organization skill to use?

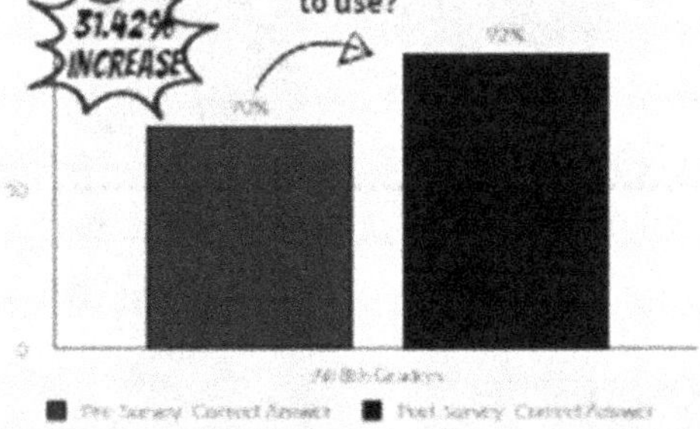

GROUP COUNSELING TOPICS

- 4 Student Success Skills Groups
- Attendance Group

** Zangle Q Data was used to select all group participants.

ACADEMIC ADVISEMENT & APPRAISAL/ PARENT MEETINGS / INDIVIDUAL LEARNING PLANS/ TEACHER COLLABORATION

- Parent/student meetings were held for all 8th graders who failed one or more classes Q1D. During the meeting, academic expectations were reviewed, and all students completed an Individual Learning Plan and signed their 8th grade Academic Contract.
- All 8th-grade students failing were assigned Grade Recovery after school and Saturday School.
- All 8th-grade students failing had check-ins at least 3 times in the semester to check on academic progress and set goals.
- Collaborated with teachers on student grades and improvement.

OUTCOME DATA

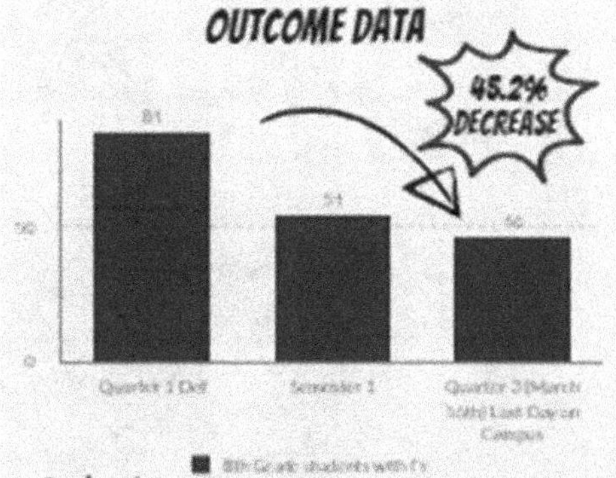

- **Goal met.**
- 38 students raised all Fs they had at Q1D to passing grades by the last day we were on campus.
- Grades only reflected till the last day we were on campus, because grading policy changed due to COVID-19, no student was allowed to fail a class.

Exhibit 6.11 (*continued*)

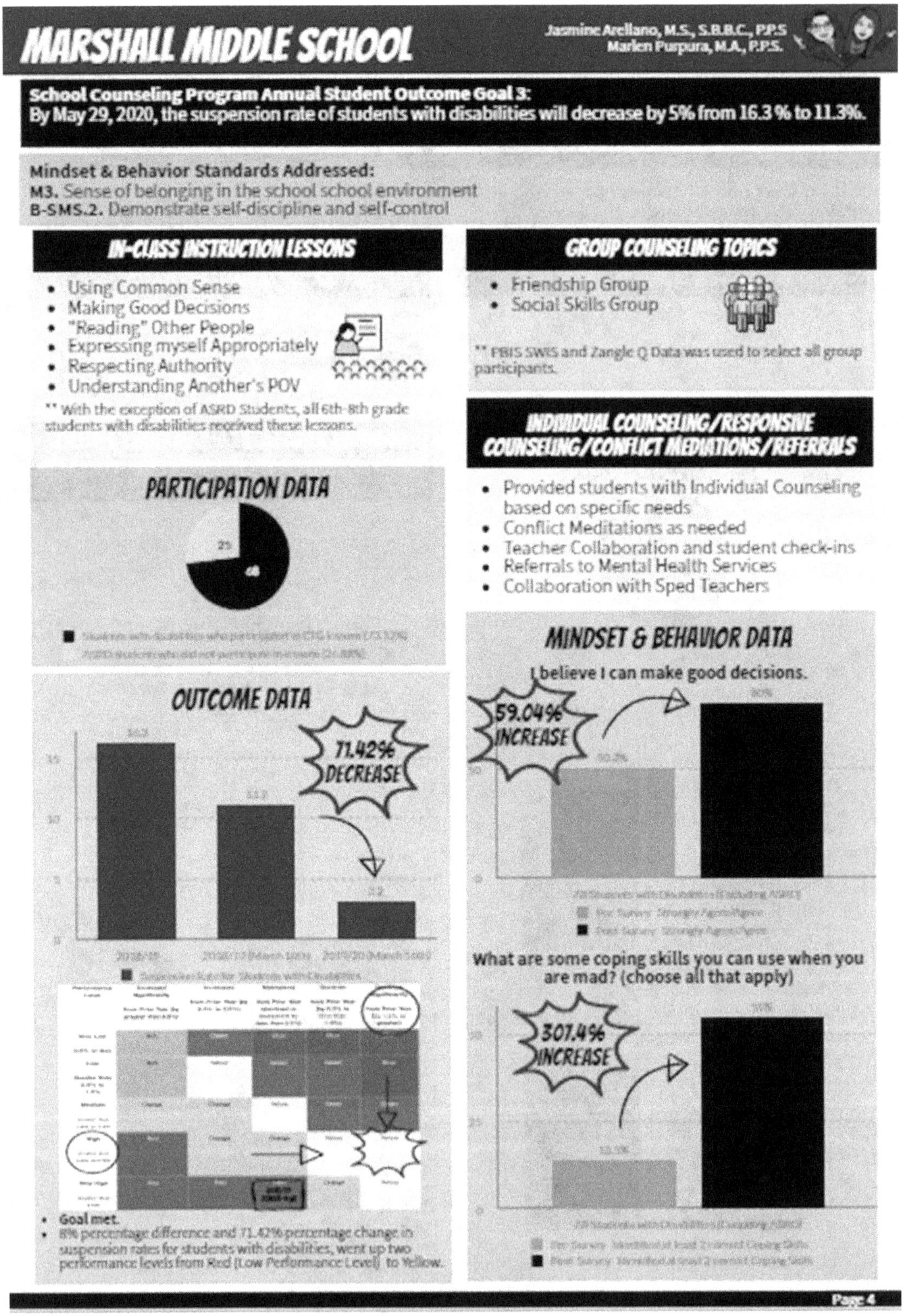

MARSHALL MIDDLE SCHOOL

Jasmine Arellano, M.S., S.B.B.C., P.P.S
Marlen Purpura, M.A., P.P.S.

School Counseling Program Annual Student Outcome Goal 3:
By May 29, 2020, the suspension rate of students with disabilities will decrease by 5% from 16.3 % to 11.3%.

Mindset & Behavior Standards Addressed:
M3. Sense of belonging in the school school environment
B-SMS.2. Demonstrate self-discipline and self-control

IN-CLASS INSTRUCTION LESSONS

- Using Common Sense
- Making Good Decisions
- "Reading" Other People
- Expressing myself Appropriately
- Respecting Authority
- Understanding Another's POV

** With the exception of ASRD Students, all 6th-8th grade students with disabilities received these lessons.

GROUP COUNSELING TOPICS

- Friendship Group
- Social Skills Group

** PBIS SWIS and Zangle Q Data was used to select all group participants.

INDIVIDUAL COUNSELING/RESPONSIVE COUNSELING/CONFLICT MEDIATIONS/REFERRALS

- Provided students with Individual Counseling based on specific needs
- Conflict Meditations as needed
- Teacher Collaboration and student check-ins
- Referrals to Mental Health Services
- Collaboration with Sped Teachers

PARTICIPATION DATA

OUTCOME DATA

- Goal met.
- 8% percentage difference and 71.42% percentage change in suspension rates for students with disabilities, went up two performance levels from Red (Low Performance Level) to Yellow.

MINDSET & BEHAVIOR DATA

I believe I can make good decisions.

What are some coping skills you can use when you are mad? (choose all that apply)

Page 4

Exhibit 6.11 (*continued*)

MARSHALL MIDDLE SCHOOL

Jasmine Arellano, M.S., S.B.B.C., P.P.S
Marlen Purpura, M.A., P.P.S.

ONLINE SCHOOL COUNSELING PROGRAM DURING COVID-19

STEPS TAKEN TO SUPPORT STUDENTS

ONLINE IN-CLASS INSTRUCTION LESSONS

- Week 1
  - Digital/Online Safety Lesson
  - Online Success Skills
  - PBIS Distance Learning Expectations
- Week 2
  - Coping Skills for COVID-19
    - Anxiety Management
- Week 3
  - Coping Skills for COVID-19
    - Stress Management
    - Self-Care Plan
- Week 4
  - Staying Motivated
- Week 5
  - Conflict Mediation Skills at Home
- Week 6
  - Community Colleges 101
  - CSUs 101
  - UCs 101
  - Private Universities 101
- Week 7
  - How to Prepare for an Interview
  - How to Dress for an Interview
  - How to fill out an Application (Mock application)

15 ONLINE SCHOOL COUNSELING LESSONS

** All these lessons were screen recorded and posted to the school counseling google classroom for ALL students to access. Participation was voluntary.

WEEKLY THEMES & ACTIVITIES

- **Week 1: Skills Skills Skills**
  - #MarshallStrongChallenge
- **Week 2: Must-Knows!**
  - Email Etiquette Challenge
  - Handwashing Challenge
- **Week 3: Mental Health 101**
  - Fortune Teller Challenge
  - Guided Meditation on Zoom
  - Stretching with your School Counselors
- **Week 4: Celebrating Diversity**
  - Flipgrid Challenges
- **Week 5: Mental Health Awareness**
  - Mental health Spirit Week Daily on Zoom with the School Counselors
- **Week 6: College Week**
  - Community Colleges Kahoot!
  - CSUs Kahoot!
  - UCs Kahoot!
  - Private Universities Kahoot!
- **Week 7: Careers Week**
  - Career Day on Zoom

14 ACTIVITIES & CHALLENGES STUDENTS COULD ENGAGE IN

** Participation in weekly themes and activities were voluntary and open to ALL students

ZOOMING WITH THE SCHOOL COUNSELORS

- **Week 1:** Initial Check-in
- **Week 2:** What's new?
- **Week 3:** Hobby Lobby
- **Week 4:** Comedy Day!
- **Week 5:** Would you Rather?
- **Week 6:** Pet Day!
- **Week 7:** Summer Plans!

56 STUDENT SCHOOL COUNSELOR REQUESTS

** Attending a zoom with the school counselor was not mandatory and not related to a group or individual counseling services. These events were facilitated by the school counselors, open to ALL students, and served as an opportunity for students to connect with their peers and staff members as they would have physically on campus.

INDIVIDUAL SCHOOL COUNSELING SUPPORT

- **Student School Counselor Request Form**
  - All students could request for school counselors to reach out through zoom, phone call, and/or email.
- **Parent School Counselor Request Form**
  - All parents could request for school counselors to reach out through zoom, phone call, and/or email.
- **Teacher School Counselor Request Form**
  - All teachers could request for school counselors to reach out to students for support
- **Responding to Securly Alerts**
  - School Counselors reached out to check in on students and support based on Securly alerts, and submitted Mental Health Referrals as needed.
- **Student and Family Check-ins**
  - Checked in with students and their families to ensure they were okay and had access to the necessary technology to be successful in distance learning.

Professionally credentialed School Counselors design and evaluate a data-informed comprehensive school counseling program by applying the ASCA standards. Marshall Middle School counselors make decisions and promote development based on ASCA's Mindset & Behavior, Ethical Standards, and through a Multi-Tier Multi-Domain System of Supports.
Pomona Unified School District's School Counseling Program is guided by ASCA.
Page 5

Exhibit 6.11 (*continued*)

POMONA UNIFIED SCHOOL DISTRICT Jasmine Arellano-Najera, M.S., P.P.S. District Middle School Counselor

MIDDLE SCHOOL/K-8 SCHOOL COUNSELING PROGRAM 20/21 MID YEAR REPORT

| August - December 18, 2020 |

MIDDLE SCHOOLS IN POMONA UNIFED

- Emerson Middle School Grades 6-8
- Lorbeer Middle School Grades 7-8
- Marshall Middle School Grades 6-8
- Simons Middle School Grades 6-8

Total Student Population: 2,499

Average School Counselor to Student Ratio: 312:1

K-8 SCHOOLS IN POMONA UNIFED

- Cortez K-8
- Harrison K-8
- Lexington K-8
- San Jose K-8
- Vejar K-8

Total Student Population: 3,185

Average School Counselor to Student Ratio: 637:1

Middle School Counselor Contacts

Total # of Documented School Counseling Contacts:	Total # of Online Class Instruction Lesson Topics (Asynchronous):	Total # of Individual Learning Plan Contacts	Total # of Tier 2 Contacts	Total # of Tier 3 Contacts	Total # of Parent/Guardian Contacts:
20,129	14	2,189	2,862	395	3,533

K-8 School Counselor Contacts

Total # of Documented School Counseling Contacts:	Total # of Online Class Instruction Lesson Topics for K-8 Schools (Asynchronous):	Total # of Individual Learning Plan (Grades 7-8) Contacts	Total # of Tier 2	Total # of Tier 3	Total # of Parent/Guardian Contacts:
70,764	32	198	411	123	9,162

MIDDLE SCHOOL COUNSELING STUDENT CONTACTS BY DOMAIN

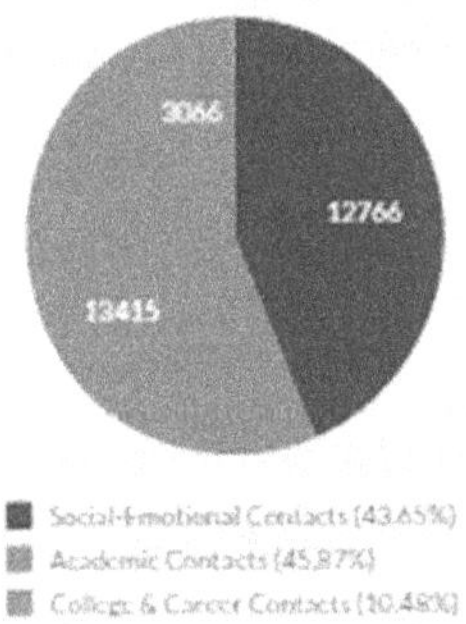

K-8 SCHOOL COUNSELING STUDENT CONTACTS BY DOMAIN

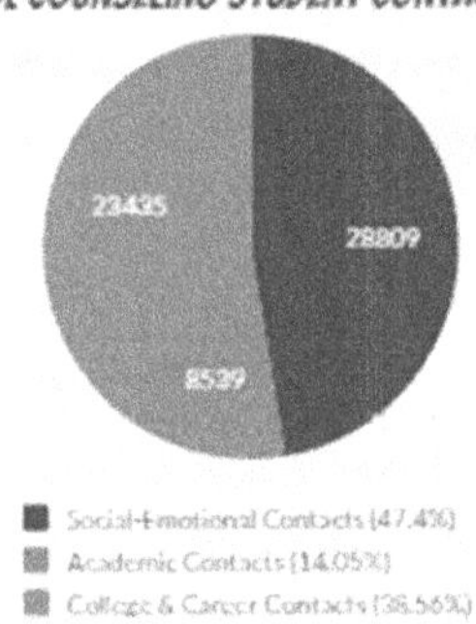

ALL MIDDLE SCHOOL AND K-8 SCHOOL COUNSELORS DEVELOPED TWO ANNUAL STUDENT OUTCOME GOALS FOR THE 2020-21 SCHOOL YEAR. GOAL #1 WAS CENTERED AROUND ATTENDANCE DATA AND BASED ON SITE-SPECIFIC DATA. GOAL #2 WAS CREATED AROUND ACHIEVEMENT DATA AND ALSO BASED ON SITE-SPECIFIC DATA.

PLEASE SEE THE FOLLOWING PAGES FOR SITE-SPECIFIC MID-YEAR REPORTS AND DATA CREATED BY EACH INDIVIDUAL SCHOOL COUNSELOR.

Exhibit 6.12 District-level midyear report illustrating participation data across schools within the district.

by me, the sole school counselor split across two school sites, serving a student population of nearly 1,300 students. I paint the picture that while I met with 94% of all my eighth graders and their parents/caregivers for individual high school planning meetings and I conducted over 13,000 minutes of individual and group counseling during this current academic year, I still fell short as I am the only school counselor with an extremely high caseload that prevented me from reaching all students across all three ASCA domains. Then I provide some personal context by sharing the stories of a few of my students that illustrate how I support them and also how I lack the opportunity to support them. These personal stories are important and impactful. Leave your school board presentation with an impression!

For those of you who work at the district office, one way to support your school counselors is to showcase their efforts by implementing campaign-like activities. For example, you might conduct a needs assessment at the beginning or end of the year to provide data about the desired professional development for your school counseling team. Accordingly, you could develop a series called "What I Wish I Knew Wednesdays," during which you address the areas most requested by highlighting the work of a school counselor who is doing exemplary work in a particular area. For example, you might have a school counselor who is quite tech savvy who has developed an extensive data-collection survey to track their daily activities. Invite this school counselor to present to their peers on the development of the online survey, such as through Google Forms, and then discuss their strategies for effective data collection. This way you are exactly addressing what your school counselors wish they knew, whether in terms of knowledge or particular skills, that can be supported through your professional development offerings.

Promoting at the Community/Public Level

As is to be expected, there is plenty of opportunity to advocate and educate the community about the critical work you do as a school counselor. To begin, consider those who serve on your school counseling advisory council. These individuals are a great place to start when it comes to educating and publicizing your work with the community. Following the recommendations in ASCA (2019), it is important to focus your presentation on clear, concise outcomes of your CSCP, making sure to highlight all three types of data (participation, Mindsets & Behaviors, outcome), and to use visual elements that describe your work. Above all, you want to communicate how students are different as a result of your efforts. Let's consider that you want to highlight the great work that you are doing among your fellow school counselor colleagues. You could consider presenting at a local, state, or national school counseling conference. This would allow you the opportunity to showcase the exemplary work of your CSCP. You could also consider presenting at other education-related conferences or events that provide you with a platform to educate and advocate about the school counselor's role and the impact of a CSCP. Look into events for which the target audience is teachers and other school personnel, such as National Association of Elementary School Principals, National Association of Secondary School Principals, and The School Superintendents Association.

In an effort to educate members of the community, think about who serves your students and families. Whether it be your local Boys & Girls Club, a Rotary Club, or other philanthropic organization, this chance to disseminate information allows you to educate others about your important work, and may serve as an opportunity for you to garner financial or other support. Let's consider that you make a presentation about the impact of your CSCP on student success and well-being to your local Rotary Club. After learning about what a difference you make the club may be willing to support your next schoolwide campaign or donate funds and other resources to help you carry out your next targeted, small-group counseling intervention. Also, it is important to realize that this can serve as an act of advocacy, in that you are advocating for your role and profession. The "what" and "why" of your accountability efforts across audiences is best summarized in Figure 6.14.

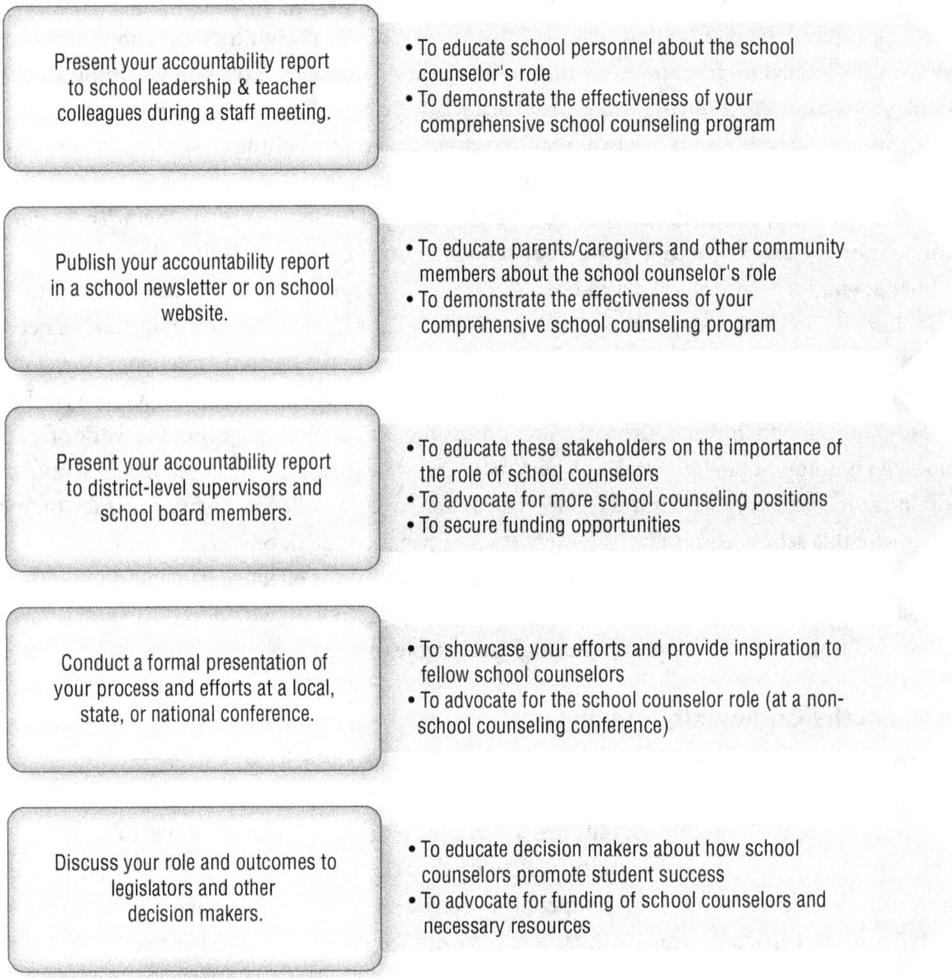

Figure 6.14 The "what" and "why" of your accountability efforts.

Conclusions

Regardless of what fashion you choose to communicate and share the successful results of your efforts, it is a powerful strategy for you to intentionally connect your CSCP to specific student outcomes that support your school's goals. Like much of what we do in our profession, there is not just one "right" way to carry out your work; rather, you must decide how you want to carry out your work, in the best interests of students, yourself, and your profession. There are numerous technological tools and strategies available to support the promotion of your CSCP. We firmly believe that every school counselor has the ability to learn the knowledge and skills necessary to develop and implement a data-driven CSCP that advocates for students and promotes the school counseling profession, especially when they are focused on assessment and data collection.

Additional Reading

Cleveland, A., & Sharp, S. (2019). 50+ tech tools for school counselors: How to be more engaging, efficient, and effective. Corwin.

Sink, C. A., Adkins, C., Cooney, M., & Garverick, T. (2019). An exploratory study of online software to support accountability practices. *Professional School Counseling, 22*(1b). https://doi.org/10.1177%2F2156759X19834443

Zyromski, B., & Mariani, M. A. (2016). *Facilitating evidence-based, data-driven school counseling: A manual for practice.* Corwin.

Tools and Resources

- ASCA RAMP offers examples (https://schoolcounselorawards.org/ramp/example) and tutorials (https://videos .schoolcounselor.org/category/ramp-library).
- Auto Closing-the-Gap (AutoCTG) is an Excel add-on to support the data collection of your closing-the-gap efforts (https://schoolcounselor.com/autoctg/).
- EZAnalyze is an Excel add-on to support your data-analysis efforts (http://www.ezanalyze.com/).
- EZAnalyze TimeTracker is an Excel add-on that allows you to track your time and efforts in providing direct counseling services (http://www.ezanalyze.com/tracktime).
- Google Workspace is an integrated workspace that provides tools for school counselor's everyday tasks (https://workspace.google.com/).
- QR Code Generator is an app that allows the user to create a QR code image that can be connected to a website, link, and other communications (https://www.qr-code-generator.com/).
- School Counseling Program Profile (SC PRO) is an accountability report format, specifically to highlight efforts in the Career Domain (https://www.schoolcounselor-ca.org/sc%20profiles%20overview).
- School Counselor's Use-of-Time Analysis (SCUTA) Lite: Provides a free account for individuals to get started using the platform (https://www.myscuta.com/tryforfree).
- School Counselor's Use-of-Time Analysis (SCUTA) University: Provides a free account/portal for school counselor educators to use for training purposes with their students (https://www.myscuta.com/partnership).
- School Personnel Accountability Report Card (SPARC), a voluntary, continuous-improvement document showcasing college and career readiness student outcomes, managed by California Career Center (https://www.calcareercenter.org/sparc).
- Time Elapsed Analysis & Reporting System (TEARS) is an Excel add-in designed to calculate and track time spent in various activities that a school counselor carries out (https://schoolcounselor.com/tears/).
- WellCheq is a research-based app that enables students to communicate with a daily check-in activity that teachers and school counselors can monitor and provide appropriate support/intervention (https://wellcheq.com/).

Key Points

- The critical work of school counselors needs to be publicized in order to educate the community and stakeholders, while also advocating for students, your role, and your profession.
- A wide variety of accountability reports are available that can illustrate the key outcomes of your CSCP, depending upon what sources of data you have and what you specifically want to promote to others.
- Extensive technological tools exist to help in your assessment and data-collection efforts, as well as when presenting your findings to stakeholders within and beyond the school counseling community.
- School counselors who design and implement exemplary CSCPs are eligible to participate in various award programs.

Questions for Reflection

- What is the most critical information that you want to share with stakeholders that highlights the outcomes of your CSCP?
- In considering your current technological competence, what skills do you need to gain and how you can go about seeking appropriate professional development opportunities?
- What type of data do I want to share? With that data in mind, what is the best format for me, given my intended audience?

References

American School Counselor Association. (2016). *ASCA ethical standards for school counselors.* https://www.schoolcounselor.org/getmedia/f041cbd0-7004-47a5-ba01-3a5d657c6743/Ethical-Standards.pdf

American School Counselor Association. (2019). *ASCA school counselor professional standards and competencies.* https://www.schoolcounselor.org/getmedia/a8d59c2c-51de-4ec3-a565-a3235f3b93c3/SC-Competencies.pdf

American Student Achievement Institute. (n.d.). *RSC: Redesigning school counseling.* http://www.asainstitute.org/rsc/

Brott, P. E. (2006). Counselor education accountability: Training the effective professional school counselor. *Professional School Counseling, 10*, 179–187. https://doi.org/10.5330/prsc.10.2.d61g0v3738863652

Cleveland, A., & Sharp, S. (2019). *50+ tech tools for school counselors: How to be more engaging, efficient, and effective.* Corwin.

Dahir, C., & Stone, C. (2003). Accountability: A M.E.A.S.U.R.E. of the impact school counselors have on student achievement. *Professional School Counseling, 6*(3), 214–221

Hatch, T., Duarte, D., & De Gregorio, L. K. (2018). *Hatching results for elementary school counseling: Implementing core curriculum, and other tier one activities.* Corwin.

Hatch, T., Triplett, W., Duarte, D., & Gomez, V. (2019). *Hatching results for secondary school counseling: Implementing core curriculum, individual student planning, and other tier one activities.* Corwin.

Mason, E. C. M., Griffith, C., & Belser, C. T. (2019). School counselors' use of technology for program management. *Professional School Counseling, 22*(1). https://doi.org/10.1177/2156759X19870794

Young, A., & Kaffenberger, C. J. (2019). *Making DATA work* (4th ed.). American School Counselor Association.

Appendix A: Figures, Exhibits, and Tables

(*continued*)

(continued)

Appendix B: Frequently Used Acronyms

Acronym	Full description
ACA	American Counseling Association
ACT	American College Testing
ADHD	Attention deficit hyperactivity disorder
ADSI	Adolescent Domain Screening Inventory
AP	Advanced placement
ASAI	American Student Achievement Institute
ASCA	American School Counselor Association
ASK	Attitudes, Skills, and Knowledge
AutoCTG	Auto Closing-the-Gap
C&CR	College and career readiness
CACREP	Council for Accreditation of Counseling and Related Educational Programs
CAEP	Council for the Accreditation of Educator Preparation
CAKE	College Admissions Knowledge Evaluation
CASC	California Association of School Counselors
CASEL	Collaborative for Academic, Social, and Emotional Learning
CAYCI-SES	Community and Youth Collaborative Institute-School Experience Surveys
CCLR	College, Career, and Life Readiness
CCRCS	College and Career Readiness Counseling Support Scales
CDC	Centers for Disease Control and Prevention
CDE	Colorado Department of Education
CFA	Confirmatory factor analysis
CRAFFT	Car, Relax, Alone, Forget, Friends, Trouble
CSCORE	Center for School Counseling Outcome Research and Evaluation
CSCP	Comprehensive school counseling program
C-SSRS	Columbia-Suicide Severity Rating Scale
CTE	Career technical education
DATA	Design, Ask, Track, Announce
DOE	Department of Education
EBP	Evidence-based practice
EDSCLS	ED School Climate Surveys
EFA	Exploratory factor analysis
EOC	End of course
FRL	Free/reduced lunch
GPA	Grade point average
GRIP	Goals, Results, Impact Statement, and Program Implications
IEP	Individualized education program
IP	Interest Profiler
KADS-6	Kutcher Adolescent Depression Scale

(*continued*)

Acronym	Full description
MAS	Motivational Assessment Scale
MCI	My Class Inventory
MCS	My Career Story
MEASURE	Mission, Elements, Analyze, Stakeholders, Unite, Reanalyze, and Educate
MTMDSS	Multi-Tiered, Multi-Domain Systems of Support
MTSS	Multi-Tiered Systems of Support
ODE	Ohio Department of Education
OIP	Ohio Improvement Process
OSCA	Ohio School Counselor Association
PBIS	Positive behavioral interventions and supports
PD	Professional development
PLC	Professional learning community
PSAT/NMSQT	Preliminary Scholastic Aptitude Test/National Merit Scholarship Qualifying Test
PTA	Parent–Teacher Association
QR code	Quick response code
RAMP	Recognized ASCA Model Program
RIASEC	Realistic, Investigative, Artistic, Social, Enterprising, and Conventional
RtI	Response to intervention
SAEBRS	Social, Academic, and Emotional Behavior Risk Screener
SAMHSA	Substance Abuse and Mental Health Services Administration
SAT	Scholastic Aptitude Test
SCPIS	School Counseling Program Implementation Survey
SC PRO	School Counseling Program Profile
SCARS	School Counselor Activity Rating Scale
SCAS	Spence Children's Anxiety Scale
SCCI	Student Career Construction Inventory
SCUTA	School Counselor Use-of-Time Analysis
SDQ	Strengths & Difficulties Questionnaire
SDS	Self-directed search
SEL	Social and emotional learning
SES	Socioeconomic status
SIP	School improvement plan
SIS	Student information system
SIT	Student intervention team
SMART goal	Specific, measurable, achievable, relevant, time-bound goal
SPA	Specialized program accreditation
SPARC	Support Personnel Accountability Report Card
SRSS-IE	Student Risk Screening Scale—Internalizing & Externalizing
SST	Student study team
TEARS	Time-Elapsed Analysis and Reporting System
YRBS	Youth Risk Behavior Survey

Appendix C: List of Assessments

Type of assessment	Full description	Acronym
Academic	American College Testing	ACT
Social–emotional	Adolescent Domain Screening Inventory	ADSI
School counselors	ASCA School Counselor Professional Standards & Competencies Assessment	n/a
College/career	College Admissions Knowledge Evaluation	CAKE
Multi-domain	Community and Youth Collaborative Institute-School Experience Surveys	CAYCI-SES
College/career	College, Career, and Life Readiness	CCLR
College/career	College and Career Readiness Counseling Support Scales	CCRCS
Social–emotional	Car, Relax, Alone, Forget, Friends, Trouble	CRAFFT
Social–emotional	Columbia-Suicide Severity Rating Scale	C-SSRS
Social–emotional	ED School Climate Surveys	EDSCLS
College/career	Interest Profiler	IP
Social–emotional	Kutcher Adolescent Depression Scale	KADS-6
Social–emotional	Motivational Assessment Scale	MAS
Social–emotional	My Class Inventory	MCI
College/career	My Career Story	MCS
Academic	Preliminary Scholastic Aptitude Test/National Merit Scholarship Qualifying Test	PSAT/NMSQT
Academic	Renaissance Star Battery of Assessments	n/a
Social–emotional	Social, Academic, and Emotional Behavior Risk Screener	SAEBRS
Academic	Scholastic Aptitude Test	SAT
School cousnselors	School Counselor Activity Rating Scale	SCARS
Social–emotional	Spence Children's Anxiety Scale	SCAS
College/career	Student Career Construction Inventory	SCCI
School counselors	School Counseling Program Implementation Survey	SCPIS
School counselors	School Counselor Use-of-Time Analysis	SCUTA
Social–emotional	Strengths & Difficulties Questionnaire	SDQ
College/career	Self-Directed Search	SDS
Social–emotional	Student Risk Screening Scale—Internalizing & Externalizing	SRSS-IE
Social–emotional	Youth Risk Behavior Survey	YRBS

INDEX

CPSIA information can be obtained
at www.ICGtesting.com
Printed in the USA
BVHW011255070122
625706BV00011B/243